Who's Afraid of Feminism?

Who's Afraid of Feminism?

Seeing through the Backlash

**EDITED BY ANN OAKLEY
AND JULIET MITCHELL**

THE NEW PRESS • NEW YORK

Library of Congress Catalog Card Number
ISBN 1-56584-384-3 HC
ISBN 1-56584-385-1 PB

Published in the United States by The New Press, New York
Distributed by W.W. Norton & Company, Inc., New York

The New Press was established in 1990 as a not-for-profit alternative to the large,
commercial publishing houses currently dominating the book publishing industry.
The New Press operates in the public interest rather than for private gain,
and is committed to publishing, in innovative ways, works of educational, cultural, and
community value that might not normally be commercially viable.

Production management by Kim Waymer
Printed in the United States of America

9 8 7 6 5 4 3 2 1

For Laura and Polly

Contents

CONTENTS

Acknowledgments

We would like above all to acknowledge and thank Sandra Stone for her perceptive criticism and remarkable efficiency and without whom we can truly say "this book would not have been produced."

We also wish to than Sue Kemsley for her exciting editorial, research and secretarial work and out editor, Margaret Bluman for unending patience and consistent support to ourselves.

Permissions

Foreword

TEMMA KAPLAN

Since the seventies, critics have been pronouncing the end of feminism. Judging from the backlash, which has never stopped scourging women, I'd say that feminism was here to stay. Certainly Ann Oakley, Juliet Mitchell, and the other contributors to this wise and provocative volume think so.

In their attempt to figure out the backlash, these essays resemble photos forming images in developing fluid: They show why women, feminism, and "the family" have become the focus of so much overheated rhetoric and why this triumvirate has been held responsible for myriad negative effects of far-reaching social and cultural change.

Whether we date the second wave of feminism to Betty Friedan's *The Feminine Mystique*, in 1963, to the awakening of black and white women in the Civil Rights movement to their own sexual abuse, or to international struggles for reproductive rights (including opposition to sterilization of poor women of color in the United States), it is important to place feminism in context. These essays do just that: They are concerned with the courage and audacity of women acting as feminists to gain rights as citizens of their countries, to redefine citizenship to include claims to racial equality and economic resources, to demand their rights as sexual beings, to win access to all institutions in their society, to relate to one another through new social practices, and to support themselves and their children. Women referring to themselves as feminists or womanists or simply as activists have been challenging those who hold power internationally. No wonder opponents want to lash these women to the masts to make them resist the sirens of freedom and to silence the voices calling out for a more just society.

This book correlates some of these developments to debates within feminism: over sexuality; over equality and difference; over identity and experience; over pornography and censorship; over social construction and essentialism; over how much feminists have advanced in social, cultural, or political institutions; over conflicts between citizenship and motherhood; over how to interpret anti-women trends even where there is no feminism (in Eastern Europe, for example); over the incompatibility of feminism and nationalism; and around the use of the term *gender* by feminists and in the culture at large.

The late, great folk singer Lee Hayes could have been talking about the backlash when he said that the past ain't what it used to be, and, what's more, it never was. Nostalgia is the fuel driving the backlash. Never mind that nostalgia is frequently more about fantasies for the future than memories of the past. When nostalgia sets the tone of debate, feminists are always at a disadvantage. Feminists don't have a utopian, idealized past and can't be nostalgic. When in history have women been equal to men in ways that guarantee them both access to food, clothing, housing, health care, and eduction, as well as meaningful sexual and intellectual lives in which they were each free to be creative in any way they chose? Those responsible for the backlash against feminism presume that women, or mothers (terms they use interchangeably), once provided all the necessities of life for their families, thereby ensuring social stability. Supposedly, the mothers of old remained loyal to their husbands, even when they beat them and had affairs. These proper mothers allegedly persuaded their children to remain celibate until or unless they married, and dissuaded their gay children from expressing their sexuality or simply didn't have gay children at all. Most of all, through cooking, sewing, and comforting their husbands and children, the good mothers prevented men from having heart attacks and the children from rebelling.

Everyone remained content with his or her lot in life, and the family remained secure. Now all feminists do is think of themselves.

Paradoxically, the backlash idealizes the powers of women, viewing them as crosses between the universal Jewish mother and the Virgin Mary (or between the Buddhist Great Bliss Queen and the Hindu Kali). If only women wanted to make their husbands and children happy, they could do so. As the myth goes, social stability depends on the happy family, and the family depends on the self-sacrificing mother who keeps her feelings and needs to herself and draws her identity from providing for others. Feminism destroyed all that.

In the place of mothers and families, feminism brought us women. But women have periodically gained advantages over men and children. Perhaps it is no coincidence that shortly after the first great influenza pandemic in the fifteenth century in Europe, when women survived at a far greater rate than men or children, large numbers of women were burned at the stake as witches. Now women in the industrial world live longer than men. In places where abortions are legal, women can sometimes decide whether and when they will bear children. In some places, women can choose their own lives over those of potential children. But apparently some of those who hold philosophical positions exalting self-interest don't approve of it for women.

It should come as no surprise, then, that the backlash has been around almost as long as feminism and often takes the form of accusing women of causing "the decline of the family."

One could say that the family has been declining for as long as the bourgeoisie has been rising, but that would be to overlook how recently the family has come to be understood anywhere as one adult woman, one adult man, and an unspecified number of children. So, what is this thing called the family? In some places, many generations of kin live together. In other areas, brothers, their wives, and children share a household. In the Mediterranean countries in the late Middle Ages, abandoned women frequently lived together and raised their children without any outside help. In the mid-nineteenth century in Cornwall, England, when the mines ran out, many men migrated to the United States, formed new families, never sent money back for their old wives and children, and left women to raise children as best they could. (So what else is new?)

To enable men to stay at home and support their wives and children, the international labor movement fought for and won (until recently, and in some places) a "family" wage, which could support a man, a woman, and some children: hence the birth of the possibility for stable families among the working classes. Married women in these families could then afford to stay in the household, working an estimated one hundred hours a week without additional wages. Some women prospered, others led lives of quiet desperation, sometimes punctuated by domestic violence or death in childbirth. As Patrizia Romito stresses in this volume, even today, the death rate for women having legal abortions at any time in their pregnancy is eleven times lower than the rate for women in childbirth. Juliet Mitchell and Jack Goody also point out that common law, not marriage vows, accounted for half of all so-called marriages in eighteenth-century England. By the mid-nineteenth century, the poorest women in Great Britain frequently had children out of wedlock.

Families formed and reformed. One prevalent form of family among the poor was what then sociologist, now senator, Daniel Patrick Moynahan, called "the black family," single mothers raising children on their own, getting help wherever they can. All over the world, the rich have been able to afford retinues; the poor may always have needed a village to raise a child (as Hillary Clinton claims), but they didn't always have one.

Leaving aside those beset by battering and child abuse, families are generally regarded as good things, particularly in their capacity as the only remaining social institutions to mediate between the individual and the state. But do they? In Argentina during the Dirty War between 1976 and 1982, the government didn't respect families. They kidnapped and murdered children and other relatives, frequently raping them in front of family members. Then they called the mothers who sought their children *Locas* "crazy women." Had the mothers simply deferred to the government and disowned their children, they would have been "good" citizens and bad mothers. In fact, as we learn in this collection, governments often don't recognize separations between individuals, families, and the state, and feminists are themselves divided over whether laws—promoted by some—for the control of pornography or around child support, for example, would adversely affect other rights women have fought to achieve. Dissidents in Eastern Europe called for a civil society separate from the state, but in practice, they have wound up democratizing male control over women and robbing women of their universal citizenship, according to Peggy Watson's account in this volume. Even in Western Europe and North America, the family, especially those headed by single mothers or lesbian couples, seems to be powerless either to protect its members against the state or to make them feel confidence in the good will of governments toward them as individual citizens or members of families. The backlash says women—and particularly feminists—bear responsibility; these essays say something else is afoot.

Shifts worldwide since the recession of the early seventies have reduced the number of high-paying manufacturing jobs in all the industrialized countries, north and south. Increased employment of young women for low wages on the U.S.-Mexican border and in the factories of the emerging economic powers in Asia, part-time work for women in Europe, and high unemployment among the best-paid union workers in all the industrial countries coexist with reduction of government social services everywhere and have placed additional burdens on the one social institution to which people recall belonging: some sort of family. The inability of this one remaining institution to sustain whole communities (the subject of several essays in this book) in the face of governmental retreat has been blamed on bad mothers. And in the United States, poor mothers who try to fulfill traditional roles by remaining at home to care for their children are called Welfare Queens.

The essays in this book, whether they focus on child support, nationalism, reproductive rights, sexual preferences, or academic shenanigans, seem to converge on the fact that the backlash is all around us. But instead of lamenting this onslaught, the book shows that feminists have been fighting back in forceful and creative ways. And because the authors of the articles in this collection hold such varied views, this volume reveals again that feminism is anything but monolithic. What is conclusive here is that feminism is alive and well, free floating and free spirited, and never more so than in these essays.

Introduction to the American Edition

ANN OAKLEY AND JULIET MITCHELL

This book is the third in a series of collected essays we have edited together. The first was published in 1976, the second in 1986. The aim of the collections is to reflect on three decades of change, stabilization, or regression. The broad purpose of the book is to assess the cadences and sources of the one cultural saga through which we are now living—the political response to the voice of "second wave" feminism, which from the late 1960s through most of the 1970s asserted women's right to be liberated from the straightjacket of traditional gender stereotypes and social arrangements. We were, and (to a degree) still are, uncertain whether the "backlash" is against women or against feminism. Attacks on feminism frequently merge into a wider misogyny and the term *feminist* is the name now given to the disliked or despised woman, much as *man-hater, castrating bitch, harridan,* or *witch* were used before the advent of second wave feminism in the 1960s. As far as a backlash against feminism is a part of a more generalized misogyny, it is not surprising that feminism itself contains anti-feminism; varying degrees of misogyny are part of the general culture shared by women and men. The politics of feminism has to expose and eradicate the misogyny that is inherent within feminism itself. Yet this is a complex task in the time of a backlash. However, one must also wonder about the relationship of feminism and the backlash. Looking at a general history of women in the Western world—on both sides of the Atlantic—the alternations of feminism and the opposition to it seem to be pulsations of the same problematic: something pushing forward always encounters something pushing backward, so that feminism never achieves an ultimate goal but rather takes a rest after some successes until the backlash spurs it into action again.

There are, however, differences between the United States and Europe in the background to the present backlash and hence in the nature of the backlash itself. In the 1960s, few campaigners for women's rights and freedoms in the United States eschewed the term *feminism*, but in Europe there was considerable opposition and distrust of its use. This was not accidental. The main thrust of what was called, in various European languages, the *women's liberation movement*, (before it was the *women's movement*) was variously socialist. By and large, particularly after McCarthyism, America was innocent of a widespread socialist tradition and although there were, of course, important groups of socialist-feminists, they stood out against a very different background. The history of what was known as feminism was of women first and foremost, irrespective of other political practices. In Europe, as our perception of the strength of the opposition to women's liberation grew clearer and the sense of an unexplored history grew more startling, the term and the practice of feminism was adopted gradually. Nevertheless, the initial European resistance had an effect—both to the women and to the nature of the backlash on the two continents. The nature of feminism was more syntonic with dominant ideologies in America than it was in Europe. A country with a Bill of Rights and a committed individualism makes a space for change within those terms. An almost all-pervasive free-market mentality allows the free-enterprise of feminism. This is not to say that American feminism has had an easy ride at any level—Caroline Heilbrun's account of academia dispels any such notion—but rather that the United States offers an inclusiveness to feminism (or any movement). The individual's culture and the opposition to it share a common language: the language of power. Historically, socialist feminists in Europe were more concerned with how to think about women within class systems that within terms of power. By now, as with the concept and term *feminism*, *power* and *empowerment* are in general use by feminists. In this volume, Nira Yuval-Davis examines the concept of empowerment within a more global context. But the strength of the American emphasis on power has enabled a right-wing free-market feminism to prosper in a way that has not been possible—nor, we would strongly argue, desirable—in Europe. This means that something antagonistic to women, a political or social group, can lurk within the very walls that frame the feminist appeal. Margaret Walters shows how the difference between the overtly anti-feminist and the overtly feminist Paglia and MacKinnon translates as sameness. Here we will simply suggest that to be anti-women in Europe necessitates being anti-feminist; feminism in Europe is immune from anti-women positions.

For young women in Europe it is often difficult to ally themselves with feminism not because of a repudiation of its aims, nor simply because the backlash has made it hard to assume an opprobrious designation, but also because they may wish to advance women differently from the earlier generation. There has never been in Europe the same absolute confidence in feminism as there has been in the United States and this weakness has begotten weakness.

There is no one position maintained within this volume. In fact its range is, in a sense, its argument. The decade intervening since the last volume saw the successes and excesses of post-modernist analyses in which the only universal truth seemed to be that everything was different. This stance was in sharp contrast to the originating drive of feminism to find what was common. What this collection stresses is that there are, of course, aspects of oppression that women share, but there are also differences and these must be told from within. It is not enough for the observer to participate, the participant must observe—and part of that observation is for us as feminists to analyze the impasses of our own positions. In addition to Margaret Walter's essay on that theme, Peggy Watson looks at the conditions of incomprehension that confront feminists if they assume that former-communist countries have conditions of gendered citizenship similar to those of the Western democracies. It is important that we do not have feminism only in one country or on one continent. It is essential to comprehend the diversity of the experiences that women have.

This collection of essays focuses on the struggles of feminism during a period of backlash. The selection of topics represented in the essays reflects our interest in the general theme, but does not aim to include all relevant areas of concern. The project of this third collection is connected to those of the earlier two, but its distinctive differences also mark the impact of time on the framing of questions about women's position. When we edited *The Rights and Wrongs of Women,* in 1976, we saw the book as a response to the gap between the revolutionary practices of the women's liberation movement and the existence of academic texts from which women's voices were missing. There was little empirical evidence then on which to base "the case for or against feminism."[1] Ten years later, when we edited *What is Feminism?,* a substantial literature had accumulated. This included statistics on women's position and demonstrations of the ways in which the voices of women have been systematically silenced in the study of human culture.[2] But feminism itself had by then begun a period of discredidation as a political identity. Young women, in particular, doubted its relevance to them. Looking back, we can now see this moment as hovering on the edge of time. To borrow Marge Piercy's phrase, Could feminism be resuscitated (this was what we hoped *What Is Feminism?* might help to do) or were we doomed to winter a phase of unreconstructed reaction in which the moral right cast feminism as the evil responsible for (almost) all social ills?

The case against feminism is clearly more complex than that, as the essays in this volume testify. Just what the backlash is, where it comes from, and what it means can be partly judged by the chapters that follow. But most importantly, the backlash is itself a cultural construction. It is a moment in the long history of the relationship between personal identity and civil rights—the fabric of which economic production and social reproduction are woven. It is not peculiar to women's place, but can be found in the dialectic generated by many revolutionary movements. Having said that, there is also something unique in the counterpoint of today's arguments about feminism and women, for the whole subject of who women are and what they want challenges our division between public life and private life. Again there are important differences as well as similaries here among the continents. The tension between individual rights and social duties slants the problem: American women have a long history of rights to appeal to, but in Europe, although we have made marked progress with such institutions as the European Commissions and Equal Opportunities legislation, there seems to be an erosion of earlier notions of social duties without a commensurate gain in citizen's rights—especially for citizens in the margins. Agneta Stark shows how concerted action has enabled Swedish feminists not to renege on a concern with social responsibility. Their strategy is clearly dependent on the small and relatively homogeneous population, but this should not allow us to underestimate how it also results from a sustained sense of women as a collective entity and a refusal to let women drop back into the enclosure of the unpoliticized world.

The historical facility with which the division between the two spheres of public and private has been maintained owes much to the way in which political knowledge has excluded women's perspectives. In the first chapter, Carol Gilligan examines how the voices of women articulated by feminism and by a substantial body of research undertaken over the last thirty years, is both heard and not heard. She writes of women's double vision as insiders and outsiders, and of the phenomena of blind eyes and deaf ears, both of which are necessary to the exclusionary project. Applying the understandings developed in her research with adolescent girls. Gilligan sees the feminist movement as itself undergoing a relational crisis—in letting go of its past, it runs the risk of forgetting what it knows. But women are actively pursuing strategies to make sure this does not happen. Agneta Stark, in her chapter, provides an optimistic counterpoint with her description of a feminist network—the "Support Stockings"—aimed at promoting women's involvement in political decision-making. The war—if it is a war—is not easy to win, even in Sweden; in may places the backlash of media caricatures and counter-organizations (in Stark's example, the "Sports Socks") absorb a good deal of energy. It is the agents of the backlash rather than the injustices against women that can then become the focus.

To speak of the backlash against feminism implies a need, at least by exponents of the backlash, to counteract the power feminism has exercised in changing women's lives. Women's lives have changed, but the backlash is as much against the threat of change as it is a marker of transformations actually accomplished. There is, as Helen Haste has noted, an important difference between dissent and backlash. Dissent is disagreement but implies respect for the other position, or at least the acknowledgment that another position exists independently of the opposition to it. Backlash is primarily "a reactive position, defending something that is perceived either to have been lost, or to be under threat."[3] A backlash must formulate the case that it is oppositional; with respect to feminism, it must characterize feminism in a particular way in order to convince us of its basically misguided, damaging nature. In this, feminism becomes a kind of generic ragbag, a collection of subjectively perceived disruptive social elements. Nostalgia for a golden past of fixed (unequal) gender identities tends to prevail.[4] The time we live in is renamed *post-feminism*, implying both that feminism is a passe label, and that everything women could reasonably want has already been accomplished. Feminism—sometimes an aspect of it that really does or did exist, sometimes a fabrication dreamt up to explain our discontents—becomes the enemy, because the supposed disempowering of men is seen to have prevented the development of new masculinities which will replace the older repressive forms.

Has feminism changed women's lives? There are really two questions here, one about the extent and direction of change and one about its causes. Of course, the question we have to ask: which women? Judith Stacey (a contributor to *What Is Feminism?*) prefaces her study of the changing family in a Silicone Valley with a long account of how feminist demands have helped feminists (like herself) and hindered women (like many of those she was studying). It may be pertinent to recall that the period that saw the very beginnings of the women's liberation movement in Europe was a period of relatively high employment—as in so much else, we have followed America into serious unemployment and declining welfare services. In fact, America itself is reversing this trend and

INTRODUCTION

the backlash there has to be read against a relatively more optimistic general situation. In Europe, the statistics on women's gains reflect some of the weaknesses of feminism and the entrenchment of sexist discrimination in the context of rising unemployment. Nevertheless, while in many respects (such as the family change charted by Goody and Mitchell in this volume) we in Europe can use the American experience as a useful predictor it is also relevant for American feminists to see the slow pace of change in Europe as an index of difficulties that appear to have been overcome but which are in fact supremely vulnerable to the backlash. On both continents what second wave feminism attained through its fight for sexual rights is under attack. However, the moral right gives a particular emphasis to the American backlash on these issues so that the bedeviling of such social phenomenons as teenage motherhood has no real equivalent to the anxiety with which it is regarded in Europe. The right to choice in the matter of retaining or losing a fetus is under assault from right-wing fundamentalism in America as nowhere else. From a European perspective, the virulence seems staggering with anti-choice campaigners (the so-called "right-to-lifers") bombing abortion clinics. The case of *Roe v. Wade* in 1973 made abortion legal in the United States; it is used as an illustration of the problem of winning rights without a race and class struggle. It is now almost impossible for poor women to exercise the right to choice. Although the right to choice is certainly under attack in Europe, the opposition is not making much ground. Histories are uneven: it was in France that they carried out the last execution, in 1943, for offering a safe abortion. There is a lot to be learned from these differing experiences, as there is, of course, from more comparable ones. In other words, it is necessary for there to be an exchange of awareness between the two continents. The cover of a U.K. government report on women published in 1995, *Social Focus on Women*, shows a woman executive or secretary balancing a baby with a bottle in one arm and a bunch of office files in the other.[5] She wears a smart office suit and a smile fixed by a thick mask of makeup. The figures inside the report (and elsewhere) suggest an extent of change that is also cosmetic. In the United Kingdom, the

XXV

proportion of women in full-time paid work has remained static for several decades.[6] Women's earnings as a percentage of men's have been stable at about 56-60 percent for most of this century; a sharp rise followed the Equal Pay Act in 1970, but the trend had started to reverse by 1977.[7] One of the main processes underlying this tradition of difference is occupational segregation between men and women. Women tend to work in jobs and occupations dominated by women , and men in ones dominated by men. This segregation, dubbed the "central feature" of gender inequality in the world of paid work,[8] is strongly related to inequalities in pay, career prospects, and employment protection.

The United Kingdom is a world leader in the field of part-time work for women, described many years ago as a "false panacea for avoiding a more basic change in the relations between men and women."[9] Part-time work is five times as common among women as among men; twice as many men as women work full time.[10] Much of women's part-time work is "explained" by motherhood, whereas the opposite is true for men. Even though the number of children per woman has declined dramatically and the number of child-free women has risen, motherhood—actual or potential—is the single most cited "cause" of paid work inequality for women. Yet contraception and the right to (conditional) abortion have changed women's situation.

When the women's movement arouse in the 1960s, abortion was illegal in all Western European countries; divorce, contraception, and abortion were illegal in Italy. Second wave feminism fought for women's sexual and familial rights; the attainment of these rights is a main target of the backlash on both continents.

Italy provides an interesting case study of the backlash in relation to motherhood. Patrizia Romito's chapter explores the contradiction inherent in pro-motherhood feminism there. Italy now has one of the lowest birth-rates in the world (little over one child per couple), but is famous for its archetype Mediterranean motherhood. This offers an exemplary case study for feminists of the contradictions inherent in motherhood. "Difference" feminism—that is feminism which wants women valued for the ways in which they are different from men—has invested this maternal archetype with a new power, and may seem sometimes hardly distinguishable from the morality which deems as criminal both abortion and contraception. Social policies in Italy support motherhood and mothers' rights in a way they do not elsewhere. Although France is now considering "wages for motherhood" to combat the low birth rate. Romito's research shows that Italian women resist the self-sacrificial Madonna image by having paid work and liking it. This does not prevent both material and ideological attacks on "working mothers." There is a reasonable level of child care for infants and young children, but there seems to be a very widespread refusal of Italian men to lessen women's double burden of entire responsibility for the home while also engaging in paid work. As Romito shows, part-time work and extended parental leave are primarily strategies designed to lead women back into the family. They rationalize women's exploitation.

These features of women's position vary strikingly even across the older European democracies. In terms of women's earnings as a percentage of men's, Spain, Portugal, and the United Kinddom are at the bottom. Denmark leads with 85 percent. Female labor market actively rates are 44 percent in Italy and 77 percnet in Denmark.[11] The availability of publicly funded child care, which helps to explain these differences, varies from 2 percent to 44 percent of newborns through two-year-olds (with the United Kingdom providing the lowest and Denmark the highest) and from 44 percent to 95 percent of three- to five-year-olds (with the United Kingdom again at the bottom and France at the top).[12]

Research has shown that the effects of different social policies toward families and different welfare regimes are critical in explaining these social facts about women's position. American attempts at public welfare, such as Hillary Clinton's plans for public health care, have been failures—stones against a relentless tide of privatization and individualization that is the hallmark of contemporary capitalism. But European governments have also differed in their attitudes toward both public welfare and the private welfare that is mainly undertaken by women in families. Women's relationship to the state has also been very varied. For example, in Western, Northern, and Southern Europe, women's right to paid work has been conceptualized as a condition for their personal liberation whereas in Eastern Europe, women have seen work as an unquestioned duty to the state. Peggy Watson analyses the paradoxes of feminism for Eastern European countries. In the Nordic countries, it can be argued that women have moved from a private to a public dependency because of their modern relation to the state, whereas women in Eastern Europe are moving the other way.[13] A recent study of women and social policy in Europe concluded that the tensions in women's relation to the state have been greatest in Britain, where the government has promoted women's freedom to work, but also increased—and is continuing to increase—the burden of the unpaid care work they do.[14] Demographic factors are of immense importance; with the great rise in longevity, it often falls to women to be care takers of both their children and of their elderly parents. With smaller families there can be little or no sharing of tasks among siblings.

While the United States and Europe still differ in their overall relation to public welfare, they are more alike in the private sphere of care giving. If one of the myths about women's place in the post-feminist world is that women are out there working on the same terms as men, the other myth is the one about the domesticated man. Cross-cultural studies show an impressive resistance of men to an equal amount in domestic work. In China, Japan, Britain, and the United States, for example, core domestic tasks in dual earner households continue to be done mainly by women. In only 7 percent of Japanese households with two breadwinners, do men and women share house cleaning; the figure is 27 percent of households in Britain, 36 percent in the United States, and 39 percent in China.[15]

The conclusion of many studies of domestic work and gender demonstrate that men have not made great strides in this direction. The male contribution increases marginally when there are young children and/or women have full-time jobs; but there is no direct relationship between women's labor force participation and men's involvement in housework.[16] A common finding is the divergence between the actual sharing of household tasks and the declared belief that they ought to be shared This discrepancy between practice and ideology is paralleled by a consistent finding of many studies, which is that men are likely to say they do more in the home than women say they do.[17]

Feminism has been the target of the backlash because of certain general changes in women's lives in the Western world. It us hard to assess responsibility, of course, though some changes are clearly undesirable (whether or not others are depends on one's perspective). Feminism both initiated changes and also simply tried to put politics in command of a shifting economic situation. Some antifeminists ascribe the rising crime rate in the advanced world on the deracination of youth, which they contend has been brought about by women failing to play traditional roles of wife and mother. Interestingly, at a recent conference discussing the staggering rise in murders in Central and Latin America emphacized as the most likely cause the widening chasm between the top and bottom in free-market consumer economies. The lower 30 percent are likely not to simply fail to be employed but are born into the reality of crime rather than the illusion of work. In contexts where consumption—what one has—rather than work—what one does—is a definition of identity, crime rather than unemployment may be a relevant marker of deprivation. But that feminism, or any one factor, should be blamed for crime rates at all tells us more about the tactics of the backlash than it does about the actual situation. There are social changes in women's position but, by and large, it is too early to assess their significance in terms of more general effects. One general trend is that women in their early thirties are now more likely to give birth than those in their early twenties. Another is that the proportion of women remaining childless/child-free has increased steadily as has the number of single mothers. More women cohabit and marry later; more divorce and separate; and more women are bringing divorce suits. More women die of lung cancer than in 1971. Although the gender division in crime and mental health still exists, the number of women in post-compulsory education has increased at a faster rate than that for men. Yet educationally girls are doing better that boys at higher levels where once it was only at younger ages. This is usually presented as an alarming fact that boys are doing worse. They are not; girls are simply doing better than hitherto.

It is clear then that while such "facts" are irrefutable, their meaning and approximate causes may be less clear. Women, like men, are affected by long-term changes in the structure of employment and family life. This is the context for the particular social policy Juliet Mitchell and Jack Goody analyze in their chapter on the Child Support Agency (CSA) established by the British Government in 1991. The two authors use a particular child welfare provision precision as a case-study to look at larger changes. They are thus deploying the British experience in the context of the wider Western World—not only America and the rest of Europe, but Australia and New Zealand as well. The CSA offers a focal point for examining feminism and its effect on women's lives. The agency and its activities have been hailed as both pro- and anti-women. Whatever the extent of its impact on the material situation of mothers and fathers and the welfare of children—an intended object of the Act—there seems no doubt that women in general, and feminists in particular, have borne the blame for a wider social crisis.

The impact of feminist activity itself may be hard to hear against all this background noise. An example here is the effort to prove a positive impact on women's position of the 1970's equal opportunities legislation. Much tortuous statistical manipulation is required to establish a general effect on women's occupational status. Interestingly, the female-to-male earnings ratio does not seem to be affected, largely because of occupational gender segregation.[18]

The media noise that we do hear is a cannon of mixed messages. On the one hand, there are stories such as "Feminism has been such a disaster for women," calling it "a giant cancer that has dug its deem crab legs into every area of society"[19] and features on such topics as "The Descent of Man" which lists men's ailments in modern society ranging from having to share the labor market with women to not being allowed to share parenthood, from an increase in eating disorders to falling sperm counts caused by the "castrating" efforts of feminists or by too many female hormones in the water supply.[20] On the other hand, there is the constant recitation of discrimination: "Secret report condemns sex harassment by barristers"[21]; "Wider pay gap for women in top jobs"[22]; "Women in professions fighting sex war"[23]; "Male bias in TV news and sport attacked."[24] This is sometimes personalized in the language of victim blaming; for example, "Women still fail promotion race."[25]

It is the function of the media to make a drama out of a crisis, but feminism has contributed to the melodrama, as Margaret Walters contends in her analysis of the work of anti-feminist media star Camille Paglia and "feminist" Catherine MacKinnon. There is a backlash within feminism, as well as against it, which makes it hard, as Margaret Walters shows (and Gilligan warns), to hold onto the optimistic knowledge of 1960s and 1970s feminism. But the pro- and anti-backlash media stars both close down discussion by simplifying feminism's essential contradictions; the easier you make it seem, the more difficult advance will be. But Margaret Walter's chapter points to something more disturbing: to a misogyny inherent within certain forms of female success, to an exploitation of oppressive practices in the name of their overthrow. Media stars, feminist or anti-feminist, flourish by exploiting the media hallmark of over-sexualizing women so that anti-pornography trades on the rhetoric of pornography.

The daily onslaught of contradiction and ambiguity makes the project of this book especially relevant. In order to understand what is happening and what is being said, we must probe beneath the surface of media characterizations and fashionable hyperbole and dissect the structures of both commercial anti-feminism and commercial feminism. It is important to grasp how the ideological links are made between what has happened to women, and what is said to be happening to the family; between the voice of women and the construction of knowledge about them and the world; between "woman" as a mythic unitary category and the multiple social groups of women existing in different political regimes and cultural identities. As the chapters by Peggy Watson, Nira Yuval-Davis, and Parminder Bhachu detail, both feminism and the reaction against it represent specific cultural formations. As Peggy Watson points out, the rise of masculinism in Easter Europe can hardly be called an anti-feminist response because feminism itself was never itself claimed as a political identity by Eastern European women. Women are differently located in communist and democratic societies. Under communism, citizenship is not a function of difference, but the politicization of difference is crucial to the democratic project. Despite an earlier history of heroic struggles and gains for women's rights on all fronts both from within and against the state, the recent democratization of the Soviet bloc and its relationship to political practices within older democracies means that a newly divisive voice has entered the dialectic of gender relations. In Eastern Europe, pro-masculinism cannot be counted as a backlash until or unless feminism takes root there. And here again it may turn out to be feminism with another face.

Other contradictions inherent in the goals of anti-oppression politics are explored by Yuval-Davis, particularly with respect to the key notions of *empowerment* and *community* which may be used to homogenize and naturalize social categories and groupings. Advocating that we abandon the earlier feminist notion of a "universal" condition of womanhood in favor of a more "behavioral" one, and a notion of the "transversal" which inscribes variety at the center of unity, Yuval-Davis demonstrates how "identity politics" can deny differences between women in an unhelpful way. The argument that not all the forces hostile to feminism come from outside is developed by Parminder Bhachu, who shows how Asian women's cultural practices have existed independently of both feminism and the reaction against it. In anticipating a future for feminism, Bhachu argues that we need to develop a new kind of feminist politics which works at what women actively do in interpreting their lives and cultural locations, rather than sticking with a rhetoric which may then to oversimplify or ignore this all-important agenda of agency. It is interesting that previous book have not included analyses from minority groups despite lip-service being paid to their importance. One reading of the 1995 Beijing conference might suggest that ten years hence (if not before—indeed is it happening now?) women on the margins will have moved to the feminist center displacing white First World feminists both in their practices and theories.

An understanding of gender as the social construction of apparently natural sex differences was an essential analytic tool of second wave feminism. One of us (Ann Oakley) played a major role in the introduction of the concept of gender and the other (Juliet Mitchell) has been inclined to contest the term (arguing that feminine and masculine are relational terms dependent on sexuality; the terms *sexuality* and *sex* respect this, while gende r ignores it). Ann Oakley takes a critical look at dualism, which is often assigned to the conception of gender—may be as much of an inconvenience as the model of the two sexes the term *gender* was originally developed to contest. But, and most significantly, a major accomplishment of backlash rhetoric is the dismantling of gender. Women can be successfully returned to the home once gender differences are re-naturalized, and women are re-burdened with their traditional role as carriers of the moral order. For what the backlash most of all demands is a return to naive masculinist understandings of women's place. Thus, and unsurprisingly, the moral right's achievement in condemning homosexuality in both men and women is accomplished by returning it to the world of "unnatural" deviation in which it started, as Joanna Ryan argues in her contribution. Joanna Ryan criticizes the practice of psychoanalysis for its attitude to lesbian motherhood. The lesbian mother or couple does not fit the central tenet of psychoanalysis which emphasizes the importance of fantasies about the primal scene of a female mother and male father.

Attacks on Freud and psychoanalysis were de rigueur in the first writings of second wave feminism. Indeed, one could almost say that feminism first carved out a place for its analysis of women's psychology and sexuality by using its opposition to psychoanalysis as its defining boundaries. This changed later to a more positive use of psychoanalysis, so that in America, France, Italy, and, to a somewhat lesser extent, Britain and Spain, a feminist re-reading of Freud produced a major contribution to understanding femininity and its representations. But the exercise of redeploying psychoanalysis to chart the central terrain of difference between femininity and masculinity produced new margins. Joanna Ryan argues that so long as psychoanalysis excludes diverse forms of parenting, it can be used to defend traditional nuclear families, and anti-feminist forms of exploitation.

From the outset lesbianism was an important vanguard of feminist positions, particularly in the United States. But a political program does not protect a personal experience. Writing from within the American context, Susan Heath recounts what it is like to live on or move across the divide of a heterosexual position and lesbian position—to shift from the hegemonic center of white middle-class wife and mother to the edges of lesbian partnership when the revolutionary heyday has passed and the revolutionary future seems reluctant to arrive. Addressing not only the backlash by the reactionary common-sense assumptions of heterosexual unity—"heterosexuality." Women (and men) can move between other-sex and same-sex relationships and object choices and subjecthood are not cast in stone.

The chapters of *Who's Afraid of Feminism?* celebrate the continued diversity of women's writing on women. Two have the particular personal perspective that was initiated by second wave feminism: Susan Heath's on the comforts and discomforts of living as a lesbian with the accelerating influence of the homophobia of the moral right, and Carolyn Heilbrun's on the romance of women's relationships with literature suffering the insults of masculinist academia—or "the tree house gang" as she calls it. Heilbrun's experience of institutional sexism is paralleled by many other cases.[26] Her account of how female sexuality is seen and abused in the male dominated academe is the material of which many sex discrimination cases are made,[27] and even more not made, because of the institutional structures that prevent women being able to take themselves seriously.

We hope that this collection of essays will make a contribution to the debate about how culture and knowledge and the social structures that carry these can be made more representative of the polarities and involvements of both sexes' experiences. Predictably, the backlash has made use of feminist understandings of differences between women and men to attack feminism. Women are socially and psychologically constructed as different, but their difference has been systematically opposed. This difference needs to be rescued from its social oppression and psychological repression; women's values must be given an equal voice; women must be allowed to know what they know. The backlash wants women's and men's differences to be fixed, unchanging entities; feminism wants women's values to affect men's as men's have affected women's. This will always be an historically specific task. The danger is that both the backlash and feminism come to speak each other's language; wherever and whenever this happens, the language is one that takes women and men out of the social context within which they relate to each other. This collection has inevitably selected some specific contexts and omitted others, but its overall intention is not simply to be a voice against the backlash but rather a sharing of feminism's successes and failures from different experiences and standpoints. It is during a backlash that we urgently need to know other experiences than our own; an ignorance of these fuels the opposition just as it weakens the struggle. The emphasis in this book on context is intended to contribute to disentangling feminism from the backlash that depends on it.

To a certain extent, because the backlash of the Western world is the topic of this collection, there is a sense of pervasive anxiety in a number of chapters. It would, however, be false both to personal experience and to a wider global and historical analysis to allow the backlash to dictate a note of pessimism. In a recent collection of essays that had nothing to do with feminism, the editor, a highly respected senior psychologist, concluded with the reflection that the judgment of history would probably award the laurels of the greatest important movement of the twentieth century to the women's movement. Who knows? It is nevertheless pleasing when such assessments come from outside. From within, we only have to reflect on the United Nations Conferences on Women that have run parallel with these volumes: Mexico City in 1975, Copenhagen in 1980, Nairobi in 1985, and, above all, the NGO that met at the same time as the official congress in Beijing, 1995. While we face a backlash in the old worlds, women from the new worlds are on the move.

Notes

INTRODUCTION

1. J. Mitchell and A. Oakley (1976). *The Rights and Wrongs of Women*. Harmondsworth, Penguin, p. 7.
2. J. Mitchell and A. Oakley (1986). *What Is Feminism?* Oxford, Basil Blackwell.
3. H. Haste (1993). *The Sexual Metaphor*. Hemel Hempstead, Harvester Wheatsheaf, p. 267.
4. J. Doane and D. Hodges (1987). *Nostalgia and Sexual Difference*. New York, Methuen.
5. Central Statistical Office (1995). *Social Focus on Women*. London, H.M.S.O.
6. N. Stockman, N. Bonney and S. Xuewen (1995). *Women's Work in East and West*. London, UCL Press, p. 81.
7. B. Bagihole (1994). *Women, Work and Equal Opportunity*. Aldershot, Hants., Avebury, p. 1.
8. A. M. Scott (ed.) (1994). *Gender Segregation and Social Change*. Oxford, Oxford University Press, p. 32.
9. A. S. Rossi (1965). Barriers to the career choice of engineering, medicine or science among American women. In J. A. Mattfield and C.G. van Aken (eds). *Women and the Scientific Professions*. Cambridge, MIT Press, p. 53.
10. Central Statistical Office, op. cit., p. 25.
11. J. Lewis (ed.) (1993). *Women and Social Policies in Europe*. Aldershot, Hants., Edward Elgar.

12. Ibid.
13. N. Lykke, A-B Ravin, and B. Sim (1994). Images from women in a changing Europe. *Women's Studies International Forum.* 17(2/3): 111–116.
14. Lewis, op. cit.
15. Stockman et al., op. cit., p. 107.
16. D. Dahlerup (1994). Learning to live with the state—state, market and civil society: Women's need for state intervention in East and West. *Women's Studies International Forum.* 17(2/3): 117–127.
17. Central Statistical Office, op. cit.
18. S. Dex and R. Sewell (1995). Equal opportunities policies and women's labor market status in industrialized countries. In J. Humphries and J. Rubery (eds.). *The Economics of Equal Opportunities.* Manchester, Equal Opportunities Commission.
19. *Daily Mail,* 5.2.96.
20. *Independent,* 17.6.96.
21. *Guardian,* 4.5.95.
22. *Independent,* 23.9.93.
23. *Independent,* 14.11.94.
24. *Independent,* 3.3.95.
25. *Independent,* 17.10.94.
26. See, e.g., W. Savage (1986). *A Savage Enquiry: Who Controls Childbirth?* London, Virago.
27. Equal Opportunities Commission (1989). *Towards Equality: A Casebook of on Sex and Equal Pay, 1976-1988.* Manchester, Equal Opportunities Commission.

Who's Afraid of Feminism?

I

Getting Civilized[1]

CAROL GILLIGAN

In the autumn of 1991, the house across the street from mine was being painted, and the painters brought their radio to work each day, placing it alongside them on the scaffold. At the time, the United States Senate Judiciary Committee, acting under pressure, had called Professor Anita Hill to testify about the nomination of Clarence Thomas for Supreme Court Justice.[2] The radio was turned up and Anita Hill's voice was riveting. The calm, steady sound of her speaking flowed through everyone's life like a river. And then her voice was filtered through the responses of the senators and their expert witnesses. I remembered the two-step process of listening to Anita Hill – hearing her, and then hearing her not being heard.

At the time I began writing my book *In a Different Voice*,[3] twenty years ago, women's voices were conspicuously missing from the psychology that I was teaching. Or rather, women's voices were inconspicuously missing. The inconspicuousness of an omission so huge as to be monumental led me to write. Like clowns looking for elephants under cars, psychologists were saying that we do not know about women, do not know what women want or how women feel, cannot understand what women mean, or follow the logic of women's thought.[4] Something was clearly askew. A societal and cultural disconnection was being maintained by a psychological dissociation. Thus, when *In a Different Voice* was

13

published, broadcasting women's voices into a world half-composed of women, and changing the interpretative framework from one that highlighted separation to one that picked up connections, the response was astonishing. In many ways, it replicated the process that I went through over and over again in the course of my writing: hearing something, and then not hearing it; understanding, and then becoming confused. Because the problem – the disconnection from women on the part of both women and men – was at the centre of people's lives and relationships. It was built into the world in which we were living. It was/is at the heart of patriarchy or civilization.

But it is not the same problem for women and men. Men's psychological disconnection from women has been built into the cultural framework, and called the separation of 'the self' from 'relationships'. For women to separate their sense of self from women requires a psychological process of dissociation – the creation of an inner chasm or split within oneself. This dissociation has been the psychological price for women entering patriarchy.

Shortly after *In a Different Voice* was published, I went into the local store to get coffee. The woman behind the counter asked if I was the one who wrote 'that book'. 'You have explained my marriage,' she said. On the street one day, I was stopped by a newspaper editor. He said that I had explained his divorce. Women from India wrote to thank me, in essence for providing a resonance, making it easier for them to hear themselves against the noise of their education. I received similar letters from women throughout the United States; often people called on the phone. A General Practitioner from England wrote an elegantly hand-written letter saying that now he understood his practice. I say all this because these strong resonances in the lives of what in the university world are often called 'real people' led to a defence of the very framework – the theories and the methods – which my work called into question. How could I say that women's and men's lives or voices were different? What was my sample? How could I be objective? What were my methods? I found these questions astonishing, not because they were invalid, but because they again ignored the huge methodological error with which I began: leaving out women from studies of humans. Theories of adult development were based on studies which included no women. Girls were missing from studies of adolescence.[5] Men's and boys' lives had served as the basis for theories of identity, morality, creativity, motivation and, most ironically, 'social perspective-taking'.[6] Yet, women were consuming this psychology, taking it into themselves and their lives. These studies of humans, which included no girls or women, were passing what were said to be the most stringent and objective processes of peer and editorial review.[7] They were lavishly funded and published in the most prestigious journals. In the process, they were passing the scrutiny of both women and men.

This, in one sense, explains how it was possible for therapists to spend hour after hour with women and men in psychotherapy or psychoanalysis, focusing on family relationships, and still not know about the incidence of incest or the prevalence of domestic violence, now deemed epidemic in US society by the conservative American Medical Association.[8] The field of psychology, in its research and clinical practices, was seriously disconnected from reality, and women's voices were revealing the disconnection. The question of difference in women's voices became so contentious in part for this reason. If women's voices are no different from men's, then leaving out women is no problem. If women's voices are different from men's, then listening to women will change the voice which we hear and name as human.

This has become most acutely clear in the current debates about sexual abuse and trauma. The women who have spoken or written about their experiences of violation have been followed by men speaking out as well.[9] A voice that had sounded 'unmanly' in revealing vulnerability and connecting feelings with thoughts – self with relationships – began instead to sound simply human. The psychological dimensions of knowing became more apparent, and the understanding of relationships consequently changed.

But hope is perhaps the most dangerous emotion, because it creates such vulnerability to disappointment and despair. In psychotherapy people often turn back just at the point where they can see the possibility of something new. This may be true in politics as well. Faced with the new, people often feel the pull of the familiar. The old acts as a beacon leading back into a world where even the worst at least is known. When women's voices revealed that psychology was disconnected from reality, a backlash was inevitable, especially as the outlines of the 'new' psychology and the sounds of a different voice became clearer. To understand that research on knowing previously did not include women is one thing. To say that women's ways of knowing change our understanding of knowing and knowledge is more difficult to accept.[10] Yet, if the second sentence is not true, the first is inconsequential. To say that mothers are not 'objects', but people with voices, feelings and thoughts is one thing. To say that maternal thinking offers a key to the politics of peace is another.[11] To say that the culture of violence is for the most part a men's culture, and that men are the main perpetrators of violence against women and men, is to say something that is historically true. And yet at a time when newspapers were filled with reports of men killing men and raping women in Bosnia, the *Nation* ran a cover story in which Katha Pollit took exception to those women who said or implied that women were less violent or more non-violent than men.[12]

What is going on here? At best, objections to the focus on evidence of gender differences represents an appreciation of the difference – the complexity and variability, the psychological, cultural and historical specificity of human lives. Statements about women or men readily admit exceptions, and findings of sex differences have been used to justify injustice or oppression, or to minimize the effects of societal and cultural forces. At worst, attacks on those who bring news of difference are an example of 'killing the messenger'.

Unless 'equality feminism'[13] joins with 'difference feminism',[14] being equal means being like men. That women can think like men and can fight like men is undoubtedly true, given the instruction women receive in men's ways of knowing and men's practices. For men to think and act like women, men need to know what women want, how women feel, how women know and what women do. Just as the Renaissance and the Reformation reconnected European cultures with their origins in ancient Greece, North Africa and south-western Asia, and by doing so changed the social construction of authority and belief, so the present moment holds the potential for a similar reconnection on a psychological level – a reconnection with women on the part of both women and men that will change the social construction of love and work.

Currently, there is serious controversy in the universities about the foundations of knowledge. What is truth? How is truth established? What is taken as evidence that something actually happened – like the Holocaust or the Middle Passage or an incestuous act? How can the effects of actions be determined? Can one know another person or oneself? What are the channels connecting inner and outer worlds? Less abstractedly, this controversy is about voice and relationship. Who is speaking to whom? Who is being heard by whom? What is the relationship of the voice to the body – is the voice not part of the body, part of the physical world of breath and sound, vibrations and resonance? What is the relationship between voice and culture – is the voice not in language and culture, carrying its sounds, rhythms, intonations, syntax and words?

In contrast to those who ask whether psychological differences are a function of nature or nurture, I have chosen to speak of voice because this reveals a psyche in connection with both the natural and the social world. Listening to voice reveals the relation of the person speaking to what is being said, because voice carries the tell-tale signs of where a person is in relation to what he or she, or she/he, is saying. The resonances, or lack of resonances, reveal the societal and cultural frameworks, and also the connections or disconnections of the voice with breath or sound. The 'talking cure' is potentially radical because it offers a way of addressing the problems of relationship and difference which have now become so pressing and acute.

The creation of a new psychology seems an inevitable response to the discovery of the problems in the old, and yet, the old goes on. The new psychology is a relational psychology, because the old psychology was out of relationship – with women, with people of colour, with gays and lesbians, with the world. Its dynamic was about separation: how to achieve and maintain a separate self.[15] Ironically, in separating powerful men from those with less power, and thus maintaining existing power relationships, it also separated men from their bodies, their families, their communities – or in short, from large parts of themselves.

I have chosen to speak of voice rather than talk about 'the self' because voice is an instrument of relationship. The self, in contrast, is an image characterized by borders and boundaries. The move from a visual to an auditory discourse leads to the construction of a more fluid or relational psychology – a psychology that is intrinsically in relation with physical and social/cultural realities, and yet which has a dynamic of its own. Just as women's voices reveal that men are not in fact separate or independent, that we do not live alone, gender studies and gay and lesbian studies make it clear that male and female are more limited categories than they have sometimes seemed. Just as women and men are of women born, so neither sex reproduces itself; both sexes contain and infuse one another, much in the way people's voices flow in and out of one another, carrying psychology and also culture, mixing inner and outer worlds.

The cultural meanings of 'masculinity' and 'femininity' are socially constructed and far more changeable than they may seem at any given time. The psychology of gender is only beginning to be developed,[16] but its development depends on learning from women as well as from men, and also from people who define themselves outside of these oppositional categories. Again, the problem of difference returns. Despite Deborah Tannen's even-handed book, *You Just Don't Understand*,[17] which equalizes mis-understanding between women and men, most women are schooled in understanding men and live under threat if they do not do so. The converse is not true for men. Or at least it was not until Anita Hill. Anita Hill was the Rosa Parks of 1990s feminism in waking people from their dogmatic slumber, as Kant said about Hume. Kant's *Critique of Pure Reason*[18] has an analogue in the feminist critique of pure knowledge. Kant said that we cannot know things in and of themselves, apart from our perceptions and categories.[19] We can only know through our experience of the world – we cannot know through reason alone.[20] The feminist critique is that we know in relationship – that we cannot know apart from relationship. It is a profoundly psychological point.[21]

One reason why the subjects of race and gender, and class and sexuality, have now become so loud is that they all affect relationships. Unvoiced, they act like a slow burn. Voiced, they bring conflict into the open, where it can be talked about and seen. A relational psychology is a talking/listening cure. The greatest difficulty is finding a way to speak that does not silence others by insult, by violation, by the threat or the use of force. The search for such a way explains some of the cacophony of this time, including the fight over political correctness. The image of feminists taking over the universities is so far from any reality that I have seen that the threat must be reinterpreted in other terms – as a change in voice which goes to the very foundations of knowledge and affects the structure of teaching and learning relationships.

Freud's famous summation of the goal of psychoanalysis – 'where *it* was, there shall *I* be'[22] – now applies on a societal and cultural scale, as women move out of objectification and into voice. Major contributions to this societal and cultural shift have been made by those who have taken the lead in bringing in women's voices, including: Mary Belenky, Blythe Clinchy, Nancy Goldberger and Jill Tarule, the authors of *Women's Ways of Knowing*;[23] Dana Jack, the author of *Silencing the Self – Women and Depression*;[24] Sara Ruddick, the author of *Maternal Thinking: Toward a Politics of Peace*;[25] and Jane Roland Martin, the author of *Reclaiming a Conversation*.[26] My list is not intended as exhaustive, but rather as illustrative of radical theoretical moves that follow from bringing women's voices in the fields of psychology, politics and education. An especially long list could be made in the area of law and legal thinking, where there is such a large, growing literature. Our ability now to hear a greater range of women's voices, and to hear these voices more clearly, is profoundly indebted also to poets, novelists and dramatists, to the many women who have spoken courageously about their lives, and to the scholars responsible for the current recovery of women's history and women's writing, which tends to be buried with sobering regularity in each generational break.

A relational restructuring of psychology changes the practices of both research and psychotherapy so as to prevent the separations which underlie disconnection and dissociation. The work of Jean Baker Miller and her colleagues at the Stone Center at Wellesley College, and the work which I have done with my colleagues on the Harvard Project,[27] provide the outlines of a new theory of psychological development. This work has been grounded in listening to women and learning from women about what previously was silenced. Judith Herman and her colleagues on the Victims of Violence Project at Cambridge Hospital[28] have broken the silence of dissociation which surrounds what many women and men otherwise know. It is striking to me, in retrospect, to realize that incest, domestic violence, rape and other forms of sexual violence were never mentioned in research or theories about moral development. The gap between hypothetical ethical dilemmas and real human problems has never seemed more huge, or the absence of women more telling.

In the course of our research, Jean Baker Miller and I came to essentially the same formulation of a central paradox in women's psychology: that girls and women, in their efforts to make and maintain relationships, take large parts of themselves out of relationship. This research is situated historically and culturally, but its claim to generality rests on the ubiquity of patriarchal societies and cultures. A key observation, made in clinical research and educational settings, is that women often keep out of relationships those parts of themselves which they most want to bring into relationships – their voice, their creativity, their brilliance, their vitality. The move out of relationships is thus, in part, a protective move designed to preserve from invalidation or attack those parts of themselves which women feel are most essential to preserve, which they most love and value. One of the most startling discoveries of the Harvard Project research was that girls, at adolescence, describe the relational impasse which forces dissociation: that if they speak they will lose relationships, but if they do not speak, they will also lose relationship.[29] Consequently some compromise between voice and relationship is struck. Girls' awareness at the time of dissociation of what they are doing and why they are doing it reveals an effort on girls' part not to lose relationship. Underlying this effort is a profound optimism that constitutes hope in the face of despair – a belief that someday things will change for the better. This vision of relationship goes against the course of culturally inscribed voices that deny the possibility of human connection, and this hope – that someday, if one keeps part of oneself out of relationship, it will be possible to bring it into relationship – may explain women's surprising resilience in the face of loss.

The understanding of dissociation as a common feature of the psychology of women living in patriarchal settings leads to a reformulation of hysteria or borderline personality syndromes, or multiple personality, as extreme manifestations of what is commonplace in many women's lives. Girls and women who participated in the Harvard Project research tended to mark dissociation verbally by saying, 'I don't know.' Because the research was longitudinal and involved clinical interviews, it was possible to observe, both over time and within the time of a given interview session, how girls and women come not to know what they have demonstrably known. Instead of signifying ignorance or humility, the phrase 'I don't know' often signified knowledge – that is, thoughts and feelings which girls were covering over. Pressed slightly, the cover opened to reveal what they knew about the human world in which they were living – their families, their schools, their communities and the larger worlds of sexuality and politics which they were entering as young women and seeing, in some sense, for the first time. Girls and women know, we were astonished to discover, a human world which is said to be unknowable. And then they 'don't know'. An obvious question is whether boys and men know as well.

Conversations between girls and women often become volatile at the precipice of adolescence, when girls become acutely concerned with what women know. The contrapuntal phrase 'you know' was often used by girls at this time as a way of taking relational soundings, or testing the depths at which it is possible for them to speak without losing connection with women, or silencing parts of themselves. Spoken half in the form of a question, the tag-phrase 'you know?' is one way girls assess what they can say in relationships without losing their sense of psychological balance or jeopardizing their sense of what is real or true. In the course of our work with girls and women, I found myself thinking about political resistance as I observed the struggle on girls' part to maintain relationships in the face of physical and psychological threat. As I watched girls continuing to speak what they were feeling and thinking, and to talk about what they were seeing and hearing when it went against the grain of what was socially constructed or generally accepted as true, I conceptualized a healthy resistance – that is a kind of psychological immunity – coming into tension with the maintenance of the *status quo*. Many of the girls whom I came to think of as political resisters were girls for whom difference was doubled in the way that Carolyn Heilbrun[30] described as protective – a kind of double-waterproofing against the dangers of drowning psychologically in patriarchy. Girls who could not fit themselves into culturally monitored ideals of womanhood – of female beauty, of sexual purity or of feminine goodness – by virtue of their race or class or sexuality or culture, were in some sense protected from the deforming effects of the patriarchy's images and ideals.

This was especially true for girls who had close, confiding relationships with women – most often, but not necessarily, their mothers.[31] In our studies, there were girls for whom trauma had left a shard of bitterness and a resistance which combined clear-sighted descriptions of hypocrisy and brittleness in others with a vulnerability that was painful to witness because it was so unprotected. Such girls often showed an acute sensitivity to relational realities, and they often were in real danger.

The reality of violence and violation in girls' and women's lives has generated a discourse of survivor and victim which many people find offensive because it implies a comparison which often is not developed: between domestic violence and political violence, between incest and murder, between racism and genocide, between living in late-twentieth-century America and living in a concentration camp or a slave plantation. Judith Herman, following Elaine Showalter, has explored the connections between the trauma of women who have suffered at home and the trauma that men suffer in war. In *Trauma and Recovery*,[32] Herman connects women's experience of domestic violence with soldiers' accounts of the battlefield and studies of post-traumatic stress in veterans. While at first sight the situation of women seems less dire, the very dailiness of their experience and the seeming ordinariness of the surroundings in which the attacks are happening, together with the mixing of love and violence, make women's and girls' experiences in some ways more confusing and terrifying, because they can leave the impression that there is no place or no one with whom they can be safe.

The sense of division which is prevalent now in many areas of the human and social sciences comes from the fact that there is real disagreement, not about interpretation, but about reality. Thus people are speaking and writing about different worlds. The experience of double-vision, which W. E. B. DuBois described as necessary for blacks living in white America, is also common among women living in patriarchy.[33] In the course of our research on women's psychological development, we have heard girls doubling their voices as they became young women, and we witnessed the development of a dizzying double- or triple-vision in the face of disparities that seemed to the girls impossible to reconcile between what was felt to be happening and what was said to be happening, what seemed real and what was socially constructed or institutionalized as 'reality'. For privileged white women who are the daughters and wives and mothers of privileged white men, this double-vision often turns into seeing double because they are standing so close.

Virginia Woolf saw the daughters of educated men as the vanguard – like Marx's vanguard of the proletariat – because they are at once inside and outside of patriarchal structures.[34] Woolf saw this as the group that had the means to get in, which then raises the persisting question: once in, can women keep their double voice and vision? Ellen Snee studied women who were at the top of institutional structures and in positions of leadership with, or over, other women.[35] In her research, she documents the strain women experience when they are continually seeing double and speaking in different voices.[36] The brilliance of her conceptualization of these women's psychological situation is caught in her metaphorical use of the phenomenon of 'blind eye' – when the eyes do not focus, one eye goes blind, if it is not patched, in order to preserve the ability to see. Snee documents this tendency towards monocular vision among women in positions of authority with women. In her interviews, she heard the same contrapuntal phrases, 'I don't know' and 'you know', that marked relational crises and dissociative moves among girls at adolescence. She also found these same words used by women in the midst of marital crises.[37]

The experience of double-vision or double-hearing and the phenomenon of blind-eye and deaf-ear have spread through US society in response to a series of relational crises which have now become full-scale societal drama. Listening to Anita Hill and then listening to the senators and their expert witnesses was a revelation for many people at the time. 'They just don't get it,' people said to one another in amazement, as they heard experiences familiar to many women being talked about in ways that sounded truly bizarre. There was real disagreement among women about Anita Hill, as there is at present about almost every aspect of women's and men's changing lives. But there was enough consensus about the need for more women in the Senate to influence election results, and for the first time women's votes elected the President. Women's voices are now entering the public world with effect. Emily's List,[38] Take Our Daughters to Work,[39] and the Company of Women[40] are among many creative efforts to make this process explicit and carry it across generations.

24

The feminist movement in the United States has reached a moment of relational crisis. If we use the map which illuminates the paradox of going out of relationship in order to keep relationships, some sense can be made of the fears and attacks which are being joined in feminist circles. In some sense the feminist movement has come of age. Like girls at the point where they are mature enough and have the words enough to actually articulate the difference between what they know from experience and what is said to be true in the world which they are about to enter into as young women, like people in psychotherapy who move to psychological breakthrough, the feminist movement has reached a moment of potentially transforming a patriarchal world. And it is at this very moment that girls get silenced or silence themselves, that people in therapy tend to retreat and retract, that the feminist movement is beset by internal fighting and attacks from outside. How do we keep our relationships with the power structures of the world and also stay in relationship with one another and ourselves?

In this sense, the feminist movement has come of age and faces the paradoxical tension between voice and relationship that leads girls to let go of the truth of their past and begin not to know what they know. Relationships among women are crucial at such times, and the scenes of love and betrayal that are played out among women in a variety of arenas indicate the potential and the volatility of this moment as a turning point in women's lives, in the feminist movement, and in the history of patriarchy.

From my experience with girls, I do not find the current conflicts, differences and disagreements among women troubling in themselves. For girls, such bad weather is as much part of relationship as the good. But for women, and especially women like myself, who live with men and work in men's institutions, relational conflict among women becomes alarming when it provides the rationale for stopping or undoing a process of radical change. It threatens to shut women out just when women are getting in, and, more pernicious, because less obvious, it threatens at the very moment when women are finding their voices to shut women up by reimposing the voices of the disciplines – the old patriarchal voices which are well-known to all natural and adopted daughters of educated men.

The publication of *Meeting at the Crossroads*[41] supports a different voice in the culture by encouraging women and girls to speak and listen to each other at the very moment when girls resist not knowing what they know – before the onset of dissociation and the appearance of psychological symptoms. Reviews of the book initially stressed the revolutionary potential in this meeting to prevent or undo disconnections and dissociations that have felt necessary or been taken as inevitable. These reviews, however, were rapidly followed by a series of articles which renewed the stress on similarities between women and men, specifically countering the evidence and significance of differences. During the year following the publication of *Meeting at the Crossroads, In a Different Voice* became the centrepiece for an attack on difference feminism. An attempt was made to distort or forget (in a process that has a remarkable parallel in the girls' not knowing) the context and history behind *In a Different Voice*, and in turn undermine an entire intellectual movement. Finding my work labelled 'pious maternalism' by Wendy Kaminer in the *Atlantic*,[42] or hearing the 'different voice' more generally associated with the voice of the Victorian 'angel in the house',[43] I saw the extent of the dissociation. Hearing these descriptions of my work, you would never guess that the two central chapters of *In a Different Voice* are about women considering and for the most part having abortions in the years immediately following Roe v. Wade.[44] The phrase 'pious maternalism' reminded me of pious Aeneas, who becomes savage Aeneas in Virgil's epic[45] as he moves towards fulfilling his mission of founding Rome. And I wondered, are some contemporary feminists becoming savage for similar reasons?

Maybe cynicism is easier than hope, maybe attack is safer than relationship – a better raincoat against the weather of disappointment and loss. Following the elections of 1992, the American climate looks hopeful. There were seven women in the Senate, thanks in part to Anita Hill.[46] We had a President who was raised by an unconventional mother, who defended his mother against a step-father's violence and who has presented a different image of marriage by giving his wife a central and public voice in his administration. The process of decision-making currently being followed is one of open conversation and discussion. It is called indecisive and naïve, in much the same way that I remember from people's comments about eleven-year-old Amy in *In a Different Voice*, who also thought that talking is a good way to solve entrenched and difficult problems – that it opens up the possibility of arriving at something new, a solution that was not imagined when the conversation began. The world, I thought, may be coming around to Amy.

Clarence Thomas is sitting on the Supreme Court, while Anita Hill continues to be attacked. African-American studies are flourishing at Harvard, while women's studies remain a poor sister. It is as if there is a contest between race and gender, so that the one must win out at the other's expense. 'Whose construction is this?' I wondered. 'Whose interest does this serve?' In reality, the two issues are intertwined: you cannot speak about one – race or gender – without talking about the other, as the situation of black women makes plain. Both race and gender imply radical changes in the ways in which we live with one another; both go beyond the righting of past atrocity or injustice to the very fundament of life: the way we live with others who are different, the way we live with one another in private as well as in public life. Is this in part the power and the threat of black women – that they challenge this retrograde splitting of race and gender, that they hold both cards?

In Toni Morrison's novel *The Bluest Eye*,[47] two girls set out to take things into their own hands and change the course of events. At the beginning of this novel, which focuses on father–daughter incest and racism, the narrator says that her question is not *why* things happen in the way things do, but *how*.[48] 'Why is difficult to handle,' she explains.[49] But to explain the 'how' of black women's development reveals an opening for a profound cultural transformation. 'How' is the naturalist's question, and also the novelist's question. It is deeply scientific and creative. To understand how something happens may point to how it could *not* happen. The growing body of work on women's psychological development, when joined with the burgeoning knowledge about race and gender, has opened to our inspection a central paradox of human development: the tendency to give up relationship for the sake of having 'relationships'. This paradox explains how psychological health, which depends on relationship, comes into tension with the reproduction of patriarchal and racist societies and cultures, which depend on disconnection and dissociation.

We come now to the framing of the next question: what if girls and women of all races and cultures do not give up relationship for the sake of 'relationships'? What if their resistance is joined? What if relationships are formed so that young women do not face the impasse of choosing between voice and relationship, or facing political, psychological and physical attack – or, at least, do not face it alone? It seems a safe bet that there would be a sharp drop in depression, eating disorders, suicide attempts – all of which rise precipitously among girls in adolescence. It is predictable that what is happening now should be happening: that relationships between women and men are becoming, at least temporarily, more turbulent and more resonant, that education is becoming more vital and more hotly contested, that more women are doing creative work, and that the vision of a transformed society and culture that has hovered around feminism from *Lysistrata*[50] to *Three Guineas*[51] is beginning to turn into a reality as more women use their voices and their votes to bring about political and economic change.

The world will change as everyone 'gets it' – that women are half the population in every generation, and that undoing men's disconnection from women and women's dissociation from themselves does mean the end of patriarchy and the beginning of something which we have barely imagined – something that wholeheartedly could be called Civilization.

2

A Brief History of Gender

ANN OAKLEY

Whereas first-wave feminism focused on the question of women's civil and legal rights, second-wave feminism is distinguished for taking up the challenge contained in Simone de Beauvoir's famous assertion that women are not born, but made. But if women are made, *how* are they made? What are the cultural processes and contexts which produce femininity and masculinity as social forms? The answer to this question demanded a way of separating the bodies of human beings from their social fates. This was how the idea of 'gender' as a cultural product came to be an essential tool of modern feminist analysis.

But, just as time has moved on for feminism and women since the beginning of second-wave feminism, so it has moved on for gender, too. The purpose of this chapter is to trace the rise and fall of gender as a tool for understanding women's position. Such a history must also engage with what is argued about the family, for in an important sense the family 'is' gender: mothers, fathers and children may stand in a biological relationship to one another, but their behaviour is largely shaped by cultural factors. Because the history of feminism and the history of gender are so intertwined, I also argue that the backlash against feminism cannot be understood without noticing what has happened to gender.

My basic thesis goes as follows: gender performs an invaluable function in analysing how women and men are made rather than born; these processes cannot be understood in terms of sex and sexuality as attributes of the natural body. But the strength of gender may also be its weakness. To speak of men and women as 'engendered' implies difference, rather than power inequality. The distinction between sex and gender does not call into question how society constructs the natural body itself. Ultimately, sex is no more natural than gender, given that our speaking of both is mediated by our existence as social beings. What is most notable, however, is that these problems with gender have been identified largely by feminists. The 'backlash' literature – that body of texts which both contests the facts of women's oppression and argues in favour of it – has its way only by forgetting gender altogether. This is because most of the backlash's preposterous arguments can only be put by ignoring much of the evidence about how social processes 'make' men and women.

In what follows I test my thesis by drawing on three particular areas of work. Firstly, there are those who argue not principally about feminism or women, but about the family. Secondly, there are the revised positions of feminists themselves – often misinterpreted but certainly there. Thirdly, there is a more definite body of literature which sets itself tight-fistedly against feminism as the main evil. So far as the uses and abuses of gender are concerned, there is a good deal of overlapping between these categories.

Today, gender slips uneasily between being merely another word for sex and being a contested political term. The history of gender is actually quite like the history of women, and this is, of course, no accident, as in one of its guises 'gender' is simply another word for 'women'. Academic feminists gain respectability by naming what they do as 'about gender' rather than as 'about women' (because the study of man remains the only really respectable tradition). Such a strategy only works because gender was invented to help explain women's position: men neither wonder about theirs nor need to explain it. This means that 'Women alone appear to have gender . . .';[1] or gender 'leads more directly to women than to men'.[2]

'A Man is What His Sex is'

When Shulamith Firestone published her case for feminist revolution, *The Dialectic of Sex*, in 1970, the concept of 'gender' had not yet emerged as a feminist conceptual tool. Firestone made do instead with the idea of 'sex class'. Taking Engels to task for a class analysis that, despite being 'a beautiful piece of work',[3] ignored 'a whole sexual substratum of the historical dialectic', she showed how women are culturally distinguished from 'human' as they are biologically distinguished from 'man'.[4] But her analysis was largely silent on the question of just *how* the cultural distinction of woman is accomplished. This is perhaps one reason why she was led to her much-criticized conclusion about the way forward for women being the abolition of their role in *biological* reproduction.

Germaine Greer's *The Female Eunuch*[5] was published the same year as Firestone's book. In a play on the ideas of sexuality, biological sex and cultural oppression, Greer's argument that society castrates women began with a chapter called 'Gender'. Here she used the term simply to mean the polarity of the sexes in nature. Around the same time as Greer's and Firestone's texts came Kate Millett's *Sexual Politics*. Seeking to explain the epidemic of sexual politics in literature, Millett drew on the beginnings of a new usage in medical science of the binary terms 'sex' and 'gender'.[6] In 1968 a professor of psychiatry at UCLA School of Medicine, Robert Stoller, had published a book called *Sex and Gender*, which took as its subject an increasingly recognized clinical condition in which children of one chromosomal sex appeared to belong to the other. The most common of these conditions, something called the adrenogenital syndrome, led to genetically female babies being born with masculinized external genitalia. Such babies could be brought up as either girls or boys, and would then develop what Stoller called the appropriate 'gender identity'. According to Stoller, gender refers to 'tremendous areas of behavior, feelings, thoughts and fantasies that are related to the sexes and yet do not have primary biological connotations'.[7] Although this was the route that stimulated the feminist takeover of gender, the term had actually appeared earlier in the work of psychologists during the 1930s who wanted to describe psychological attributes of people without linking these to physiological differences between men and women.[8]

'Sex' has a biological referent as female or male: the chromosomal differentiation of body cells, and all that emanates therefrom. 'Gender' – femininity and masculinity – is the parallel cultural term. It was originally a grammatical one, referring to the sex of words, and linked to the term 'genus', though it also had another meaning to do with copulation and generation.[9] In modern usage, gender refers to the multiple differentiations of bodies that occur in social space and are mapped on to the biological ground-plan. As one psychology text puts it, 'Domestic animals, newborn infants and Olympic athletes are divided into two sexes; but when we are introduced to a stranger, a *gender* is attributed to us on the basis of a variety of bodily and behavioural cues.'[10]

From the late 1960s on, when feminists sought to explain why women's situation was so different from men's, they found a huge repository of cultural arguments about the lives of men and women, most of which were thinly based on any differences that might be said to result from nature. Nurture became second nature. Biological explanations of female–male differences had actually started to wane somewhat earlier in the century, contemporaneously with the growth of social science and first-wave feminism and the breaking down of some of the institutional barriers to women's advance in public life.[11] But the need for gender as an analytic tool was especially highlighted with the retrenchment of post-war culture and the feminist mystique so ably complained about by Betty Friedan in 1963.[12] My own *Sex, Gender and Society*, published in 1972,[13] is credited with being the first text to introduce the term gender into the discourse of social science.[14] The distinction between sex and gender was subsequently taken up and used by many feminists and other writers as a useful tool in both the epidemiology of women's position and its epistemology: both causes, and ways of knowing. Many classics of feminist writing during this period are hard-hitting elaborations on the basic theme of social construction; society, psychology, sociology, literature, medicine, science, all 'construct' women differently, slipping cultural rhetoric in under the heading of biological fact. It is cultural prescription – gender, not sex – which explains why women fail to have proper orgasms, are ill-fitted to be brain surgeons, suffer from depressive illness, cannot reach the literary heights of Shakespeare, and so on and so forth. Equally importantly, it is the failure to understand that women are primarily human beings which gives rise to misleading theories about the causes of their behaviour.[15] During this period, even/especially influential theories such as Freud's about the origins of 'sexual' difference came to be restated in the language of 'gender development'.[16]

And so we all came to understand that everything is a matter of gender. Women's oppression owes its particular nature to the ways in which society has built up layers of cultural expectation and prescription and has constructed material and political edifices to support these. Women, in the sense of woman, are indeed cultural artefacts. Without gender, they are nothing.

Gender and the Sociology of the Backlash

If it was women who posed the problem gender was devised to explain, then it would be logical to suppose that any move to do away with women as the problem would also have to take on gender. Such a strategy is, indeed, an important weapon in the current armoury of the backlash. Backlash texts convince us in part because they discard the conceptual insights of 1960s and 1970s feminism. They return us to a world of naïve understandings about the origin of social differences between men and women, which in turn permit naïve conclusions about the nature and implications of some of the most significant social changes of the last thirty years.

Backlash literature contains variants of all the following themes: that women are no longer discriminated against; that feminists exaggerate(d) the extent of such discrimination; that feminism has never represented the interests of women as a group; that feminism

33

is principally, and unhelpfully, a language of victimization; that feminism ignores the social and personal importance of the family, including to women; and that feminists inaccurately portray discrimination against women as a male conspiracy. Most of these contentions involve returning gender to sex: making social inequalities disappear inside the body.

Prime among the texts that take feminism to task for failing to respect the family are the works of historian Christopher Lasch – *Haven in a Heartless World*[17] and *The Culture of Narcissism*[18] – which are joined to the voices of other male critics such as George Gilder (*Sexual Suicide*[19] and *Men and Marriage)*[20] and of sociologists Peter and Brigitte Berger in their *The War Over the Family*.[21] Books which accuse feminism of failing to address the question of practical support structures for the family include Sylvia Hewlett's *A Lesser Life*,[22] and others which bang feminism's head against the door of either the Family or The family – most notably, Betty Friedan in *The Second Stage*[23] and Germaine Greer's powerful pro-feminist argument in her *Sex and Destiny*.[24] Then, in the category of arguments that discrimination against women is much less than it used to be, and the main problem now is not so much the *feminine* mystique as the *feminist* one, there are texts such as Christine Sommers's *Who Stole Feminism?*[25] Thirdly, there is a category of books, of which Rosalind Coward's *Our Treacherous Hearts*[26] and Lynne Segal's *Is the Future Female?*[27] are the best known in the UK, which focus on the failings of feminism's new celebration of difference and consequent inability to take forward a materialist–socialist programme of reform. (These are, of course, feminist texts in a key sense – their project is the unification of feminism around an agenda of socialist reform.) Fourthly, there are the arguments against 'victim' feminism; these include Naomi Wolf's *Fire with Fire*,[28] the works of younger feminists such as Katie Roiphe in *The Morning After*[29] and Rene Denfeld in her *The New Victorians*,[30] and the work of Camille Paglia, who, as self-appointed media star of backlash feminism, joins her critique of the notion of women as victims to a ragbag of other tactics, including a general rubbishing of the personal qualities and qualifications of well-known feminists, and a celebration of men as the primary founders of human culture.[31]

At the Heart of It All: The Family

Much early second-wave feminist analysis identified families as the primary sources of gender inequality. It is within families that children become boys and girls. Mothers and fathers treat female and male babies differently, and a main reason for this is that they are themselves different. The great power of the family as a gender system lies in its self-perpetuating character; the psychology of parenthood and the sociology of gender are inescapably joined.[32]

Because the family is important in producing gender, *defending* the family as a sex/gender system is a significant way of contesting feminism. However, the arguments can be both subtle and complicated. There is often an emotional appeal to a higher good – usually that of 'society' or children. Historian Christopher Lasch, for example, sees the central problem of modern culture as the decline in internalized authority and the domination of the pleasure principle by the separation of love from discipline. Both of these have their origins in the new form of the family, which is characterized by father absence and the dissolution of other-centred moral values. Such a standpoint would seem to have little to do with feminism, but feminism, like other cultural radicalisms of the 1960s, has failed to understand the importance of the family: 'The trouble with the feminist program is not that economic self-sufficiency for women is an unworthy goal but that its realization . . . would undermine equally important values associated with the family. Feminists have not answered the argument that day care provides no substitute for the family. They have not answered the argument that indifference to the needs of the young has become one of the distinguishing characteristics of a society that lives for the moment [and], defines the consumption of commodities as the highest form of personal satisfaction . . .'[33]

Lasch condemns those who find in his book a reactionary glorification of the old-style bourgeois family; this is not what he intends. But his view rides blithely over the analysis of the family as a/the sex/gender system in microcosm – that social structure which, above all, acts to produce man and woman as cultural forms. It is this sense of the family as the repository and source of gender division and inequality which the sexual politics of the 1960s and 1970s entered into the cultural frame: not 'the' family itself, but what is allowed to happen *inside families*.

In *Sexual Suicide*, George Gilder takes a less subtle line, interpreting the feminist argument about processes of discrimination against women as a call for the abolition of 'biological' differences between men and women. In their *War Over the Family*, Peter and Brigitte Berger's representation of the anti-family argument depends, like Lasch's and Gilder's, on the exhumation of families as 'natural' forms. What was, was better; 'the' family is best understood as existing in history as some kind of essence, rather than as shaped by cultural influences which turn it into a theatrical battleground for the enactment of 'gender' roles whose scripts are written largely by the combined forces of capitalism and patriarchy. Starting from the assertion that 'the family is a problem', the Bergers pick apart the use of gender as an analytic tool by noting that the concept of 'gender roles' is merely 'femspeak' – a technique for arguing that the assignment of roles within the family is arbitrary and that it can/should be changed, so as to advance women's welfare.[34] This denial of natural differences, say the Bergers, unhelpfully undermines the democratic and nurturant functions of the family.

But women cannot be returned to the family in any obviously oppressive way. A cleaner device is to juxtapose the modern self-seeking family (with the modern self-seeking woman inside it) with a vision of an organic community which manages to be anti-materialistic as well as altruistic. Amitai Etzioni in *The Spirit of Community* expresses it neatly when he de-genders the family and motherhood by speaking of the 'communitarian family' and 'the parenting deficit'.[35] It is crucial to his argument that two-parent families are better for children because of the division of labour that is possible between mothers, who give emotional security,

36

and fathers, who provide an 'achievement-oriented' push away from 'the comfortable cradle of love'.[36] This view is essentially the same as sociological functionalism in the 1950s, according to which women perform 'expressive' and men 'instrumental' roles within the family.[37]

A more veiled version of the same theme is provided by Ivan Illich in *Gender*, published in 1983. Illich's argument involves an unconventional usage of both sex and gender. In his view, pre-capitalist societies were based on 'vernacular gender' – a general (better) art of living in which men and women accepted their differences, and society was organized in a nurturing and altruistic manner. Then came the commercial culture of industrial capitalism which created new images of men and women as economic players in a theatre of self-seeking commodification. Vernacular gender became economic sex, and women suffered because they lost their traditional role within a system of masculine privilege and power. Whereas the old asymmetry of gender was not hierarchical, the new asymmetry of sex is. In this usage, sex and gender are almost reversed in meaning. Gender becomes a form of cultural nostalgia for a mythic and more moral past. This reversal is only achieved because for Illich 'Both gender and sex are social realities with only a tenuous connection to anatomy.'[38]

The Problem of the Masculine Gender

The essence of the backlash lies in the contention that the nuclear family has been unreasonably attacked. Whether this is dressed up as a defence of men or a defence of children/pro-family mother-hood, the result is the same; the historical conflict between femin-ism and the family is foregrounded as the basic issue of women's rights. Feminists dispute 'The Family' for many reasons, but one is because it is the site of male (hetero)sexuality, a phenomenon in which, as Lynne Segal argues in her *Straight Sex*,[39] sex and gender are hopelessly conflated. This is one explanation of femin-ism's constant equation with 'man-hating'. Its 'antiphallic' tenden-cies are applied to sex as well as to gender. Women become the defenders of men and children, just as men are defenders of themselves as fathers and/or patriarchs. Texts such as Maureen Freely's *What About Us? An Open Letter to the Mothers Feminism Forgot* are less about motherhood than about a form of male identification which ignores the 'truths' about women's experiences. Freely's book attacks 'femstars' for being mostly childfree; 'The feminist canon has it that we are the great beneficiaries if we can escape Biological Destiny.'[40] On the contrary, says Freely, bodies have their own laws; the real problem is parenthood, not women. What is important is control over the process of being a mother, not its repudiation. Such an oversimplified case is, of course, only possible because the texts of feminism are selectively chosen, and because the saga of problems is spun from the centrifuge of a middle-class kitchen.

In a related vein, Julia Neuberger's *Whatever's Happening to Women?* contends the middle ground of the relevance of some feminist arguments, at the same time as the widespread damage feminism in general has done to women's lives by insisting on a rhetoric of male oppression and unreasonable standards of gender equality: '. . . women who stayed at home felt inadequate; women who worked but who did not reach real seniority hit what has been described as the glass ceiling, felt angry and betrayed; women were exhausted rather than fulfilled; and whole tracts of female experience and female desires, the nurturing we were brought up to do and the sense of duty we feel to our loved ones, have been jettisoned for some apparently nobler cause, self-fulfilment in the workplace, alongside men.'[41]

Unsurprisingly, the case for men as a sex rather than as a gender is most forcefully stated by men themselves. Nicholas Davidson's *The Failure of Feminism* is the open letter to men that parallels Freely's to mothers. Its central dogma is akin to those of backlash media star Camille Paglia's: that women's rights are too important to be left to feminists, as indeed are all 'gender' issues. Gender here is used to depoliticize the word 'women'; what Davidson is interested in is not women's rights but 'the future of gender'.[42] As he puts it, 'Men have no place in feminist discourse except as the objects of scrutiny and attack.'[43] What feminism is about is the devaluation of the 'feminine'; equal pay would make it difficult for men to support families on their own and would force women to go out to work; day care is bad for children because they catch respiratory infections. Most critically, feminism is to blame for inventing the prescriptive idea of gender roles as arbitrary impositions on human personality. Feminism has relied totally on this assailable truth – that most of the observable differences between the sexes are culturally imposed. To unmask feminism, therefore, the belief in gender must itself be abolished.

Davidson's attack on cultural determination exposes a large hole that is conveniently filled by sociobiology, and by an ever-expanding cascade of 'scientific' discoveries about sex differences. Robert Pool's *The New Sexual Revolution*[44] is an example of how old Victorian ideas about biological essentialism can be dressed up in modern scientific armour and then presented as 'factoids'[45] which produce the inexorable conclusion that the sexes are, after all, different, and it is only on this magnificently shifting ground that they can ever hope to be equal.

Losing Gender

As Janice Doane and Devon Hodges argue in their *Nostalgia and Sexual Difference*,[46] a vision of a golden past which authenticates a traditional domestic role for women is the other side of the coin of the backlash against feminism. Feminism is seen to fail because it has produced a present for women which is qualitatively (subjectively) worse. Probably even more important is the measurable decline in the welfare of men and children. In times of cultural change, the idea of a fixed essential identity is attractive. The easiest route is therefore to forget about gender altogether.

Forgetting gender and remembering 'The Family' appear as linked devices for stating that most persuasive of all cultural concerns: the need for altruism, particularly as regards children. Ten years ago Judith Stacey provided a detailed analysis of the meaning of what she called 'conservative pro-family feminism'.[47] Looking closely at such texts as Friedan's *The Second Stage*, Greer's *Sex and Destiny* and Jean Bethke Elshtain's *Public Man, Private Woman*,[48] Stacey concluded that the main failing of this position is the loss of the conceptual framework of gender, because what happens is that the structural processes differentiating male and female roles both inside and outside the family then simply disappear. For example, when Betty Friedan changed from emphasizing the feminine mystique to noting the excesses of the feminist one in *The Second Stage*, she drew our attention away from the engendering that takes place within the family as the source of both 'feminine' and 'feminist' discontents. In the feminine mystique, the mirage of female satisfaction held up by traditional wife–mother–housewife roles could only be dissolved by making women the equals of men in the public sphere. In the feminist one the problem is the feminist longing for the public sphere itself. A very important strand in this argument is that feminists supposedly derogate motherhood along with everything else about the family. The baby gets thrown out with the bathwater because the plug of gender has been pulled out.

Greer's position on the family is more complex than Friedan's. *Sex and Destiny* is an intelligent argument about sex in the sense of sexuality rather than gender: in a series of linked contentions about the 'irrationality' of modern culture, Greer argues that the ideologies and practices surrounding sexuality and reproduction are often not in women's best interests. We cannot conclude, for example, that because motherhood is an inferior social status in our society, it is necessarily bad to define women by their mothering function: 'We have at least to consider the possibility that a successful matriarch might well pity Western females for having been duped into futile competition with men in exchange for the companionship and love of children and other women.'[49] While all this seems eminently sensible, Greer's espousal of the extended, non-biological, child-centred family does ring with a tone of nostalgia that is in some ways similar to that of Lasch *et al.*

These revised concerns of 'older' feminists may partly reflect their own changed personal concerns.[50] What was once an overriding interest in avoiding enforced motherhood has become a nostalgia for motherhood as a lost and undervalued opportunity. Feminists who had children might look back with a sense of how they might have made better mothers without feminism; feminists who remained childfree might wonder whether they should have done. A concern with sexual liberation in the sense of liberation to be sexual becomes an understanding that sexuality need not be the driving force of human conduct after all, particularly once the menopause arrives to tame the power of all those raging hormones. In her *Revolution from Within*, Gloria Steinem's brain cells celebrate[51] when she realizes there is no longer any imperative to be sexual all the time. Does this sudden new experience of the body restore a (reluctant) belief in biology where faith in gender had taken firm political root?[52]

The Problem of 'Gender' Feminism

Because gender as a concept was a basic building block of second-wave feminism, there is probably no better way to undermine feminism than by discrediting the very idea of gender. The neatest, most double-handed manoeuvre here is to accomplish this by tarring gender with feminism's own brush. In *Who Stole Feminism?* American philosopher Christine Sommers points the finger unequivocally at a group she calls 'gender feminists'. These are people who believe that 'our society is best described as a patriarchy, a "male hegemony", a "sex/gender system" in which the dominant gender works to keep women cowering and submissive. The feminists who hold this divisive view of our social and political reality believe we are in a gender war . . .'[53] Gender feminists are distinguished from women who are active in helping the real victims of real abuse and discrimination. They are also juxtaposed unflatteringly with 'equity feminists', who believe that women 'have made great progress' and who do not believe that they are 'socially subordinate'.[54] While 'equity feminists' point proudly to the gains women have made towards achieving parity in the workplace, 'gender feminists' disparage these gains as small and illusory.

Gender feminism attacks men and therefore makes the signal mistake of attacking the women who like men, and who enjoy the traditional *mélange* of differences from men, including the 'right' to stay at home and raise children. Some 'gender feminists' are also 'resenter feminists' who are personally 'convinced that men generally take every opportunity to exploit women and that they often delight in humiliating them physically and mentally'.[55] Sommers herself is a feminist[56] – though not of the 'gender' or 'resenter' kind.

Significantly, Sommers never defines her use of the term 'gender'. Implicit in her use of the term is an equation between an analysis of women's situation, which sees this as one of political oppression on the one hand, and a theory which says that most socially observable differences between men and women are a social product, on the other.

But the best-publicized proponent of this point of view is probably Camille Paglia. Paglia's opinion is that feminists cannot be trusted with sex – they will turn it into gender. 'There are some things we cannot change,' she asserts. 'There are sexual differences that are based in biology. Academic feminism is lost in a fog of social constructionism . . . leaving sex to the feminists is like letting your dog vacation at the taxidermists.'[57] In this much-quoted statement, social constructionism is some sort of death-knell, trapping men and women into a web of lies about their true nature and deceiving them about the possibility of a gender transformation.

The sense of 'gender' to mean 'politically unequal' is, however, not how *most* people have used the term. Indeed, it is because gender lacks this signifier of power relations that some other 'feminists' have complained about it.

The Errors of Celebrating Difference

If we strip away the veil of gender, people are once again allowed to assume their 'natural' identities. Differences reign; hierarchy is in the eye of the beholder. One problem here is that feminists may value difference differently from one another. The valorization of women's particular biological and social strengths is a prominent strand of modern feminism. Women are celebrated for their distinctive approach to knowledge,[58] emotion,[59] moral choice,[60] parental thinking,[61] and diverse forms of nurturance and altruism.[62] In Marilyn French's *Beyond Power*,[63] as in many other texts, these 'feminine' values are recast as human ones. Gloria Steinem's parody of Freud's thinking on gender difference, 'What if Freud were Phyllis?' demonstrates some of the political and personal implications that might result from a widespread cultural appreciation of women's reproductive superiority.[64] Actually, the tradition of celebrating women's difference from men goes right back to first-wave feminism, which was divided on the question as to whether women should have the vote because they were *like* men or because they were *unlike* them.[65] Some of the early sociologists also stressed women's reproductive and moral superiority.[66]

None the less, it is true to say that second-wave feminism began with an insistent denial of fundamental differences between the sexes – it was this that gave political birth to the idea of gender. A celebration of difference instead of a denial turns the old argument on its head. The theme of celebrating difference is interwoven with other motifs in the backlash literature; there is, in particular, a very close connection with a liberal defence of the family. Perhaps this is unsurprising, given that it is the family that institutionalizes a gendered division of labour in the first place. After all, we know from very many studies that, when domestic roles and tasks are gendered, women do most of the work.[67] Some celebration of women's contribution as morally important is probably necessary in order to avoid the charge of exploitation.

In *Our Treacherous Hearts*, Rosalind Coward accepts that as a result of feminist activity, women's lives have dramatically improved: '. . . the chaos and confusion caused by feminism has abated. That chaos – the chaos of changing sexual roles, the antagonism of angry women – belongs to a different era. The battles have been fought and won.'[68] When she goes on to ask why women are not happy with their new lot, her answer is that women stubbornly continue to value their traditional family roles, and are reluctant to challenge the linked tradition of male power. Social and political solutions to the problems women individually confront are impossible, because feminism has disappeared – due mainly to divisions within itself. Women battle alone with the guilt and the overload of being expected to be like men and benefit from the new forms of equality, while at the same time shouldering all the conventional burden of responsibility for family life. Coward views the discovery of women's greater 'decency' and the power of the mother–infant bond as detrimental to the pursuit of a *social* solution, which is what she considers to be most important. The essential point about gender here is that if inequalities between men and women are returned to the domain of the apparently 'natural', a *political* response is ruled out. Natural differences cannot provide the organizing topic for revolution. Revolutionary agendas need differences attributable to preventable causes.

Six years before *Our Treacherous Hearts* came Lynne Segal's *Is the Future Female? Troubled Thoughts on Contemporary Feminism*, which is a diatribe against the development in modern feminist thinking of polarized views of men and women – this emphasis 'on natural or psychological gender *difference*'.[69] Segal sees this development as giving rise to 'an apocalyptic feminism . . . which portrays a Manichean struggle between female virtue and male vice, with ensuing catastrophe and doom unless "female" morality and values prevail'.[70] She comments on the irony whereby 'traditional gender ideology' has become the 'new commonsense' of feminism,[71] and on the political stasis that results from emphasizing the 'totality' of 'the sex-gender system'. Such a theory allows the material exploitation of women to slip from view. The argument that 'the future is female' is a form of useless essentialism which distracts from the a priori politics needed to abolish all the social distinctions between men and women. 'Essentialist' thinking grows stronger as the feminist movement itself becomes progressively weaker organizationally, and as feminist perspectives become more fragmented. But one question here is whether such a celebration of difference truly constitutes a repudiation of *gender* – that is, of the *social* explanation of sex differences – or whether (somewhat

44

less malignantly) it can be conceived as a *political* attempt to value some aspects of the feminine gender role. Perhaps the concept of 'gender', by implying equal status for the gender differences to which men and women find themselves heir, itself carried a fundamental flaw along with it?

Segal's own nostalgia leads her back to a past of socialist feminism, when feminism's clear project was the removal of material and therefore ideological barriers to women's unequal treatment. Like Lasch, though with a different objective in sight, she tries to recreate this nobler political past as objectively true rather than as simply validating what she wants to argue about the faults of feminism now.

Victim Feminism

A central plank of backlash ideology takes issue with the political portrayal of women as victims. Much of 1960s and 1970s feminism conveyed the idea that women are victims not only of patriarchy and capitalism but of men and the entire gender system. In one sense, the invention of gender provided an excuse for women not taking responsibility; all the excesses and deficits of their lives could be attributed to the overwhelming power of gender as a culturally deterministic force. There are two basic counter-contentions in the backlash position here. The first is that men are as much victims as women. The second is that to see women as victims deprives them of agency – of the proper autonomy and responsibility they ought to have if they are truly to be the equals of men.

Naomi Wolf's contrast between 'victim' and 'power' feminism highlights the weakness of gender on the power front. In *Fire with Fire*, she contends that most women do not champion the cause of gender equity, because of the disservices feminism has done itself by allowing victim feminism to dominate public debate. In victim feminism, women were seen as 'sexually pure and mystically nurturing', and as powerless in asserting their rights in a system which assigns power *per se* to men. This is distinct from the more reasonable power feminism, which decrees that women have rights simply because they are human beings, and not because of any special characteristics they have as women.[72] Significantly, also, victim feminism sees men as the enemy, while power feminism does not.

According to Wolf, victim feminism was helped along by theories developed from the 1970s on, which served to alienate most women further from any identification with feminism. These theories include: all men are rapists, all heterosexual sex is rape, all women are lesbians, and all sex differences are only 'the social fiction of gender'.[73] The problem is that it is essentially unattractive to suggest banishing *sexual differentiation* as the principal form of gender difference. What ordinary woman wants to blame men for everything and/or to lose her womanliness in the process? It did not help, as Wolf observes, that at this point along came the French post-structuralist feminists who obscured the framework of sex/gender analysis even further by using an extremely dense technical language to beat the male academics at their own game.

Victim feminism invites women to seek power as a collectivity through an identity as powerless people. The backlash caricature of victim feminism depends for much of its strength on a version of male–female sexual relations which does 'something slick and dangerous with the notion of victimization'.[74] Katie Roiphe in *The Morning After*[75] and Camille Paglia in *Sex, Art and American Culture*[76] parade the excesses of the rape crisis movement, rather than confront the statistics of male violence against women in order to argue that women's worst enemy is their own attribution of sexual power to men.

The reaction against victim feminism is said to be the reason why young women in particular are unable to identify with feminism as a political movement. Roiphe's book is an angry rejection of North American 'campus' feminism, as ruled by unacceptable orthodoxies, workshops on date rape and sexual harassment, and miserably biased theses about 'the colonialist appropriation of the female discourse'.[77] For Roiphe, feminism has caricatured women as humourless victims, who see offence where none is intended, because of a misguided, almost 'feminine' sensibility. The truth is more, as Camille Paglia has asserted, that women walk with their eyes wide open into Testosterone Territory and ought to know and arm themselves against this.

For Rene Denfeld, feminists are like 'new' Victorians in seeing women as chaste victims of predatory males; there is even something very *anti-feminist* about this view (if feminism means insisting women be the same as men). But the basic problem for Denfeld is the same as it is for Sommers and Paglia and Coward and Segal: the 'antiphallic campaign'[78] – the identification of male sexuality as the root cause of women's oppression. In suggesting that lesbian relationships may be less oppressive, that women can be raped in other ways than by penile penetration, and that the images of women in pornography are explicit about more than just sex, the morality of much feminism today is unfashionably out of tune with the original notion of feminism as 'sexual' liberation.

Many young people probably do grow up believing that their right to use their bodies for sex with men without running the risk of unintended motherhood is the single most important heritage of 1960s feminism. Given this, the suggestion that sex with men is sex with the enemy may be hard to take. There is much concentration in these texts,[79] not on this central tenet, but on the details of the methodologies used by feminists to contend the widespread nature of rape and sexual assault on women. Deflating the statistics so that they seem to mean much less than they are said to mean involves taking issue with other feminists. Internal disagreement about what feminism 'is' is, of course, another feature of how the backlash constructs feminism. The backlash is attributed to feminists' inability to agree about feminism, in much the same way as the decline in any political position is caused by internal squabbling. Healthy disagreement has no place on the political stage when there are forces out there whose main goal is discrediting the players' performance anyway.

Histories of Sex and Gender

The first usage of the term 'gender' in the 1970s took cultural variability as its main difference from sex. Sex was the fixed star; the emphasis was on the non-essentialism of gender. Gender differences were/are not 'true' differences;[80] they were/are not 'absolute, abstract or irreducible'; no 'essence' is involved.[81] Another interesting twist to the sex–gender argument is provided by recent historical and sociological work showing that cultural construction applies also to sex. This means that the essential distinction between sex and gender collapses. Even the binary distinction of sex itself – female or male – disappears when you look hard enough.

Thomas Laqueur found it difficult to read ancient, medieval and Renaissance texts about the body through the epistemological lens of the Enlightenment, which says the physical world of the body is 'real', while its cultural meanings are epiphenomenal.[82] Before the seventeenth century, sex (the body) was the epiphenomenon and gender was 'real'; sex was a sociological and not an ontological category. For 2000 years, female and male bodies were not conceptualized in terms of difference. Medical texts described female and male bodies as fundamentally the same, with one difference: women's genitals were inside their bodies and men's were outside. In this 'one sex' model women were simply men turned inside out and the lack of specific terms for women's organs (vagina, ovary, clitoris) reflected not a disregard for their importance, but an assumption that in this men and women were equal, that is like men. One consequence of understanding the way in which sex is culturally constructed is that 'almost everything one wants to say about sex . . . already has in it a claim about gender. Sex . . . is explicable only within the context of battles over gender and power.'[83]

Laqueur's elegant exposition of the transition from a 'one sex' to a 'two sex' model is the kind of history one needs to give depth to naïve understandings. The same could be said of Vern and Bonnie Bullough's treatise on *Cross-dressing, Sex and Gender*,[84] which exposes the fiction of transgenderism as a modern phenomenon. They show that gender-crossing is so historically and cross-culturally ubiquitous that genitalia can hardly be considered essential insignia of gender. As with everything else, however, there is little symmetry here. Women cross-dressers assume the characteristics of men as the norm, whereas male cross-dressers fit themselves into the residual category of what is left once men have defined masculinity.

Because 'gender' was originally the inverse of the essentialist term 'sex', its own usage was bound to iterate the intellectual shifts in how people perceived nature.[85] In her book on the archaeology of sex hormones, Nellie Oudshoorn[86] points out another important problem with gender; that it left sex to the medical scientists. The social scientists dealt with gender, and the asocial scientists with sex. A further, unhelpful binary distinction was created.

These arguments about the shifting stars of both sex and gender were prefigured in American anthropologist Sherry Ortner's well-known paper 'Is Female to Male as Nature is to Culture?', which was first published in 1974. Ortner contended that the sociology of women's bodies suggests a position closer to the natural world than to the cultural one. She remarked that 'the whole schema is a construct of culture rather than a fact of nature'.[87] This is another way of expressing the sentiment that gender leads directly to women rather than men, and/but most statements about women's sex are also statements about gender.

The feminist discovery of gender in the 1970s saw biological essentialism as a primary legacy of Western culture. What Sandra Bem[88] has deemed 'gender polarization' gives to cultural processes and factors the same dichotomy with which culture constructs biology: because there are two sexes, there must be two genders. There is a whole set of dualisms here: nature/culture, sex/gender, private/public, reproduction/production. Dualistic assumptions about gender can preclude consideration of other relevant categories (race, class, age, etc.). In other words, gender as an 'untheorized binary variable' is not helpful.[89] As Barrie Thorne notes, the evidence is persuasive for distinguishing conceptually between biological sex, cultural gender and sexuality (desire), but it should not be assumed that these are easily separable: 'One of our central tasks is to clarify their complex, often ambiguous relationships . . . We should muse about why, after all our careful distinctions, *we so easily slip into interchangeable use of sex, gender and sexual.*'[90] (Italics added.)

This is an extremely important question, particularly today, when we have both the prominence of the body in the new discipline of the sociology of the body, and its partial disappearance under the influence of Foucault, Lacanian psychoanalysis and post-structuralism. The social construction of sex/the body is different for the two genders, with women's bodies/sex seen as being much more controlled by hormones than men's and therefore as fragile and altogether less stable biological products. The role of hormones in constructing women's natural bodies is paralleled by their cultural use as strategies for adjusting women to both biology and society – the hormones oestrogen and progesterone are the most widely used drugs in the entire history of medicine.[91]

Using the Tools of the Master's House

While most feminists used to like gender, many today dislike it. The most fully developed 'complaint' about gender as a concept is to be found in the work of Catharine MacKinnon. A critical element in MacKinnon's position is that 'If a concept like difference is a conceptual tool of gender and of inequality, it cannot deconstruct the master's house because it has built it.'[92] In *Feminism Unmodified: Discourses on Life and Law*, a set of essays addressing the fact that 'Feminism has not changed the status of women,'[93] MacKinnon argues that the language of gender has served to obscure the truth that inequality is fundamentally sexualized. Sex is inequality and inequality is sex. The gender 'differences' from which women suffer are imposed by force. Hence, the idea of gender difference as a set of bipolar distinctions helps to sustain the reality of male dominance. Or as MacKinnon puts it, 'One of the most deceptive antifeminisms in society, scholarship, politics and law is the persistent treatment of gender as if it truly is a question of difference, rather than treating the gender difference as a construct of the difference gender makes.'[94] A further charge is that, because inequalities between men and women include the inequalities of their sexual relationship, and these are socially defined as enjoyed by both men and women, gender inequality appears to be consensual when actually it is not, most of the time.

MacKinnon, like Sommers, leaves the definition of the term 'gender' itself open. Her usage of it suggests that the things she calls 'gender' differences may be equally traceable to biology, society, god and/or the cosmos. Gender is the sexualization of inequality between men and women, rather than an explanation of this inequality itself. The cultural referent has been lost; gender has been returned to sex. In her later *Toward a Feminist Theory of the State*, MacKinnon equates a theory of gender with a theory of male dominance – that is, 'an account of its key concrete sites and laws of motion, an analysis of why and how it happened and why (perhaps even how) it could be ended'.[95] Gender is to feminism what class is to Marxism: the essential political tool. This position seemingly contradicts her earlier view that gender lets women down because it is at root an apolitical concept. Gender becomes instead the thing that occupies the space between men and women; the experiential aspect, or adjectival form, of sex. 'I use sex and gender relatively interchangeably,' MacKinnon concludes.[96]

The concept of 'relative' interchangeability may be a little muddling, but MacKinnon definitely has popular usage on her side. By the late 1980s, gender had become a substitute for sex in much public and scientific debate. Perhaps gender has a ring of up-to-dateness about it; an aura of political correctness derived from its frequent usage by feminists? Someone who speaks of gender rather than sex intimates a seductive familiarity with social analyses of oppression, whatever is really going on. Thus, application forms ask people their 'gender' along with their age and 'marital status'; scientists speak of 'gender' differences in the womb and even the chromosomes themselves; some even claim to detect gender in sperm.[97] Doctors reserve the right to choose babies' gender[98] by refusing parents' rights to selective abortion. The end result of such conventions is to defuse the power of the concept of gender to explain men and women's different social situations; gender becomes as useless as sex.

Conclusion

This chapter has argued that the political power of the distinction between sex and gender has been largely made to disappear in both pro- and anti-backlash texts. On the one hand, authors like MacKinnon argue that because gender attributes both femininity and masculinity in seemingly equal measure to the influence of culture, the *inequalities* of power evident in the social relations of the sexes appear to be denied. Because the language of gender assumes the source of women's oppression to be cultural, any particular power and responsibility of men as oppressors fades, or is made to pass only momentarily, like the shadow of a puppet, on the social stage where men and women dance their more politically comfortable ballet of *difference*. Structures which discriminate against women hide behind gender differences; this is not helpful to the feminist project.

On the other hand, however, writers such as Denfeld, Roiphe and Paglia accuse gender of the opposite sin: of postulating a hierarchical system of difference which privileges male power. Again, this is condemned as countering a necessary progress towards equal rights for women. Yet a third litany on gender differences permits the valorization of those – motherhood, nurturance, connected thinking, emotionality, ecological concerns – developed particularly in women. Some have countered by arguing that this celebration of women's difference succeeds only in unproductively returning them to the domain of nature. It also gets in the way of the *real* issues, which remain what they were in the beginning: inferior civil and political rights, economic dependency, lack of freely available and safe abortion and contraception, and inadequate material and social support for motherhood.

The important question is not whether gender is appealed to or used as a concept in the analysis, but *how* it is used. There was nothing wrong with its original usage – to map a domain of cultural perspectives on the natural body which would help people to develop both personal and political understandings of important aspects of their own and other people's identities. There is still a need for this usage today. After all, the notion of 'truth' as nothing more than fluidity and subjectivity – nothing is true except at the personal moment of its perception – is beginning to be widely resisted; for this is simply not how most human beings experience their everyday lives.

But at the same time matters have grown more complicated. Gender has collected a history of both uses and abuses, of political purposes and deviations, of slippages and confusions; and it brings this history along with it wherever it goes. Because gender is a linguistic marker for women, what has happened to women is bound to be reflected in what has happened to gender. Because 'women' always signifies feminism on one level or another – feminism is a permanent possibility but requires specific historical circumstances to manifest itself politically[99] – the fate of gender is also bound to follow feminism's destiny. Finally, we can see how 'The Family' holds gender, women and the feminist struggle jealously within itself, so that any argument about any of these must take this as a primary site.

The relation of gender to power is one of the most problematic aspects of its history. Initially, analyses of difference in terms of gender offered a placatory suggestion of equal oppression: both men and women might be equally shaped by cultural prescriptions not of their own choosing. But as evidence of unequal treatment mounted, it became clear that not much about women's situation could be explained without reference to what happens to them in the family. It was a short step from here to the charge that gender feminism fails because it conceives men (and children) as the enemy. The recurring problem for feminism is that men *are* the enemy politically, but for many women they are not so personally – or are only so intermittently. Love is always most likely to be brandished when inequalities of power intrude.[100] Motherhood has always been the best argument for altruism, although there is little evidence that women have ever been self-seeking in relation to their children. On the contrary, altruism fails mainly in men, who abandon their children in droves.

The other central problem for feminism is what to do about women's agency. It is obvious that women cannot merely be the victims of gender, or of men. But it is equally obvious that being expected to conform to a fairly strait-jacketed gender role formula of domesticity, wifehood and motherhood, and having various inducements to, and penalties against, this put in one's path, is a powerful fact of everyday life for many women. Just as in recognizing women's agency it is not helpful to celebrate femininity in any simple-minded way, so it cannot be useful to deny gender. It is a pity that younger feminists have concentrated their attacks on what they call victim feminism, because this deflects attention from the place where important changes most need to occur: in our cultural thinking about the proper roles of men and women, and the manifestations of this both in the 'haven' of the home and the market-place of the world beyond. Of course, we also now need to think about how we view sex and sexuality, and about the misleadingness of binary thinking altogether (sex *and* gender, male *and* female, nature *and* culture, homo- *and* hetero-sexuality).

The backlash is a recurring phenomenon. There is absolutely nothing new about a widespread cultural reaction to the prospect of women gaining rights some of them wish to have. All radical movements are liable to generate this kind of response; but there is something always archaically different about women, not only because of sex, but because of gender. The ineluctable confusion between the sociology and biology of women's bodies – their use both for biological reproduction and as a metaphor for systems of social/material discrimination – makes women, and therefore feminism, a critical part of the counterpoint about what is happening, on a general political and moral level, to 'society'.

The backlash as a project is more about a response to too little change than to too much. In all the prolegomena penned over the last decade, there is, startlingly, no authoritative text which examines carefully and in detail the statistics of just what has happened to women's social position since second-wave feminism got off the ground.[101] A comparison of what happened in the decade up to the end of the 1970s and in the one that followed might show interesting patterns in the relative speed of advance. While no one doubts that there have been real gains, these need to be set against any losses. The losses include temporary set-backs in the move towards equality, as well as those brought about directly by a reactive public policy, and especially one that increasingly targets women as lone mothers and as beneficiaries of state welfare systems in the guise of defending 'The Family' and providing a vaccine against widespread moral degeneracy. Now, as always, women are charged with being the carriers of culture and morality in a way that men, for all their claimed machismo, have managed to escape. In this new ideological warfare, it seems attractive to pursue the *natural* causes of social ills, because these lie within the dominion of a science that is not about gender. Removing the political weight of gender from the reactionary wagon is therefore an essential part of the whole reactionary ideological project.

3

American Gothic: Feminism, Melodrama and the Backlash

MARGARET WALTERS

In the last few years, melodrama – with its hyperbole, its cut and dried morals and its obsession with sexualized violence – seems to have invaded feminist thinking. If an interest in women's sexual experience – in the widest sense of the word – was the distinctive contribution of second-wave feminism, it has become pat and reductive. We're offered a world that resembles a Bosch painting, pervaded and perverted by sexuality. Too many feminists cast themselves as heroines of melodrama, beating off the forces of darkness, demonic rapists and pornographers – or teachers, doctors, class mates, colleagues and husbands. There's an insistent note of strident self-righteousness that seems to spring from unexamined anger and frustration; it actually makes it harder to think or act about urgent issues like rape and domestic violence. The media – always responsive to sexy simplifications – delights in cartoon scenarios about date rape and sexual harassment and pornography. It has made stars of fanatical puritans like Andrea Dworkin and Catharine A. MacKinnon on the one hand, setting them against a let-it-all-hang-out libertarian like Camille Paglia, who defiantly styles herself a pornographer, and twirls imaginary moustaches like a pantomime villain. Both form part of a backlash *within* feminism, that's perhaps as great a threat as any backlash against it. From opposite ends of the moral spectrum, puritans and libertarians alike jettison complexities; they cut through the difficulties and disagreements – yes, the confusions – that keep feminism alive.

Melodrama has always been a chameleon form, frequently rigidly conservative, as often unexpectedly subversive. It nearly always sides with the weak against the powerful and it offers metaphors that dramatize what's consciously denied. At the same time it works in exaggerated black and white terms; it can encourage self-righteousness, and very often betrays a sneaky enjoyment of what's openly condemned. Overt pornographers make themselves at home in this world of monstrous villains and fragile victims. Rape, actual or metaphoric, is at the heart of the form, its defining metaphor.[1] In fact, the earliest and the greatest (perhaps the only truly great) melodramatic novel, Samuel Richardson's *Clarissa*, dwells for more than a thousand pages on a single rape and its aftermath. Richardson transcends the clichés of his sensational plot, to explore the personal, political, social, familial and psychological meanings of this single act. The story is intensely relevant to those contemporary feminists preoccupied with rape as both symbol and primary cause of women's oppression. But they'd probably want to ban Richardson out of hand for the ambiguity of his sympathies, his recognition of the intense and complicated ties between Clarissa and her rapist, Lovelace.

Melodrama has always tempted women writers. Gothic storytellers in the late eighteenth century and sensation novelists at the end of the nineteenth century seized on it as a way of articulating their hidden desires and dissatisfactions. Its tuppenny-coloured images helped crystallize feelings repressed by bourgeois society. Just before she died in 1797, the first great feminist Mary Wollstonecraft was working on a Gothic novel called *The Wrongs of Women, or Maria*. She had already couched her plea for equality in the language of human rights learned from the American and French revolutions. Romantic melodrama (her letters suggest an easy familiarity with *Clarissa*) offered her images that would tap into a deeper level of feeling. The novel is a cry of rage at the way men ignore or trivialize the 'misery and oppression peculiar to women'. The 'horrid' decaying madhouse where the heroine has been incarcerated by her heartless husband becomes the symbol of a world which treats all women as slaves. Women are imprisoned all their lives. If they dream of fulfilment in romantic love or seek an outlet for their sexual longings, they are caught in an even deadlier trap. Wollstonecraft planned a courtroom ending, with the heroine making a public protest about the way law itself contributes to the oppressed situation of all women. It is a passionate piece of theatrical pleading – and it leaves heroine, writer and reader still trapped.[2] It's intriguing to set *Maria* against *Northanger Abbey*, written only a few years later, by Jane Austen. She knew and thoroughly enjoyed Gothic extravaganzas; but her own book is a cool, comic reminder of how easily melodrama can distract us from the things that really matter. The naïve heroine, Catherine, imagines that her future father-in-law is a monster, who has incarcerated and probably murdered his wife. Her gruesomely enjoyable fantasies blind her to everyday cruelties, and to the less spectacular but painful working of class and gender inequalities in her society – inequalities, she discovers, that threaten her own prospects of happiness.

Towards the close of another century, more and more feminist writers seem to have adopted – unconsciously – the heated, heightened tone of melodrama, its histrionic simplifications, and its typecasting. The average office or college campus is as full of perils as any Gothic ruin. The fragile *fin de siècle* feminist looks more and more like a throwback to another century, under threat from cradle to grave. That may be unfair to the Victorians. When Florence Nightingale, say, or Charlotte Brontë visited the great European galleries they were by turns alarmed, and shocked, and aroused by the blatant nudity that confronted them – but always set thinking. How much more open they seem than the late-twentieth-century students and their professor at Pennsylvania State University, who were made 'embarrassed' and 'uncomfortable' by a reproduction of Goya's *Naked Maja* hanging in their classroom and insisted it be removed under sexual harassment regulations.[3] How much more thoughtful than that mature and well-travelled novelist, Marilyn French, who felt 'assaulted' on a visit to the

Pompidou Centre in Paris by 'twentieth-century abstract sculpture that resembles exaggerated female body parts, mainly breasts'.[4]

It is hard, in this climate, to recall the optimism and the robustness of the women's movement of the late 1960s and early 1970s. A concern with how we lived our lives sexually was central; at their best, consciousness-raising groups gave women a chance to talk together about domestic violence and rape and child abuse, to give names to subtler and grosser forms of denigration and harassment, to examine and try to get beyond the old divisive sexual stereotypes – Madonna, mother, whore. It was no idyll: we pontificated about 'sexual liberation' as if it were there for the taking; we were naïve about political power, about our relationships with men and with each other, and about our own darker selves. We were muddled and inconsistent: how could we not be, trying to articulate what we felt, what we needed, what we could just about imagine? But what happened to the vitality of that attempt to examine and explode the clichés we had grown up with – that men are active, women are passive, and that nice girls don't? What happened to the optimistic energy – and at times, the angry panic – of trying new ways of living, talking, making relationships? If consciousness-raising groups often ended in tears, if experiments in communal living collapsed acrimoniously, there was enough support to, as it were, pick yourself up, brush yourself off and start all over again.

What malignant fairy godmother turned that 1970s feminist, confused perhaps, but optimistic about changing her own sexual life as well as changing the world, back into an unwitting victim? Or worse, a collaborator, a masochist who insists on sleeping with the enemy? Or, to bring back Germaine Greer's term, a eunuch? Her 1970 warning seems far more relevant today.

It is falsely assumed, even by feminists, that sexuality is the enemy of the female who really wants to develop . . . in fact the chief instrument in the deflection and perversion of female energy is the denial of female sexuality for the substitution of femininity or sexlessness.[5]

But even in the mid-1970s sexual issues were becoming a battleground. Bitter squabbles between homosexual and heterosexual feminists disintegrated the British movement and drained away its energy for urgent social and political issues. But it was Americans – bred to an explosive combination of puritanism rooted deep in both WASP and immigrant populations, and a popular culture saturated with sexually explicit and often violent imagery – who began to insist, obsessively, on sexuality as the sole source and symptom of women's oppression. In 1981 a Barnard College conference hopefully titled 'Towards a Politics of Sexuality' marked a point of no return. Carol Vance presented a paper setting out a hopeful agenda that offered a chance to reconsider and ask questions about women's sexual situation:

> To focus only on pleasure and gratification ignores the patriarchal structure in which women act, yet to speak only of sexual violence and oppression ignores women's experience of sexual agency and choice and unwittingly increases the sexual terror and despair in which women live.[6]

But the proceedings were disrupted by pickets: Women against Violence against Women, Women against Pornography, New York Radical Feminists. Many speakers complained that opponents persecuted them, and by all accounts the conference ended bitterly, with impassable gulfs that have yawned wider with the years. Increasingly, Lynne Segal argues, a large part of the American movement directed its 'individual fears, anxiety, guilt, frustration and personal unhappiness back to what it saw as the main agenda: men's abuse of power symbolized in pornography'. Disappointed by the inevitable failure of the utopian dream that all women are potential sisters, upset by the failure to ensure passage of the Equal Rights Amendment and by threats to welfare and abortion rights, many American feminists seized on a single, all-explaining theory – one that, ironically, bred further, and bitter, divisions. As Segal puts it:

> With poorer women facing greater hardship, welfare services being removed, and the conservative backlash against radical politics in the ascendancy everywhere, 'pornography' served for some women as the symbol of women's defeat. From that time on many feminists would become less confidently on the offensive, less able to celebrate women's

potential strength, less concerned with wider issues of equality, more concerned with a narrower, defensive politics linking sex and violence. Pornography provided its authorization.[7]

It would also, ironically, lead many feminists into strategic alliance with the religious right, who were some of feminism's most vocal enemies.

The groundwork for the new puritanism was laid as early as 1975 in Susan Brownmiller's scholarly, ground-breaking and influential study of rape, *Against Our Will*. She argued that rape is universal, and the primary way in which men have subordinated women throughout history. Prehistoric gang rapes were probably the first examples of male bonding. Rape is the ultimate test of the male's superior strength, 'nothing more or less than a conscious process of intimidation by which *all men* keep *all women* in a state of fear'[8] (her italics). Rape is already on the way to becoming a paradigm for every sexual encounter. Indeed, four years earlier, Susan Griffin had suggested that 'the basic elements of rape are involved in all heterosexual relationships' though her later book, *Pornography and Silence*, makes subtler distinctions with a serious critique of the far-too-easy assumption that pornography is 'liberating'. Rather than freeing eroticism, it expresses 'a fear of bodily knowledge and a desire to silence eros'.[9] Robin Morgan – though she too would later take up a more complex position – was one of the first to argue that 'the violation of an individual woman is the metaphor for man's forcing himself on whole nations . . . on non-human creatures . . . and on the planet itself'. 'Pornography is sexist propaganda,' she argued, and coined what became a slogan, 'Pornography is the theory and rape the practice.'[10] In the hands of writers like Andrea Dworkin and Catharine MacKinnon, these early thought-provoking generalizations harden into dogma.

Dworkin, in *Pornography: Men Possessing Women*, *Intercourse* and *Letters from a War Zone*, circles obsessively around the image of man as sadistic rapist. She occasionally jokes about it: 'Romance is . . . rape embellished by meaningful looks,' 'In seduction, the rapist bothers to buy a bottle of wine.'[11] More often she describes 'intercourse in a man-made world' as pure nightmare. Aggression is at the core of all sexuality, but it's wholly one way; woman is passive, childlike, victimized. *All* penetrative intercourse is inherently and *always* a violation for Dworkin; indeed, at the end of *Intercourse*, she suggests that 'incestuous rape is becoming a central paradigm for intercourse in our time'. In everyday sex 'men use the penis to deliver death to women'. And she compares 'normal' sex with the sadism of guards at Treblinka, who 'slashed open bellies of living women' then forced prisoners to 'simulate the act of love' with the disembowelled victims snatched from the gas chambers. 'Penetration was never meant to be kind,' she asserts. 'A sabre penetrating a vagina is a weapon; so is the camera or pen that renders it; so is the penis for which it substitutes.' Dworkin deploys military similes at great length: woman is invaded and occupied by men; she is occupied 'even if there has been no resistance', even if the occupied person said, 'Yes, please, yes, hurry, yes, more.' Women saying yes in this way are particularly base collaborators, who 'experience pleasure in their own inferiority; calling intercourse freedom'.[12] One particularly nasty passage in *Pornography* ostensibly attacks the overuse of Caesarean sections in American maternity wards; the point may be a valid one, but listen to her rhetoric. The woman giving birth is 'a whore, there to be used, the uterus of the whore entered directly by the new rapist, the surgeon, the vagina saved to serve the husband'.[13] The baby never gets a mention. In Dworkin's fiction – as in this passage from her 1987 novel, *Ice and Fire* – the fantasies seething beneath her puritan self-righteousness emerge with embarrassing clarity. She is simultaneously sadist and masochist – and her prose is wholly, and nastily, pornographic.

He tears into me. He bites my clitoris and bites it and bites it until I wish I was dead. He fucks. He bites my clitoris more, over and over, for hours, I want to die. The pain is shooting through my brain. I am chewed and He tears into me bitten and maimed. I am bleeding. He leaves. I hurt so bad I can't even crawl.[14]

It's ironic but hardly surprising that two of her books were seized at the Canadian border under anti-pornography laws that she and Catharine MacKinnon drafted. But this brand of sexual politics offers far more excitement than the slow slog to get a better deal for women in the workplace, at home, in politics, or the equally slow struggle to explore the ambiguities of our own sexual feelings, to recognize the points where we do collude with oppression, the complex (sadistic, masochistic) fantasies that shape our experience. Sex, Catharine MacKinnon rightly argues, shouldn't be seen as something separate from society. But her crude version of social construction – social *conditioning* – leaves us flat, cartoon characters leading narrow and one-dimensional lives, smug about our innocence, our victim status, because we've never had to look at our own cruelties and aggressions, or at the two-way nature of all sexual relationships. Indignant puritanism provides its own dubious excitement – the lascivious preacher is a cliché – and indeed, in the age of AIDS, *talking* about sex may be the quickest, safest fix of all.

And an obsession with sex makes for good soundbites; you may not be doing much for women, but you'll certainly get media space. So much prominence is given to two women, who are both skilled exponents of what I call feminist melodrama – Catharine MacKinnon and Camille Paglia. On the face of it they are polar opposites. Camille Paglia does a cabaret turn, Catharine MacKinnon comes on like Cassandra. They are both grandstanding individualists, aggressively narcissistic performers, who deploy simplified ideas with theatrical – with sexy – gusto. Neither leaves room for disagreement, or even questioning. Paglia – whose big book is titled *Sexual Personae* – plays the bad girl, setting out to provoke, jeering at rigorous puritans like Dworkin and MacKinnon. A self-styled vamp and tramp, a streetwise academic who constantly invokes a 1960s dreamtime of sex and drugs and rock and roll, she insists on her Mediterranean origins and proletarian sympathies. She defends pornography, even child pornography, and poses happily, if not very convincingly, outside a sex store, decked out in chains and jackboots. The austerely legalistic

MacKinnon, on the other hand, sworn enemy of all pornographers, is the high-minded high priestess of political correctness. Anyone who is not with her is against her; audiences and readers are swept away by her charismatic fervour. British academic Catherine Itzin refers to her as 'an intellectual giant of the twentieth century' and staid academics treat her lectures as 'a religious experience' and hail her as a prophet. MacKinnon's fiancé, Jeffrey Masson, reportedly said that living with Catharine was like 'living with God'. They are no longer engaged.[15]

Libertarian seems on the face of it to have nothing in common with puritan. But if Paglia and MacKinnon detest each other, they also need each other. The personae they project are eerie mirror opposites; it's as if each has conjured up her lost, suppressed self. Both cut through the infuriating, essential contradictions of feminism, and close down discussion from opposite positions. Paglia mythologizes, MacKinnon moralizes feminism out of existence. Paglia is notorious for her trashing of other feminists, and her non-stop chatter. MacKinnon invites questions from an audience then steamrollers right over them; any woman who disagrees is a fraud, and worse, a traitor. How dare you claim, she rages at an audience of feminist lawyers, that 'your liberalism with its élitism, your Freudianism with its sexualized misogyny has anything in common with feminism'.[16]

Paglia and MacKinnon both inhabit closed, claustrophobic worlds where sexuality rules, unaffected by time or social change. MacKinnon's insistence that gender is socially constructed remains just that – a theoretical ploy, unsullied by any specific understanding of her own or any other society, and undermined by her own remark that 'our status as a group relative to men has almost never, if ever, been changed from what it is . . .'[17] Paglia juggles with archetypes, and boasts that 'when I think about anything in culture I'm thinking about a 10,000 year time span'.[18] Both take the old feminist graffito 'all men are rapists' as literal truth, though Paglia celebrates it, while MacKinnon sees it as woman's tragedy. The sub-text of everything they say is more disturbing: I would argue that both, at heart, are deeply contemptuous of women.

MacKinnon is the more formidable speaker and writer, with an enormous following, particularly in the universities. Her lectures have been collected in *Feminism Unmodified*, and she is the author of the long, scholarly and intermittently brilliant *Towards a Feminist Theory of the State*. Her most recent book *Only Words* is structured as a serious argument about the conflict in United States law between the First Amendment to the Constitution, which protects free speech, and the Fourteenth, which aims to ensure equality. But MacKinnon is a great stump orator, and her prose – raw, sensational, occasionally frenetic – grabs us by the throat. Take the opening of *Only Words*:

Imagine that for hundreds of years your most formative traumas, your daily suffering and pain, the abuse you live through, the terror you live with, are unspeakable – not the basis of literature. You grow up with your father holding you down and covering your mouth so another man can make a horrible searing pain between your legs. When you are older, your husband ties you to a bed and drips hot wax on your nipples and brings in other men to watch and makes you smile through it. Your doctor will not give you drugs he has addicted you to unless you suck his penis . . . In this thousand years of silence, the camera is invented and pictures are made of you while these things are being done . . . In them, what was done to you is immortal. He has them; someone, anyone, has seen you there, that way. This is unbearable.[19]

'Imagine,' she commands us – but MacKinnon's prose leaves no space for reverie, for thought, for true imagining. She aims to shock; her tone is uncomfortably close to that of pornographers whom she demonizes; she, like them, demands a single, simple and sexualized response. The moralist becomes a distorted echo of the sinners she castigates. There's a note, surely, of sadistic pleasure in the physical specificity of the details she assembles. (The paragraph, she acknowledges in her footnote, has been con- structed from a variety of sources, from confidential conversations, from Linda Lovelace's account of filming *Deep Throat*, as well as two court cases.) MacKinnon doesn't just remind us that these horrors can and do happen; she betrays no sympathy or fellow- feeling for the victims of rape and violence. MacKinnon tries to strong-arm us *all* into recognizing ourselves in this primary victim. That repeated, bullying 'you' leaves us no alternative. Her rhetoric melodramatically, literally, victimizes us. In fact, you could claim, using MacKinnon's own argument – that *words* damage and violate, that 'to say it is to do it' – her prose rapes us.

Being a woman is a perilous business. 'To be about to be raped is to be gender female in the process of going about life as usual,' MacKinnon remarks. If a child abuser or rapist doesn't get you, a necrophiliac may: '. . . one never knows for sure that one is not next on the list of victims until the moment one dies (and then who knows?)'; words and acts of sexual abuse threaten 'from birth to after death'.[20] But like her friend and colleague Andrea Dworkin she goes further. Sex *is* rape, and any woman who claims sexual pleasure, let alone sexual equality, is kidding herself. Women who are 'compromised, cajoled, pressured, tricked, blackmailed or out-right forced into sex (or pornography) often respond to the unspeakable humiliation . . . by claiming that sexuality as their own'.[21]

Freud is MacKinnon's special bogey. She brushes aside, with contemptuous brevity, those feminists who have made such fruitful use of psychoanalysis, who have found it an essential tool, in Juliet Mitchell's words, in the task of analysing 'how men and women live *as men and women* within the material conditions of their existence', of understanding 'how femininity is lived in the mind'.[22] Freud is simply the man who 'disbelieved' women's stories of being sexually abused, dismissed them, peremptorily, as fantasy – i.e. in MacKinnon's vocabulary, unreal. ('Check it out,' she orders readers, though I can find no evidence in any of her writing that she has read a word of Freud. Her claims that Freud advocated 'de-repression' are unfootnoted, and the footnotes on Freud on sexual abuse refer us to Jeffrey Masson's crude and paranoid attack on psychoanalysis, *The Assault on Truth*.)[23] She simply asserts that psychoanalysis and pornography become mirrors of each other, 'male supremacist sexuality looking at itself looking at itself'. Freud should have asked, she argues, what do *men* want? Pornography provides the answer: men want 'women bound, battered, tortured, humiliated, degraded and defiled, killed'.[24] And what men want, women have been conditioned to want too.

Working with the crudest model of social conditioning, she denies the very existence of an unconscious that shapes the way each of us lives as women. She divides women into sheep or goats, victims on the one side, on the other the fools who disagree with her. The word erotic hardly exists for her; like certain feminist art historians, she posits a continuum between the 'art' nude, pin-ups, hardcore imagery and 'snuff' films, where someone is actually killed for sexual excitement. The many feminists interested in creating or viewing, reading or writing, their own erotic, or even pornographic images are of course beyond the pale. Camille Paglia, whose glamorized view of pornography is an eerie reverse image of MacKinnon's doom-laden anathemas, need not be taken seriously at this level. It's hard to believe that she has looked at much hard-core pornography lately when she argues that it 'shows us nature's daemonic heart', 'a pagan arena of beauty, vitality and brutality', where 'the lush disorderliness of the flesh' is celebrated.[25] But writers like Susan Sontag and Angela Carter in *The Sadeian Woman* at least deserve serious hearing when they argue that pornography is necessary because it reminds us of the further reaches of experience. Subversive and transgressive, it breaks down the contained, the social self and offers us glimpses of extreme and ecstatic states.[26] Simone de Beauvoir herself wrote an essay called *Must We Burn Sade?* I have never found their arguments wholly convincing; even the most subversive pornographic texts rarely get beyond a thoroughly conventional view of gender. And even if Angela Carter's dream of a 'moral' pornography could be achieved in literature, it might prove more difficult on film. A pornographic photograph or movie always raises awkward questions about the relationship of the real model and the photographer.

But there are no pat answers, as the novelist Jeanette Winterson discovered when she was photographed nude herself and talked to regular soft-core models, who were cheerfully matter-of-fact about it all.

They were all in it for the money, making the most of their assets before gravity took its toll. They had learned to cut themselves up, to split themselves off, in order to do the job at all. The ritual of dressing and undressing had become the doorway from one world into another; from the world of ordinary concerns, where they went shopping and saw their friends, to the hyperbole of soft porn, where the simplest things are overstated.[27]

The commonplace little scene that Winterson describes so vividly is a complicated one. At some level, the models are indeed colluding in an act of violence against themselves: they are splitting, cutting off, something vital. Living in a world where we're constantly assaulted by images trading in knowing perversities of all kinds, it's easy to become blunted, to stop noticing the sexualized violence that surrounds us. But how would MacKinnon's patronizing censorship help the models? How do her doom-laden generalities help us make sense of their world, or of ours?

For MacKinnon *you* – we – are all sleepwalkers in a nightmare world created and structured by abuse. She plays on the double implications of the term, as speech and as action. Pornography works on the penis not the mind; it sets up an endless circle of victims: women who – even if they've gone into the business with their eyes open – are abused in making it, merge with the women who are abused by the *effects* of pornography. And that, in the long run, means all of us. 'Sooner or later, the consumers want to live out the pornography further in three dimensions. Sooner or later, in one way or another, they do.'[28]

But what on earth does she mean when she remarks that 'even Hitler didn't know how to make killing into sex the way the pornography industry does'?[29] MacKinnon's version of pornography, becoming pornographic itself, traps *you* – us all – in a pornographic nightmare. All distinction between fantasy and action, representation and reality is collapsed. *Only Words* evokes a masturbator's paradise where a 'real' rape filmed, equals a simulated rape made 'real' by the camera, equals a 'real' rape that's copycat from a filmed rape. MacKinnon's fevered prose matches Susan Sontag's description of the characteristic pornographic style:

'There are no gratuitous or non-functioning feelings, no musings, whether speculative or imagistic . . . everything must bear upon the erotic situation.'[30] *Only Words* reproduces the atmosphere of that late twentieth-century version of melodrama, the horror movie. Her rapist resembles the indestructible bogeyman of, say, *Nightmare on Elm Street*. We, the readers, are cast as the classic movie woman-in-jeopardy, whose screams of terror go unnoticed. 'Your relation to speech is like shouting at a movie. Somebody stop that man, you scream. The audience acts as though nothing has been said, keeps watching fixedly or turns slightly, embarrassed for you. The action on screen continues as if nothing has been said.'[31]

There is no doubt that MacKinnon dramatizes a very real problem. Most pornography is demeaning, some is truly vicious; it eroticizes violence and degradation, expects its models to smile even while they're apparently being hurt and certainly humiliated. None of us can afford to ignore its prevalence, or brush it aside as quite irrelevant to her life. But MacKinnon makes it harder and her Manichaean extremism seems to push many of her American critics, particularly, into opposite simplifications. In *Defending Pornography* the American Civil Liberties Union lawyer, Nadine Strossen, falls over backwards trying to be fair to the women who go into the sex industries with their eyes open – and makes the whole business sound cheery, cosy, the sort of fulfilling career option you might consider for your teenage daughter. Strossen ignores the brutal nastiness of many freely available images, their sadism and their racism, and never considers their surely conceivable links with discrimination and violence. Hot in defence of the cherished American principle of free speech, she never discusses the irony to which MacKinnon returns again and again: that even the ugliest pornography is legally protected 'speech', while abused women often go unheard, discounted by judges and juries. She was on more convincing ground when she claimed that censorship is always, in the end, used to suppress dissenters; indeed, she argues that the MacKinnon-Dworkin laws passed in Canada have already been turned against feminists and homosexuals.[32]

Many British reviewers of *Only Words* – coming from a

traditionally more repressive, even coercive, society – have written favourably, though in terms that MacKinnon would hardly approve. Bernard Williams in the *London Review of Books* engages seriously with her argument that 'the law of equality and the law of free speech are on a collision course' in liberal democracies, and that speech inciting contempt and discrimination may actually injure groups of people. But Williams feels that this timely analysis is 'overlaid by an oration about pornography which is rhetorically spectacular and in that line sometimes quite enjoyable, but which systematically runs together most of the distinctions that are needed if one is to make sense of the problems of controlling pornography'. Williams – who chaired the 1979 Committee on Obscenity and Film Censorship – points out that MacKinnon wrongly assumes that all pornography is heterosexual and sadistic, for example, and assumes that it has been proved beyond doubt that pornography leads straightforwardly to rape.

She should reflect who are her real allies; who would use the vague and moralistic laws she wishes to introduce and to do what? She will be lucky if they are the friends of women's freedom ... She quotes her friend Andrea Dworkin as saying, 'pornography is the law for women'. This seems to me an insult to women, who have more to fear from the law, and more to hope from it than this would allow.[33]

Indeed, when Catharine MacKinnon and Andrea Dworkin drafted their model ordinances against pornography as 'a practice of sex discrimination', defining it as 'graphic sexually explicit subordination of women through pictures and/or words' for the Minneapolis City Council in 1983, their allies, according to Nadine Strossen, were conservative Republicans and right-wingers, who had fought hard against the ERA. In Indianapolis in 1994, every Democratic member of the city council voted against their law, and every Republican for it. (The laws were struck down first in a series of higher court rulings and finally by the Supreme Court on the grounds that they violated the First Amendment's guarantee of free speech.)[34]

Camille Paglia simplifies the issue from an opposite direction in

Sexual Personae and her collection of essays *Sex, Art and American Culture*. In the journalistic *Vamps and Tramps* she quarrels directly with MacKinnon, labelling her a casuist, a totalitarian who wants a risk-free world, 'a Stalinist who believes that art must serve a political agenda, and that all opposing voices are enemies of humanity who must be silenced'.[35] Flashing her street-smart credentials, Paglia mocks feminists who see a rapist lurking under every bed and cry rape at every unpleasant or merely embarrassing encounter. The current 'theatrics of rage', she remarks, restores the old constricting double standards that feminism has fought hard to dismantle, and she's scathing about people who turn victimhood into a vocation. (Paglia has her own brand of histrionic anger, which she vents not just at the American academy, which she insists has slighted her, but at any woman who could be conceivably viewed as a competitor.) If Paglia is at least as hectoring as her opponents, she sometimes peddles a slightly more complicated vision. 'A perfectly humane eroticism may be impossible'; sex always means taking a chance on pain and loss; the only freedom we can be guaranteed is the freedom to take our own risks. Her suggestion that rape may express desperation as well as aggression, that it may be 'a confession of envy and exclusion' is certainly worth pondering, and her insistence on the power of unconscious fantasy in our lives, her recognition that adult sex is always 'representation, a ritualistic acting out of vanished realities' lend even her more wilful exaggerations a certain resonance.[36]

But for Paglia, too, gender is a terrible (and terribly simplified) line of demarcation. 'The sexes are eternally at war,' she pontificates. 'Rape is a breaking and entering; but so is the bloody act of defloration.' But out of that war – or rather, out of male lust and aggression – comes culture. For Paglia the 1970s' slogan, 'We won't play nature to your culture,' was based on an absurd misunderstanding. Male bonding, patriarchy, civilization itself is a defence against 'woman's power, her imperviousness, her archetypal confederacy with chthonian nature'. (As she notoriously remarked, and repeats proudly, 'If civilization had been left in female hands, we would still be living in grass huts.')[37] Where MacKinnon quotes a Yiddish proverb that translates roughly as 'A stiff prick turns the mind to shit,' Paglia counter-claims that 'An erection is a thought and the orgasm an act of imagination.' Indeed, 'the male project of erection and ejaculation is the paradigm for all cultural projection and conceptualization.'[38]

Paglia approvingly quotes a (male) colleague who likes to say, 'Any woman is more powerful than any man.'[39] Women exist for her almost entirely in the realm of the archetypal, and feminists miss the point when they read archetypes as demeaning social stereotypes. Woman is nature, mystery; she is the Medusan mother, the vampire; her primary image is the *femme fatale*, who is no fiction but 'an extrapolation of biologic realities in women that remain constant'.[40] What feminist academics tend to see as dirty words – voyeurism, objectification and fetishization – are for Paglia at the root of all art. Sexual objectification is 'a supreme human talent'. The only women she writes about with real enthusiasm are those who have learned to flaunt themselves as objects, as icons; who project their faces and bodies theatrically, who inhabit one or other of her checklists of sexual personae. Princess Diana has achieved such astonishing popularity because her story taps into 'ancient archetypes of conventional womanhood' – Cinderella, princess in the tower, betrayed wife, *mater dolorosa*.[41] Philadelphia prostitutes in their miniskirts and thigh-high boots are no victims, rather 'heroines of outlaw individualism'. 'They rule the street. "Pagan goddess!" I want to call out, as I sidle reverently by.'[42] Paglia rhapsodizes about Elizabeth Taylor, 'Hollywood's pagan queen' who 'simply *is*', or about Madonna, with her 'sophisticated view of the fabrications of femininity, that exquisite theatre which feminism condemns as oppression but which I see as a supreme artifact of civilization'.[43]

There is a disquieting brittleness about all this: as if woman's highest achievement is as drag queen. She often seems to be describing a woman imitating a man imitating a woman. When Paglia invokes the 1960s, which she does often, usually nagging younger feminists about their indulgence in self-pity, she scarcely mentions the women's movement. Paglia's 1960s were less about the liberation of women than trying to live out a dream of liberation from being a woman. 'The women of my Sixties generation were the first respectable girls in history to swear like sailors, get drunk, stay out all night – in short, to act like men. We sought total sexual freedom ... we woke up to cold reality.'[44] The cold reality she woke up to is – being a woman. In a *Guardian* article, Claire Messud placed Paglia as the contemporary embodiment of a very American myth of self-invention: life and work as the projection of an idealized self, that goes back to Walt Whitman's *Song of Myself*. (It's also a very masculine myth; Paglia reminds me at moments rather of Mailer and his *Advertisements for Myself*.) Messud further points out the 'lacerating self-loathing' behind the celebration of the liberated self. 'She is a feminist who despises feminists, a lesbian who condemns lesbians, an academic who rails against the very institutions that produced her.'[45] She is also, even more powerfully, a woman who despises women, who has never recovered from that 1960s' disappointment that she can't, after all, act just like a man. She tries to make up for it by identifying with gay men – hailing the homosexual photographer Robert Mapplethorpe as a kindred spirit, a 'brother' – and rivals them in her high-camp appreciation of movie-star glamour.[46] Her writing often has the brittleness of a male impersonator: not surprisingly, as her world-view leaves no room for women to think or speak. She may argue for the androgyny of the creative impulse, or defend the bi-sexual power of the Greek goddess Athena, who 'appears in more disguises and crosses sexual borderlines more often than any other Greek god because she symbolizes the resourceful, adaptive mind, the ability to invent, plan, conspire, cope, and survive.'[47] But Athena exists in myth; in ordinary life, Paglia's creative androgyny is a one-way street. She includes only two women writers in *Sexual Personae*, Emily Brontë and Emily Dickinson; true to form, she sees them less as androgynes than as imitation men. The first 'leaps across the borderline of gender into her savage hero', Heathcliff, the second, whom she titles 'Amherst's Madame de Sade', is likened, in an extraordinary simile, to 'the homosexual cultist draping himself in black leather and chains to bring the idea of masculinity into aggressive visibility'.[48]

This profound, and never consciously recognized, contempt for woman brings MacKinnon and Paglia together. Together, they make explicit a persistent strand in feminist thinking that is rarely confronted or resolved. It's intriguing to find that both writers – almost without exception hostile to other feminists – cite Simone de Beauvoir approvingly. MacKinnon rehearses – and simplifies rather than develops – her argument that one is not born, rather one becomes a woman. Paglia seizes on and exaggerates the impassable division de Beauvoir sets between culture and nature, between man and woman. She shares de Beauvoir's belief that 'it is male activity that in creating values has made of existence itself a value; this activity has prevailed over the confused forces of life; it has subdued Nature and Woman', and echoes de Beauvoir's argument that we are human only in so far as we break the cycle of 'meaningless' biological repetition, and produce rather than reproduce. (It's startling how little interest either de Beauvoir or the contemporary writers display in reproduction, in maternity; their sexualized worlds are sterile.) MacKinnon and Paglia both share the deep pessimism at the heart of de Beauvoir's rational feminism. A man's 'vocation as a human being in no way runs counter to his destiny as a male', but woman faces an impossible dilemma. The emancipated woman 'refuses to confine herself to her role as female, because she will not accept mutilation; but it would be mutilation to repudiate her sex'.[49]

Paglia and MacKinnon come together at this point: woman as ancient mystery, or woman as victim, either way, she is condemned to rape, to mutilation and to silence. I am insistently reminded of Peter Brooks' description of how 'melodrama menacingly rehearses the effects of a menacing "primal scene"', and how often, in its 'gallery of mutilations and deprivations', it uses mute characters trapped in nightmares where they are unable to prove their innocence or name their persecutors.[50]

Paglia's version of melodrama edges towards the titillating; her non-stop chatter sounds like one more way of distancing herself from other women's silence, reassuring herself by identifying with the brutally creative male. MacKinnon's version is truly troubling. Her femininity *is* traumatized silence. Abused, 'you develop a self who is ingratiating and obsequious and imitative and aggressively passive and silent – you learn, in a word, femininity.' And we are all abused. From the opening paragraph of *Only Words* on, she offers a terrifying paradigm of female experience: a primal paternal rape that freezes woman in a state of childhood terror that is repeated again and again down the years, that traps us in the nightmare of speechlessness. She cuts back obsessively to the image of 'a violated child alone on the bed, this one wondering if she is lucky to be alive'. She – the child–victim – can never grow up: 'The aggressor gets an erection; the victim screams and struggles and bleeds and blisters and becomes five years old.' And even a woman engaged in apparently pleasurable consensual sex probably conceals the same dark secret. When an interviewer asked MacKinnon if she'd disapprove of a loving couple who, for their mutual pleasure, chose to photograph their own sexual activities, she responded that 'It would be interesting to know if the woman had been sexually abused as a child.'[51]

A child is being raped: MacKinnon's prose oddly echoes Freud's 1919 paper *A Child is Being Beaten*. Like Freud's fantasists, she seems to identify now with victim and now with the aggressor, shifting between masochism and sadism. Her flat denial of the very existence of the unconscious means that she's peculiarly at its mercy; unacknowledged fantasies shape her text, and lend it power. Her prose can't easily be dismissed because it plays upon, exploits, some of our primal terrors – whether it's fear of paternal rape, or an even more primitive terror of being physically invaded, assaulted, intruded upon – that probably go back to earliest infancy. Reading *Only Words* I found I was thinking of the ugly Greek legend about two sisters who, taken together, incarnate a terrifying image of femininity: Philomena, who was violently raped by her sister's husband, and Procne, who was imprisoned among slaves and had her tongue cut out so that she could not bear witness. Fears of rape and of castration, the horror of lifelong muteness, meet in the legend as in MacKinnon's pamphlet. An image full of horrified revulsion at the female condition, masquerading as feminism, it offers us no hope at all.

4
Women, Ethnicity and Empowerment

NIRA YUVAL-DAVIS

Any discussion on backlash against feminism cannot assume that forces undermining feminism have all come from outside and were hostile to feminism. Nor do we want to see feminism as a static 'ideal type' social phenomenon with no room for development and change. This article, rather than pondering on outside factors and attacks on feminism, is aimed at a critical evaluation of some of the central goals pursued by feminist politics – especially the notion of empowerment – but also those of community, identity politics and coalition building. The article introduces the notion of 'transversal politics' as a possible way forward for feminist activism. It is important not to treat aspects of tensions *within* feminism as though one or other of them constituted an attack from outside. This is not to argue against a backlash, but rather to see that contradictions cannot always be reconciled and if this is not grasped a space is made for reactionary politics. Elements of the backlash thus can arise not from outside but from within the processes of creating a politics of feminism.

'Empowerment' has been a central item, at least since the late 1960s, on the political agenda of all grass-roots resistance movements, whether they have called for black power, raising women's consciousness or for a more general 'return' to 'the community'.[1] One of the major issues the anti-racist and feminist movements have been struggling with has been the effects of that self-negation which powerlessness carries with it. These effects and, hence, the solutions called for often have psychological implications. For example, Frantz Fanon called on the 'Black man' to 'regain his manhood';[2] and the feminist movement has called on women to reclaim their 'womanhood' (or 'humanhood' – depending on their specific ideology). These calls are a result of the view that the internalization by the powerless of the hegemonic value system according to which they are invisible, valueless and/or 'dangerous' is a major obstacle to their ability to resist their discrimination and disadvantage. Of particular influence in this trend of thought has been the work of Paulo Freire,[3] which intimately links knowledge and power. Jill M. Bystydzienski claims:

Empowerment is taken to mean a process by which oppressed persons gain some control over their lives by taking part with others in development of activities and structures that allow people increased involvement in matters which affect them directly. In its course people become enabled to govern themselves effectively. This process involves the use of power, but not 'power over' others or power as dominance as is traditionally the case; rather, power is seen as 'power to' or power as competence which is generated and shared by the disenfranchised as they begin to shape the content and structure of their daily existence and so participate in a movement for social change.[4]

Bystydzienski and other feminists who have written about empowerment[5] see empowerment as a process which breaks the boundaries between the public and the private domain, that comes out of the personal into the social, and which connects the sense of the personal and the communal. Empowerment can be felt momentarily or can be transformative when it is linked to a permanent shift in the distribution of social power. Great emphasis is put on autonomous grass roots activity:

Offering subordinate groups new knowledge about their own experiences can be empowering. But revealing new ways of knowing that allow subordinate groups to define their own reality has far greater implications.[6]

The ideology of empowerment, however, is not without its pitfalls, as has become clearer the more successful collective empowerment resistance movements have become. The aim of this paper is to evaluate critically the ideology of empowerment and its links to debates about solidarity and difference among women, especially those from oppressed and minority collectivities. In doing so it explores themes which have relevance for feminism and psychology as well as for politics and sociology. The notions of community, identity, culture and ethnicity are examined as well as questions such as women's citizenship and coalition-politics.

'Empowerment' and the Ideology of 'the Community'

The work of Freire and those who followed him links the notion of empowerment closely to the notion of 'the community'. Its progressive political connotations of 'power of' rather than 'power over' firmly situates the individual inside a more or less egalitarian and homogenous grouping which is 'the community', the members of which share in the process of empowerment and collectively manage to fight their oppression and become the controllers of their own destiny.

The ideology of 'the community' has become popular in wide circles of the Left since, in recent years, in the Western world in general, and in Britain in particular, representations based on political parties and trade union memberships have come to be seen as less and less satisfactory, reflecting imbalances of power and access which exist within the civil society itself as well as in the state. Women and ethnic minorities have been the primal foci of attempts to create new selection mechanisms which will be more 'just' in their representative and distributive power. The notion of autonomous 'community organizations' as the basis of an alternative mechanism of representation to the more traditional ones has been promoted for that purpose.[7]

As has been elaborated elsewhere,[8] certain analytical (as well as political) problems arise with these formulations. The notion of 'the community' assumes an organic wholeness. The community is perceived as a 'natural' social unit. It is 'out there' and one can either belong to it or not. Any notion of internal difference within the 'community', therefore, is subsumed to this organic construction. It can be either a functional difference which contributes to the smooth and efficient working of 'the community', or it is an anomaly, a pathological deviation. Moreover, the 'naturalness' of the 'community' assumes a given collectivity with given boundaries – it allows for internal growth and probably differentiation, but not for ideological and material reconstructions of the boundaries themselves.[9] It does not allow for collectivities to be seen as social constructs whose boundaries, structures and norms are the result of constant processes of struggles and negotiations, or more general social developments. Indeed, as Homi Bhabha[10] and Paul Gilroy[11] have shown, the fascination of left-wing intellectuals with the 'working-class community' has resulted in their adoption of a model of 'Englishness' which is unquestionably racist, culturally discriminatory and invariably sexist. The perspective of the community as fixed can create exclusionary boundaries of 'the community' which would keep as 'the other' all those perceived different – in other words, they can become extremely conservative, racist and chauvinist (e.g. tenants' associations on some housing estates which mobilize the neighbourhood to exclude Afro-Caribbeans and Asians in Britain; and on a much more horrific scale some of the fights in Lebanon, Bosnia and other 'ethnic cleansings').

These inherent problems within the notion of 'community' are shared, in somewhat different ways, with the notion of 'empowerment'. The automatic assumption of a progressive connotation of the 'empowerment of the people' assumes a non-problematic transition from individual to collective power, as well as a pre-given, non-problematic definition of the boundaries of 'the people'. Moreover, it also assumes a non-problematic, mutually exclusive boundary between the notion of 'power of' and the notion of 'power over', as if it is always possible for some people to take more control over their lives without it sometimes having negative consequences on the lives of other powerless people. Two very different examples can demonstrate the naïvety of such an assumption – firstly, the price children often pay when their mothers break out of oppressive family situations (which is not to say that they also cannot often have real gains out of this, of course); and secondly, the destabilization and often persecution of internal minorities as a result of successful struggles of liberation and independence of oppressed and colonized people.

The automatic assumption that no inherent conflicts of interest can arise during the process of people gaining empowerment has been, as has been shown,[12] a cornerstone of the 'equal opportunity' policies. The promoters of those policies, both in formal institutions and in the voluntary sector, have assumed that the interests of all the oppressed and disadvantaged – be it women, ethnic and racial minorities, the disabled etc. – are not only always 'progressive', but also automatically shared and reconciled. The ideological construction of these policies did not allow for possible conflict of interests among them. 'White backlash' and 'working-class racism' were, therefore, never taken seriously, except as 'false consciousness' or a personal pathology of despair. Nor was 'in-fighting' and the growing clashes between 'women's units' and 'race units', between 'Afro-Caribbeans' and 'Asians' etc., taken seriously.

I am far from believing, and especially far from hoping, that solidarity among different people, as individuals and as groupings, in struggles against racism, sexism and other forms of discrimination and disadvantage, is impossible. I shall expand on this later. However, I do not believe that such struggles can be taken forward successfully by simplistic notions of empowerment of the oppressed.

Ethnicity, Culture and Identity

Some of the underlying assumptions of the ideologies of both 'the community' and of 'empowerment' relate to their analytical collapse of ethnicity into culture, on the one hand, and into identity on the other. These collapses, evident in various forms of 'identity politics' movements and 'equal opportunities' policies based on both 'multi-culturalist' and 'anti-racist' schools of thought, need examining and unpacking.

There is no space here to enter into a full elaboration of a theoretical framework on ethnicity and the ways it is linked with race and racism.[13] Ethnicity relates to the politics of collectivity boundaries, dividing the world into 'us' and 'them' around, usually, myths of common origin and/or destiny and engaging in constant processes of struggle and negotiation. These are aimed, from specific positionings within the collectivities, at promoting the collectivity or perpetuating its advantages, via access to state and civil society powers. Ethnicity, according to this definition, is, therefore, primarily a political process which constructs the collectivity and 'its interest'; not only as a result of the general positioning of the collectivity in relation to others in the society, but also as a result of the specific relations of those engaged in 'ethnic politics' with others within that collectivity. Gender, class, political and other differences play central roles in the construction of specific ethnic politics and different ethnic projects of the same collectivity can be engaged in intense competitive struggles for hegemonic positions. Some of these projects can involve different constructions of the actual boundaries of the collectivity. Ethnicity is not specific to oppressed and minority groupings. On the contrary, one of the measures of the success of hegemonic ethnicities is the extent to which they succeed in 'naturalizing' their social constructions.

Ethnic projects mobilize all available relevant resources for their promotion. Some of these resources are political, others are economic and yet others are cultural – relating to customs, language, religion etc. Class, gender, political and personal differences mean that people positioned differently within the collectivity could, while pursuing specific ethnic projects, sometimes use the same cultural resources for promoting opposite political goals (e.g. using various Koran surras to justify pro and anti legal-abortion politics, as was the case in Egypt, or using rock music to mobilize people pro and anti the extreme right in Britain). In other times, different cultural resources are used to legitimize competing ethnic projects of the collectivity – e.g. when Bundists used Yiddish as 'the' Jewish language in an ethnic-national project whose boundaries were East

European Jewry, and Zionists (re)-invented modern Hebrew (till then used basically for religious purposes) in order to include in their project Jews all over the world. Similarly, the same people can be constructed in different ethnic-racial political projects in Britain to be 'Paki', 'Black Asians' and 'Muslim fundamentalists'.

Given the above, it is clear why ethnicity cannot be reduced to culture, and why 'culture' cannot be seen as a fixed, essentialist category. As Gill Bottomley claims when discussing relationships between ethnicity and culture:

Categories and ways of knowing . . . are constructed within relations of power and maintained, reproduced and resisted in specific and sometimes contradictory ways.[14]

Different ethnic projects can also play different roles in the construction of individual identities. I have heard a presentation by a Bosnian woman refugee who described how Islam, from a virtually non-significant, if quaint, element in her background, has become, through the recent war, her primary identity. Different historical situations can enforce individual as well as collective identities, and thus promote certain ethnic projects more than others.[15] Moreover, in certain historical circumstances, certain ethnic projects can result in the construction of new collectivity boundaries which would include people who previously would not have defined themselves as being part of the same collectivities, and sometimes would have even been hostile (e.g. 'Asians' in Britain as including people from Sikh, Hindu and Muslim origins, from both Pakistan and Bangladesh, who were fighting each other on the Indian sub-continent). As Avtar Brah points out, 'Difference is constructed differently within various discourses. These different meanings signal differing political strategies and outcomes.'[16]

Moreover, because specific ethnic projects tend to suit certain members of the collectivity more than others who are positioned differently in terms of class, gender, stage in the life cycle etc., there can be no automatic assumption, as has been so prevalent within 'identity politics'[17] that specific individuals, just because they are members in certain collectivities, can automatically be considered as 'representing their community'. Only those elected in democratic ways can even partially be considered so. Otherwise, the best and most committed 'community activists' should be considered only as advocates, not as representatives of their 'community'.[18] And in terms of equal-opportunities policies, the fact that certain individuals of the groupings become employed in a category of work that previously excluded members of their grouping, although positive in itself, can by no means automatically guarantee the overall improvement in the situation of those who belong to it as a whole. The widening gap of class positions among African Americans is a case in point.

The collapse of ethnicity to culture, on the one hand, and identity, on the other hand, can also create what Kobena Mercer calls 'the burden of representation'[19] which can handicap members of groupings subject to positive actions and equal-opportunities policies. In the collection Mercer edited on this subject, Judith William remarked:

The more power any group has to create and wield representations, the less it is required to be representative ... the visible demand to 'speak for the black community' is always there behind the multi-culturalism of public funding.[20]

Moreover, specific individuals are usually, especially in contemporary urban settings, members in more than one collectivity. The boundaries of these collectivities sometimes partially overlap and often cross-cut each other. 'Identity politics', which called people to organize (and empower themselves) according to their particular identities, came up against this reality. In the 'equal opportunities' policies of the GLC and other local authorities' 'popular planning' groups, for instance, fights broke out concerning the question of whether a certain black woman worker should become part of the 'Race unit' or the 'Women's unit'. On the other hand, once the budget was tight, the same black woman would probably be asked to represent all the interests of all minority 'communities' in the area, notwithstanding conflicts and differences of interests among them.

As Kobena Mercer points out, these assumptions are part and parcel of the ideology of multi-culturalism which, with some changes, 'anti-racists' and 'popular planners' have adopted as well.[21]

'Multi-culturalism'

'Multi-culturalism' (and later on 'anti-racism') has been a major ideological response in the West to the obvious failure of previous liberal approaches which assumed that racism is caused by the 'strangeness' of the immigrants, and that with the 'acculturation' and eventual 'assimilation' of the immigrants – or their children – the issue would disappear. The 'melting-pot', however, did not make the ingredients melt, and ethnic and racial divisions got reproduced from generation to generation.[22]

Multi-culturalism constructs society as composed from basically internally homogenous units – an hegemonic majority, and small unmeltable minorities with their own essentially different communities and cultures which have to be understood, accepted, and basically left alone (since their differences are compatible with the hegemonic culture), in order for the society to have harmonious relations.

Multi-culturalist policies construct cultures as static, ahistoric and in their 'essence' mutually exclusive from other cultures, especially that of the 'host society'. Moreover, 'culture' in the multi-culturalist discourse is often collapsed to 'religion', with religious holidays becoming the signifiers of cultural difference within 'multi-cultural' school curricula.

Fundamentalist leaderships, which use religion in their ethnic political projects, have benefited from the adoption of multi-culturalist norms.[23] Within the multi-culturalist logic, their presumptions about being the keepers of the 'true' religious way of life are unanswerable. External dissent is labelled as racist and internal dissent as deviance (if not sheer pathology, as in the case of 'self-hating Jews'). In the politics of identity and representation they are perceived as the most 'authentic others' to be included in the multi-culturalist project. At the same time, they are also perceived as a threat, and their 'difference' as a basis for racist discourse and exclusion. Unlike previous proponents of multi-culturalism, fundamentalist activists refuse to respect the 'limits of multi-culturalism' which would confine 'ethnic cultures' to the private domain or to some limited cultural community spheres. Fundamentalists aim to use modern state and media powers in order to impose their version of reality on all those whom they perceive as their constituents.

This has proved to be very confusing for the Left, and impossible to grapple with within the paradigm of multi-culturalism based on identity politics. An ILEA document in 1977 promoted multi-culturalism as a policy 'which will ensure that, within a society which is cohesive though not uniform, cultures are respected, differences recognized and individual identities are ensured'. While the contents of the ideology promoted by religious fundamentalist activists are often anathema to all people on the Left generally believe in, in terms of women's equality, individual freedom etc., they are committed to 'respect different culture and ensure different identities'. The ideology of autonomous self-determination and empowerment, which is at the base of identity politics and multi-culturalism, forbids 'intervention in the internal affairs of the community' as Eurocentric and racist, part of a tradition of cultural imperialism which must be rejected.

Women have been primary victims of fundamentalist politics.[24] Nevertheless, many women have also joined fundamentalist movements and gained a certain sense of empowerment from them in spite of this.[25] Subjective feelings of empowerment and autonomy, however, cannot be the full criterion for evaluating the politics of a certain action. In a conference in Ireland on Gender and Colonialism (Dublin, Spring 1992) Gayatri Chakravorty Spivak defined 'effective gendering' as 'constructing constriction as choice', which is an accurate description of the situation of these women. Feelings and knowledge are constructed as a result of specific power relations and are not outside them.[26] As Richard Johnson points out:

Frameworks are embodied in practical strategies, tacit beliefs, detailed stories . . . I may feel empowered or disempowered, heroic, a victim, or stoical, depending on the framework.[27]

'Choosing the framework' is, therefore, not just a question of applying 'positive thinking' – as some of the more simplistic feminist and 'Human Growth' workshops on 'women and empowerment' would tend to imply. As Foucault importantly has shown us, 'Power doesn't only weigh on us as a force that says no . . . it induces pleasure, forms of knowledge, produces discourse.'[28]

These questions of women and empowerment need to be examined, therefore, in relation to the ways women affect and are affected by ethnic and national processes.

Women, Citizenship and 'the Community'

The specific ways women affect and are affected by ethnic and national processes have been elaborated elsewhere.[29] They include the roles of women as biological and cultural national reproducers; as cultural embodiments of collectivities and their boundaries; as carriers of collective 'honour' and as participants in national and ethnic struggles. All these ways are vitally important to any analysis not only of the specific position of women, but also for any adequate perspective about the ways state and society operate in general.

The construction by the state of relationships in the private domain, i.e. marriage and the family, is what has determined women's status as citizens within the public domain.[30] In some non-European countries, the right of women even to work and travel in the public domain is dependent on formal permission of her 'responsible' male relative,[31] and until 1948 women marrying 'aliens' would have lost their British citizenship altogether.

There have been attempts to explain some of the recent changes in Eastern and Central Europe in terms of the reconstruction of civil society. This is defined as a presence of a social sphere which is independent of the state. Many Western feminist analyses of the relationships between women and the state have shown this 'independence' to be largely illusory, as it is the state which constructs, and often keeps surveillance of, the private domain (especially of the lower classes).[32] However, in Third World societies there is sometimes only partial penetration of the state into civil society, especially in its rural and other peripheral sections. In these cases, gender and other social relations are determined by cultural and religious customs of the national collectivity. This may also happen in 'private domains' of ethnic and national minorities in other states.

However, it is not only in the 'private domain' that gender relations differ within different groupings. Often the citizenship rights and duties of women from different ethnic and racial groupings are different as well. They would have different legal positions and entitlements; sometimes they might be under the jurisdiction of different religious courts; they would be under different residential regulations, including rights of re-entry when leaving the country; might or might not be allowed to confer citizenship rights on their children, or – in the case of women migrant workers who had to leave their children behind – might or might not receive child and other welfare benefits as part of their social rights.

With all these differences, there is one characteristic which specifies women's citizenship. That is its dualistic nature: on the one hand women are always included, at least to some extent, in the constructions of the general body of members of national and ethnic collectivities and/or citizens of the state; on the other hand, there is always, at least to a certain extent, a separate body of regulations (legal and/or customary) which relate to them specifically as women.

Marshall[33] defines citizenship as 'full membership in the community', which includes civil, political and social dimensions of citizenship. The problematic notion of 'the community' discussed above notwithstanding, the ambivalent nature of women's citizenship creates an inherent ambivalence within women's politics vis-à-vis their collectivities, on the one hand, and vis-à-vis women from other collectivities, on the other hand. The famous quotation by

Virginia Woolf that 'As a woman I have no country' emphasizes the realization of many women that they are positioned in a different place then men *vis-à-vis* their collectivity and that the hegemonic cultural and political projects pursued in the name of their collectivities can be against their interests. On the other hand, especially among subordinated and minority women, there is a realization that to fight for their liberation as women is senseless as long as their collectivity as a whole is subordinated and oppressed.

Feminist politics are affected by this ambivalence. Many Black and minority women have pointed out the racist Eurocentric and middle-class biases which have been at the heart of most feminist agendas, at least until the last few years. As bell hooks claimed:

The vision of sisterhood evoked by women liberationists was based on the idea of common oppression – a false and corrupt platform disguising and mystifying the true nature of women's varied and complex social reality.[34]

There are many examples of this varied and complex social reality of women, which, as a result, problematize any simplistic assumptions about what is 'the feminist agenda'. Debates relating to these issues can be found in all areas of feminist politics – whether it is the debate on reproductive rights and prioritizing forbidden abortions vs. forced sterilizations; the attitudes feminists should have towards 'the family' as an oppressive or protective social institution or the extent to which women should come out against all forms of violence or should campaign for participation in the military.[35]

If we add to membership in particular ethnic, national and racial collectivities also other dimensions of identity and difference among women, such as class, sexuality, stage in the life course etc., it would be very easy to reach a post-modernist deconstructionist view and a realization that 'everyone is different'. The question, then, is whether any collective political action in general, and feminist collective action in particular, is possible once such a deconstructionist analytical point of view is conceded as valid.[36] Are effective politics and adequate theoretical analysis inherently contradictory to each other? My basic answer to this question is the same as that of Gayatri Chakravorty Spivak when she claimed:

Deconstruction does not say anything against the usefulness of mobilizing unities. All it says is that because it is useful it ought not to be monument-alized as the way things really are.[37]

Or, to put it in Stuart Hall's succinct way, 'All identity is con-structed across difference.'[38]

Women and 'Coalition Politics' – Linking Theory and Practice

Adopting such a political perspective of boundary construction of 'units' or 'unities' can keep us aware of continuous historical changes and keep our perceptions of the boundaries between col-lectivities sufficiently flexible and open so that exclusionary politics are not permitted. At the same time it still enables us not to be paralysed politically. Concretely, this means that all feminist (and other forms of democratic) politics should be viewed as a form of coalition politics in which the differences among women are recognized and given a voice, without fixing the boundaries of this coalition in terms of 'who' we are, but in terms of what we want to achieve. As Caryn McTighe Musil says:

The challenge of the 1990s is to hold on simultaneously to these two contradictory truths: as women, we are the same and we are different. The bridges, power, alliances and social change possible will be determined by how well we define ourselves through a matrix that encompasses our gendered particularities while not losing sight of our unity.[39]

The question is, of course, how to go about this task concretely. I shall now look critically at several approaches which have attempted to tackle that task – two of which, although creative and thoughtful in many ways, have, I believe, some major flaws relating to some of the issues discussed earlier in this chapter, and two of which, although very different from each other, might point the way forward in effectively tackling the problem.

The first approach has been described in the article by Gail

Pheterson in the *Bridges of Power* collection.[40] It describes an experiment in Holland in which three mixed women's groups (more or less in half and half proportions) were constructed – one of Black women and white women, one of Jews and Gentiles and one of lesbian and heterosexual women. The groups operated very much within the usual pattern of feminist consciousness-raising tradition. Pheterson found that

in every group, past experiences with oppression and domination distorted the participants' perceptions of the present and blocked their identification with people in common political situations who did not share their history.[41]

She talks about the need to recognize and interrupt how we internalize both oppression and domination in order to create successful alliances. Her position constructs ethnicity as including a power dimension – of oppression and domination and not just as made of 'cultural stuff'. She also shows that women can experience internalized oppression and domination simultaneously as a result of different experiences – people and identities are not just uni-dimensional. On the other hand her approach implies that there is such a thing as an 'objective truth' that can be discovered, rather than a constructed one. I would say that rather than using a discourse of 'distortion', one should use a discourse of ideological positioning. I will come back to this point later.

The discourse of 'distortion' creates its own distortions. Pheterson discusses, for instance, the reluctance of some women (Black women born in the colonies rather than in Holland; Jewish women who have only one Jewish parent) to identify with their groups and sees it as a distortion and 'blocked identification'. Such a perspective assumes essentialist homogeneity within each category (such as 'Blacks', 'Jews' etc.) and refuses to accept that these women are genuinely located in different positionings than other members of their groups. Moreover, it assumes that the centrality and significance of these categories would be the same to different women members and disregards differences of class, age and other social dimensions among the participants as inherently irrelevant for the group.

Such an approach is typical of the 'identity politics' which were discussed above and which have been very central to Western feminism. The whole idea of consciousness-raising techniques assumes, as a basis for political action, a reality that has to be discovered and then changed, rather than a reality which is being created and re-created when practised and discussed.[42] Moreover, this reality is assumed to be shared by all members of the social category within which the consciousness-raising movement operates, who are perceived to constitute a basically homogenous social grouping sharing the same interests. Individual identity has become equated with collective identity whereas differences, rather than being acknowledged, have been interpreted by those holding the hegemonic power within the movement as mainly reflections of different stages of raised consciousness. Although to a large extent this has been acknowledged by the women's movement(s) in recent years, the solution has often been to develop essentialist notions of difference, such as, for example, between Black women and white women, or middle-class and working-class women. Within each of these idealized groups, the assumptions about 'discovered' homogenous reality, and the other problems of 'identity politics' and the politics of 'the community' discussed above, usually continue to operate. Moreover, as Linda Gordon points out, such essentialist notions of difference are necessarily exclusive:

We are in danger of losing any ability to offer any interpretation that reaches beyond the particular groups . . . it does not capture the experience of all . . . women.[43]

Even more importantly, as Bonnie Thornton Dill points out:

As an organizing principle, difference obliterates relation . . . Difference often implies separation, but these relationships frequently involve proximity, involvement.[44]

An attempt at a more sophisticated type of identity politics was theorized by Rosalind Brunt, who writes in the influential collection *New Times*.[45] Brunt argues that

Unless the question of identity is at the heart of any transformatory project, then not only will the political agenda be inadequately rethought but more to the point, our politics aren't going to make much headway beyond the Left's own circles.[46]

Reflecting upon one's own identity, the return to the 'subjective', does not imply for Brunt withdrawal from politics, but rather the opposite – locating grids of power and resistance – in the Foucauldian way, which are horizontal and not just vertical, while keeping political frameworks of action heterogeneous and floating. She rejects the logic of 'broad democratic alliances' and 'rainbow coalitions' because, she argues, political action should be based on 'unity in diversity', which should be founded not on common denominators but on

a whole variety of heterogeneous, possibly antagonistic, maybe magnificently diverse, identities and circumstances . . . the politics of identity recognizes that there will be many struggles, and perhaps a few celebrations, and writes into all of them a welcome to contradiction and complexity.[47]

As a positive example of this type of political struggle Brunt points to the support activities which surrounded the miners' strike in 1984–5. This is, however, an unfortunate example, because, with all its positive features, the strike ended in a crushing defeat, not only of the miners and the trade union movement, but of the anti-Thatcherite movement as a whole.

Defeats and real politics aside, Brunt's model of politics can be seen as very seductive – it incorporates theoretical insights of highly sophisticated social analysis, is flexible, dynamic and is totally inclusive. However, it is in this last point that the danger lies. What ultimately lies behind Brunt's approach is a naïve populist assumption that in spite of contradictions and conflicts, in the last instance all popular struggles are inherently progressive. She shares with other multi-culturalists a belief in the inherent reconcilability and limited boundaries of interest and political difference among those who are disadvantaged and discriminated against. Such a belief, as discussed above, has created a space for fundamentalist leaderships to rise.

The next example which I want to discuss is of feminist politics which has progressed beyond such assumptions. It is that of Women Against Fundamentalism (WAF), which was organized in London in the wake of the Rushdie affair to struggle exactly against such fundamentalist leaderships of all religions as well as against expressions of racism which masqueraded themselves as anti-fundamentalism.

WAF includes women from a variety of religious and ethnic origins (Christians, Jews, Muslims, Sikhs, Hindus, etc.). Many of the members also belong to other campaigning organizations, often with a more specific ethnic affiliation – such as the Southall Black Sisters (SBS), the Jewish Socialist Group and the Irish Abortion Support Group. However, except for SBS, which has had an organizational and ideological initiatory role in establishing WAF, women come there as individuals rather than as representatives of any group or ethnic category. On the other hand, there is no attempt to 'assimilate' the women who come from the different backgrounds. Differences in ethnicity and points of view – and the resulting different agendas – are recognized and respected. But what is celebrated is the common political stance of WAF members, as advocating 'the Third Way' against fundamentalism and against racism.

In her book *Black Feminist Thought* (1990) Patricia Hill Collins discusses the importance of recognizing the different positioning from which different groupings view reality. Her analysis (which follows to a great extent the feminist epistemological perspective elaborated by Donna Harraway)[48] echoes exactly the agenda which has been guiding the members of WAF:

Each group speaks from its own standpoint and shares its own partial, situated knowledge. But because each group perceives its own truth as partial, its knowledge is **unfinished** [to differentiate from invalid – N.Y.-D.] ... Partiality and not universality is the condition of being

heard; individuals and groups forwarding knowledge claims without own-
ing their position are deemed less credible than those who do . . . Dialogue is critical to the success of this epistemological approach.[49]

In this, Hill Collins side-steps the trap that Marxists and many
sociologists of knowledge have been caught in of relativism on
the one hand, and locating specific social groupings as the epistemological 'bearers of the Truth' on the other hand. Dialogue,
rather than fixity of location, becomes the basis of empowered
knowledge. The campaigns of WAF on, for instance, state
religious education or on women's reproductive rights, have been
informed by the differential experiences of the women of different
positionings and backgrounds in the group.

The last example I want to discuss is also based on dialogue. A
dialogue which has been developed by Italian feminists (from the
movement Women in Black – especially the women from the
Bologna and Torino Women's Centres) working with feminists
who are members of conflicting national groups, like the Serbs
and the Croats, but especially Palestinian and Israeli Jewish women.
On the face of it, such a dialogue does not seem very different
from the more common 'identity politics' type of dialogue such
as was described by Gail Pheterson. However, several important
differences exist.

The boundaries of the groupings are not determined by an
essentialist notion of difference, but by a concrete and material
political reality. Also, the women involved in the different groups
are not perceived simplistically as representatives of their groupings.
While their different positioning and background is recognized
and respected – including the differential power relations inherent
in their corresponding affiliations as members of the Occupier and
the Occupied collectivities – all the women who were sought and
invited to participate in the dialogue are committed to 'refuse to
participate consciously in the reproduction of the existing power
relations' and are 'committed to finding a fair solution to the
conflict' (Italian letter of invitation, December, 1990).

The basic perspective of the dialogue is very similar to that of

Patricia Hill Collins. The terminology is somewhat different. The Italian women use as key words 'rooting' and 'shifting'. The idea is that each participant brings with her the rooting in her own membership and identity, but at the same time tries to shift in order to put herself in a situation of exchange with women who have different membership and identity. They call it 'transversalism' – to differentiate from 'universalism', which by assuming a homogenous point of departure ends up being exclusive instead of inclusive.

Two things are vital in developing the transversal perspective. Firstly, that the process of shifting would not involve self-decentring, i.e. losing one's own rooting and set of values. There is no need for it, as Elsa Barkley Brown claims:

All people can learn to center in another experience, validate it and judge it by its own standards without need of comparison or need to adopt that framework as their own . . . one has no need to 'decenter' anyone in order to center someone else; one has only to constantly pivot the center.[50]

It is vital in any form of coalition and solidarity politics to keep one's own perspective on things while empathizing with and respecting others. In multi-culturalist types of solidarity politics there can be a risk of uncritical solidarity. This was very prevalent, for instance, in the politics of some sections of the Left around the Iranian revolution or the Rushdie affair. They saw it as 'imperialist' and 'racist' to intervene in 'internal community matters'. Women are often the victims of such a perspective, which allows the so-called representatives and leaders of 'the community' to determine policies concerning women.

Secondly, and following from the first point – the process of shifting should not homogenize the 'other'. As there are diverse positions and points of view among people who are similarly rooted, so there are among the members of the other group. The transversal coming together should not be with the members of the other group *en bloc*, but with those who, in their different rooting, share compatible values and goals to one's own.

A word of caution, however, is required here. Transversal politics are not always possible, as conflicting interests of people who are situated in specific positionings are *not* always reconcilable. However, when solidarity *is* possible, it is important that it is based on transversalist principles so as not to fall into the pitfalls of 'identity politics' of the feminist, nationalist or the anti-racist kind.

Conclusion

Empowerment of the oppressed, whether one fights for it for one's own – individual or group – sake, or that of others, cannot by itself be the goal for feminist and other anti-oppression politics. Recently, for instance, memoirs by former members, especially Elaine Brown, have brought to light the 'disciplinary' practices of brutality and violence which became part of the daily reality of the American Black Panthers,[51] and the murder of the teenager to which Winnie Mandela allegedly has been party, has been one dreadful demonstration of the old truism that 'power corrupts'. And this also applies to the power of previously disempowered people, and to power which is only relative and confined to specific contingencies.

The ideology of 'empowerment' has sought to escape this dilemma by confining 'positive' power to 'power of' rather than 'power over'. However, in doing that, empowerment has been constructed as a process which breaks the boundaries between the individual and the communal. As Bookman and Morgen point out, the notion of empowerment connotes

a spectrum of political activity ranging from acts of individual resistance to mass political mobilizations that challenge the basic power relations in our society.[52]

This paper has pointed out that such constructions assume a specific 'identity politics' which homogenizes and naturalizes social categories and groupings, denying shifting boundaries and internal power differences and conflicts of interest. Also in such an approach cultures and traditions are transformed from heterogeneous, sometimes conflicting reservoirs of resources into unified, ahistorical and unchanging essence.

As an alternative to this kind of 'identity politics' the paper suggests that the idea of 'transversal politics' provides the way forward. In 'transversal politics', perceived unity and homogeneity are replaced by dialogues which give recognition to the specific positionings of those who participate in them as well as to the 'unfinished knowledge' that each such situated positioning can offer. Transversal politics, nevertheless, does not assume that the dialogue is boundaryless, and that each conflict of interest is reconcilable. However, the boundaries of such a dialogue are determined by the message, rather than the messenger. The struggle against oppression and discrimination might (and mostly does) have a specific categorical focus but is never confined just to that category.

If empowerment of women is to transcend some of the pitfalls discussed in this paper, it is perhaps wise to adhere to Gill Bottomley's warning:

The dualistic approach of a unitary Us vs. a unitary Them continues to mystify the interpenetration and intermeshing of the powerful constructs as race, class and gender and to weaken attempts at reflexivity . . . Both the subjective and the objective dimensions of experience need to be addressed as well as the thorny issue of the extent to which observers remain within the discourses they seek to criticize.[53]

The transversal pathway might be full of thorns, but at least it leads in the right direction.[54]

5

Thoughts of a Latecomer: On being a Lesbian in the Backlash

SUSAN HEATH

I write this as a truly 'respectable' lesbian. Just looking at me, you'd think I was still the proper wife I used to be; I've never managed to get rid of that old-fashioned acceptable English accent, so I don't sound belligerent when I talk about my choices in life. I don't 'sport the kind of GI Joe haircut' that Daphne Merkin homophobically associates with 'women who put their tongues in each other's mouths when they kissed instead of politely brushing the cheek' – this, in a deeply unpleasant article that positively screams her own terror of being herself a lesbian and whose title, 'A Closet of One's Own', cravenly uses Virginia Woolf to give her observations a spurious acceptability.[1]

I inhabit a world made possible by brave lesbians whose activism allows me to live relatively openly with my woman lover. In large measure because of those women, there are laws on the books now that theoretically should protect people like me, but the fight for protection and equal rights is more necessary than ever. A backlash is a response by the threatened to those who have success-fully challenged and changed the status quo. And living under a backlash as the 'other' means having to observe and craft one's own story in the context of the reality of political oppression and the excitement (and terror) of one's own struggle.

Here's some of what it's like to be a lesbian living in the backlash. You can be out of the closet if you live in the right neighbourhood in a large liberal city and you choose your friends carefully and you don't depend on anybody else's politics or ideology for your job. You can go to the bookstore and see plenty of books by and about lesbians in the couple of bookshelves at the back or off to the side of the store (next to the section on feminism), but you probably won't read any of those books on the subway in case you get harassed. Your friendly corner grocer assumes you and your lover must be sisters because you're obviously having such a good time together and because he apparently can't conceive that two such clearly 'nice' women could be in any other sort of relationship to and with each other: the notion 'lesbian' doesn't exist for him.

As you read magazines, newspapers and novels, you understand that being a lesbian is just about the last category that is unprotected by the concept of PC: demeaning lesbian stereotypes are still the fodder of unpenalized jokes and slurs. You note that a recent *New Yorker* uses the phrase 'bull dykes with serious armhair problems' to make a point not once but three times in the same article (never mind that the article was written by a long-time feminist with impeccable credentials).[2] You go to a 'lesbian' movie and you realize that the audience is mostly other gay women, who are mortified at the shallowness and stupidity of its story and characters, but who have gone to see the film anyway because how often, after all, is a lesbian even portrayed on the screen?

You can go on holiday with your lover, but if you don't go to a specifically designated 'woman's space' you feel you have to check with the hotel first to see if two women who are partners will be comfortable and safe there. Your local gay rights demonstration is shown on the evening news, but if you're a 'self-avowed practising homosexual'[3] your church won't let you minister to a congregation even if that congregation has chosen you to do so. You're still waiting for a law that makes it mandatory for your life partner's employer to include you on the company's health insurance plan at her office; and you know that if you die, there'd be a hell of a fight if she tried to hold on to your rent-controlled apartment.

Living under the backlash means being compelled to be continually aware of the complex dialectical tension between victory and defeat: between one step forward when, for instance a lesbian couple in one county in New York State wins the right to become legal co-parents by having the non-biological mother become a legally adoptive parent,[4] and one step backward when a law is passed in ten counties in that same state ruling that lesbians cannot adopt their partners' children, because they are not legally married.[5] It means rejoicing when one ruling affirms the legality of a lesbian choice, but then having to recognize with a sinking heart that it is clear that a particular judge allowed the adoption because the women were together at the time of the ruling and were viewed as part of an intact (if non-traditional) 'normal' family. Separated now, they must, if they cannot work things out between them, go to court again to figure out custody details; there is no guarantee, no precedent to assure the adoptive mother that her lesbianism will not count against her this time around. As Ruthann Robson warns, 'When we use the law against each other, we are ultimately being used by the law: to sustain its own (non-lesbian) power. We sustain the law's power when we appeal to its categories.'[6] 'And what if one of the mothers decides to enter into a relationship with a man? There is at the moment nothing to stop the court deciding that a heterosexual home (even one headed by the non-biological mother) would be more desirable for the children. For lesbians, the court itself can – and often does – become an antagonist, complicating, even jeopardizing, an already uncertain situation.

Living under the backlash means cheering when, in December 1995, the United States Courts of Appeals for the 11th Circuit 'ordered the Attorney General of Georgia to defend his withdrawal of a job offer to a lesbian who participated in a religious "commitment" ceremony with her female partner'.[7] This victory was offset, however, by a decision in Virginia's Supreme Court (where homosexual conduct remains a felony under state law) that granted custody of a lesbian's biological son to her own mother. When she learned of the decision, the grandmother told a reporter that she was 'just happy for the boy. He has a chance at a normal life;

his life would have been mighty screwed up if he'd gone back with the mother.'[8]

Being a lesbian in the backlash is to understand that the poisonous filth that goes out over the airways in the name of religion is referring to you, to your friends, to your partner and is in earnest in its intent to stamp you all out. Representatives of the religious right feel perfectly justified in preaching from their pulpits that I am the work of Satan and as such can and should be reviled and eradicated. When the Christian Coalition and seven other religious-right organizations held a gay-bashing rally in Iowa at the beginning of the 1996 presidential campaigns, they 'demonized homosexuals and the prospect of "same-sex marriage as the source of all ills in America . . . send this evil lifestyle back to Satan where it came from"'.[9] Six out of seven Republican presidential candidates endorsed the rally; the one honourable exception, Richard Lugar, dropped out of the race early on. I may not feel at risk in my own particular neighbourhood and circle in my own particular city, but such sanctioned hatred menaces us all.

If I were a schoolteacher, for instance, I would need a lot of courage to be out of the closet; it might be safe in some independent schools in large cities on the East and West coasts, but what about a public school in a small town in almost any other state? After all, in 1992, orchestrated and organized by the religious right, Colorado passed Amendment 2 to its state constitution, voiding any existing laws in Denver, Aspen and Boulder that protected homosexuals from discrimination and barring any government entity in Colorado from passing gay-rights laws in the future.

It took three years for Amendment 2 to be struck down as unconstitutional by Colorado's Supreme Court; the US Supreme Court must now decide whether it upholds the position of Colorado's Solicitor-General that, as the *Denver Post* puts it, 'gays as a group do not have the same right to protection as minorities such as blacks or women' [sic].[10] Try coming out to students and parents in a state where you have no job protection or in another state where a male fundamentalist famously warned against a proposed equal-rights amendment by characterizing its supporters as part of a movement that 'encourages women to leave their husbands, kill their children, practice witchcraft, destroy capitalism and become lesbians'.[11]

As lesbian women, we pick our way carefully through the land-mined terrain of the growing public acceptance of our homosexuality and the concurrent homophobia that proliferates in direct response to that acceptance. Take the sexual relationship out of the equation, though, and you realize that three decades of Western feminism haven't changed the simple fact that being a woman means being at risk. A man who mutters 'dyke' at a straight woman wearing cowboy boots, jeans and T-shirt will whistle, proposition or mutter 'bitch' at a lesbian woman wearing high heels, short skirt and tight sweater; it's their sexuality he is attacking, not their sexual orientation. And it is the prospect of women, lesbian or not, becoming powerful that has produced the backlash against us.

I was a housewife and a mother for thirty years before I went to college and graduate school to train as a feminist literary scholar and access my own version of power by finding a voice and acquiring a profession. I studied Freud and Lacan, among other male theorists, and though I learned much from them, I came to believe that trying to fit women's experience into the theoretical constructs of men does not serve women well. We need to do more than continue to theorize in reaction to those constructs. We must recount and validate our own intellectual and material experiences in order to theorize our particular experience. We know that stories can create and recreate history; we need to understand and believe they also provide a framework for making sense of it – as well as, of course, a framework for producing social and political change, for countering a backlash.

I don't even know if I'm a 'real' lesbian (or even if there is such a phenomenon). I lived with my husband and four sons for thirty years before I left to live with the woman with whom I hope (as all those entering new relations do) to spend the rest of my life. I fell in love with her, and though the first time we made love made me at last truly understand why men are so sexually obsessed with women (if I were a man, I too would endlessly want to make love with women, with that warmth and welcoming softness), I haven't found myself suddenly being attracted to other women in general. (The possibilities have doubled; I just don't seem to be interested in taking advantage of them.)

I did choose, however, almost eight years ago, to leave my thirty-year-old marriage and live as an openly gay woman. I have been a feminist since the early 1970s. I've lived in a private world surrounded by males and a public world where women, gay or straight, have had to struggle for every millimetre of progress that's been grudgingly 'given' to them. I've followed those fights with admiration and gratitude, and, in an admittedly small, protected way, I've tried to change the world around me. For my first forty-nine years that world was entirely heterosexual. And then I met this woman . . .

This is the first time in my life I have been responsible for myself entirely and the first time in my adult life that I am responsible for others only electively. My children are all grown up and there is no biological necessity for my continuing existence; no one is really dependent on me for anything any more. My life is my own choice; it continues only at my pleasure (a nod to the Furies – yes, I know I have no control, that I live in randomness and chaos; you could strike me down at any minute). The small amount of homophobia I experience personally is muffled and politely suppressed in my presence. I recognize my privilege in being white, educated and able to earn my own living without having to hide (or declare) my sexual orientation. The price I pay for the life I have chosen today is mostly economic; it does not result from the sex of my partner but from a nasty divorce.

Coming out as a gay woman was only exhilarating at first – I was in love, I wanted to talk about it. But it took a long time for us to be accepted as a pair; some of my former friends never have. For the first couple of years there was definitely a demeaning, hurtful feeling in the air that I was 'going through a phase', and I only understood after the fact that I had scared some people and made them have to think about their own previously unacknowledged homophobia. I'm still not sure that my choice to live with a woman was the major problem, however. Divorce has made me considerably poorer than I have ever been, which is uncomfortable, even incomprehensible for many of my old friends. It feels now as though the change in my economic status has ultimately been more difficult for them to deal with than the change in the sex of my chosen partner.

Coping with leaving my marriage, on the other hand, has only been painful. The sadness that comes from breaking up a family is hard to carry. The leaver gains little sympathy; after all, she brought the consequences upon herself, she could have stayed. And it is difficult to talk about my sons. They have had to come to terms with a profound change in someone they thought they knew, and I worried that they would (groundlessly) feel that I now valued them less because they were male. I will never know what they really think, but I believe they, and their wives and girlfriends, are fond of us. My four-year-old grandson sends cards to 'the grannies' via his parents, and at a wedding we went to after we first became a pair, my oldest son asked me to dance and his girlfriend danced with mine.

I still wonder what made a hitherto unquestioningly heterosexual woman fall in love with another woman. Why did I have no conflict, no twinge of culturally inherited guilt about going to bed with her, I who had never had even a flicker of sexual attraction to women? My life before I met her had been unflinchingly heterosexual. To paraphrase the psychoanalyst who at a Greenwich Village party was trying to find out the cause of Edna St Vincent Millay's headaches, it had never occurred to me that I might perhaps, although I was hardly conscious of it, have had an occasional impulse towards a person of my own sex.[12] I never felt that I should really be with a woman; I didn't secretly worry when I was a girl that I wasn't attracted to men – I *was* attracted to them. By the time I reached middle age, I just thought something had been left out of me; I thought passion and romantic love were gifts I had been denied – it didn't occur to me to seek a homosexual alternative. And then I saw her across the room. I was forty-nine years old, and I started to live in a song. I became a walking cliché.

Is Sandra Lipsitz Bem correct when she suggests that the sexuality of a woman like me is 'organized around dimensions other than sex'?[13] That eroticism can be ignited by a conversation, a question, a force field of desire that has nothing to do with conventional sexual difference? I think she is. But I also know that it was the expression of sadness on that stranger's face that first caught my attention and then the way her voice sounded on the telephone and the way her shirt collar stood up so bravely around her thick shiny hair and her cuffs turned back so crisply and the way she held her shoulders when she walked. That sounds like sexual attraction to me, and if it was, why did I recognize it in her particularly and feel so free to act on it?

I couldn't find an answer to my question anywhere in the many books I already had on my own shelves or in women's bookstores or in the library. So I started to interview women who had left long-term heterosexual relationships (I defined 'long-term' as ten years or more – this is after all the era of 55 per cent of American heterosexual marriages ending in divorce) to see if they could tell me what I needed to know.

When you first become a lesbian, one of the great pleasures is telling your story to other gay women and another is discussing what it means to be a 'real' lesbian and are you really one just because now you're in a relationship (i.e. sleeping with) a woman. Would you, could you, ever imagine making love with a man again? If she left you, would you look for another woman or would you look for a man? What does the word mean anyway; does it mean that you have sex with other women, is that the defining definition?

Fifteen years ago Adrienne Rich said she meant the term '*lesbian continuum* to include a range through each woman's life and throughout history – of woman-identified experience; not simply the fact that a woman has had or consciously desired genital sexual experience with another woman.'[14] I like the inclusivity of that meaning; I like the idea that one can move along a range from friendship to love to (possibly) sex and not be stuck in any one place for always.

On the other hand, Monique Wittig's definition worries me: 'The refusal to become (or remain) heterosexual always meant to refuse to become a man or a woman, consciously or not. For a lesbian, this goes further than the refusal of the *role* "woman." It is the refusal of the economic, ideological, and political power of a man.'[15] As a feminist, I've always believed in inclusiveness; as a lesbian feminist, I still think that the best way to restructure the patriarchy is to remain part of it and work for change from within. *Écriture féminine* leads ineluctably to marginalism and silence, and silence equals powerlessness.

Without exception, the women I interviewed said it was meeting a wonderful woman that had allowed them to become a lesbian. Some of them had always loved women but thought they had to marry men; some of them had always thought they loved men but had found one particular woman with whom they had fallen in love; and some of them had been able to acknowledge love and desire wherever it came to them and had switched around between the sexes. It seems to make it all so simple: love is valuable in all its forms. What *is* the problem for the knee-jerk conservative right wing with behaviour that steps outside their so straight and narrow path?

A coming-out story: A friend said to me a few weeks after I had told her about my new love, 'Susan, I know (sort of) what the two of you do in bed together, but what do you do when you're alone together in the evenings?' What she was saying is that a lesbian is defined by her sexual activity. What did she think we did; did she think we had no other connection but that of sex? We made supper, we chatted, we talked about our day, we watched television together, we cleaned our teeth and yes, when we went to bed we sometimes made love. Perhaps she wanted another story; perhaps she wanted to hear that lesbian relationships don't have the same complications that beset the heterosexual kind.

I too used to think that living with a woman would be like living with your best friend; it sounded idyllic. No quarrels, unending amounts of sympathetic listening; talking in the sureness of being heard as you mean to say it; no chasms of frozen hurt misunderstanding; no demands beyond endurance; no unkindness; no feelings of inadequacy; no wishing to be anywhere but here. It would be fun, I thought, and so easy.

But, of course, your best friend isn't your lover. It's being lovers that complicates friendship. And it's having been in love that makes it hard to come down to earth and craft and forge a substantial long-term possibility. So lesbians in a committed relationship quarrel and have misunderstandings just like men and women who live together. They bicker over who washes the dishes and when to turn off the light at night. Women who are lovers have just as much trouble over trying to control one another as a heterosexual couple; the issues may be different, but it's just as difficult to negotiate through who wants to be in charge of what. One of the dark secrets in the lesbian world is that women batter women; frustration can lead to physical violence even between women.

I want to think that two women can do it differently. After all, we both know what it's like to feel powerless. We both know what it's like to live with someone who has been endowed by the patriarchy with the idea of being the centre of the universe. Living with each other we don't have to conform to the roles to which we've been brought up. But difference requires imagination, a conscious discarding of those roles. We have to think our way through to new modes of being together that are generously and respectfully inclusive.

For whom am I writing this piece? Is it for a heterosexual audience that wants to be reassured that women like me are really the same as them, they just happen to be sexually attracted to other women (and you know, there must be a reason – did something happen to her in her childhood?)? I don't hate men, I admire and cherish my four remarkable sons; I don't want to live in a world without men (but I wish they'd understand what it is to be a woman struggling to live in *their* world). The men I know are (mostly) decent, funny, kind, sensitive, politically aware, careful not to offend their (mostly) feminist wives and women friends. But they're still in charge: for all the work of the last thirty years of feminism, the structures of male dominance have remained remarkably intransigent. So often, when a man comes into a room full of women talking, the women stop the intimate conversations and, to a woman, try to make him feel comfortable and included (usually by asking him about himself and not telling him – and certainly not being asked – anything about themselves). There are still things you just don't talk about with men because they just don't get it. Even the very best of them. If another woman comes in, however, the conversations simply open a little bit more as she adds to the stories already on the table.

The question is whether it matters if I present myself as respectable and acceptable. Even if I do, I'm still on the fringes of a heterosexual world; I jumped off that cliff when I left my husband. There's a tension between wanting to make homosexuality accepted by that world and believing fiercely that every manifestation of choice should be encouraged. So you don't make waves; you don't quarrel with an old friend when she makes an unconsciously homophobic assumption or when you notice that suddenly now you're a lesbian, people rush to assure you that they know lots of women like you and think it's fine, it's just that they like penises themselves and haven't you chosen an awfully hard path? And when they find out the terms of your divorce, they obviously have to stop themselves asking you, well, what did you expect when you left him for a woman (I didn't; she was the catalyst and that's different from being the cause). But what sort of political statement am I making by helping a heterosexual world to feel more comfortable with my lesbianism? Is that what lesbians should be fighting for? Surely in-your-face lesbians for whom heterosexual acceptability is the last thing on their minds also have the right to be the way they are without being publicly jeered at and despised.

When I heard my partner's cousin was getting married to her female lover and having a wedding ceremony, I told myself I was making fun of the idea because I considered them fools to be aping a patriarchal institution that has served women so ill. In fact, what I really felt was that two women had no business to be making public declarations about their feelings for each other; I was afraid they would make a spectacle of themselves, and I was deeply embarrassed by the idea of being a participant. I had no idea how homophobic I was being. And then we went to the wedding and watched as Chloe and Olivia claimed as their right the ceremony that patriarchy has always used to celebrate a couple's commitment and made the ritual their own. The women who are their neighbours and friends told how much the relationship between these two women meant to their community; the (female, straight) minister preached that love was too scarce and too precious in this precarious world not to be honoured when it was found; and Chloe's eighty-year-old father stood up in church and welcomed Olivia as his daughter.

Attending that ceremony didn't make me want to get married again.[16] It did, however, force me to look very closely at my own prejudices and assumptions. To denigrate choice by the use of unexamined, unanalysed stereotypes is one of the most insidious forms of backlash. The two women who married each other with such grace taught me to honour even more scrupulously the choices made by other women; they helped me to understand how carefully and consciously I have to guard against contributing to the backlash myself.

6

The End of a Long Marriage

CAROLYN HEILBRUN

Like most marriages, whether they end in divorce or continuing companionship, the marriage between women and the study of literature began as a romance. Women, in love with reading, dreamed of themselves as valued members of a community of literary scholars. James Atlas, in a recent book, remembered with passion the sense of empowerment he encountered in the depths of Harvard's library, empowerment flowing from the sacred words of Plato through Milton and beyond. Women, too, have felt the romance of that empowerment. I have memories of such fervent encounters, not in Harvard's library, which did not, in my youth, admit women, but in public libraries and those of Wellesley and Columbia. I, too, can wax nostalgic about that early romance. The joyful past, of course, is always remembered in an aura of enchantment and, for women, innocence.

But it has only been in the last twenty-five years that I and other women have come to understand how one-sided was that romance, and the marriage that followed. Maud Bodkin, whose book *Archetypal Patterns in Poetry*[1] was widely studied when I was a graduate student, noted in the 1940s that any gifted woman's 'imaginative life has been largely shaped by the thought and adventure of men'. We women, roaming the stacks in the days before paperbacks, reserving the assigned books and reading them intensely in the hours they were allotted to us, transposed our adventurous and literary selves into male minds and experiences. If it occurred to us that this was in any way an odd undertaking, we did not allow so outrageous a thought to reach the point of expression, even to ourselves. Just as I would eventually discover the difficulty of making graduate students in the late 1970s and 1980s grasp the sexual mores of an earlier time, so I could hardly make them understand that women in my youth, particularly in the terrible 1950s, never questioned our allotted roles as readers, students and assumers of a male persona. We dreamed we might become an equal among equals, hardly daring to wonder how.

Lionel Trilling, at whose feet I all unnoticed sat, could write, with no fear of contradiction, this paragraph about Jane Austen's *Emma*:

The extraordinary thing about Emma is that she has a moral life as a man has a moral life. Women in fiction only rarely have the peculiar reality of the moral life that self-love bestows. Most commonly they exist in a moon-like way, shining by the reflected moral life of men. They seldom exist as men exist – as genuine moral destinies. Nor can we say that novels are deficient in realism when they present women as they do: it is the presumption of our society that women's moral life is not as men's. No change in the modern theory of the sexes, no advances in the status that women have made, can contradict this. The self-love that we do countenance in women is of a limited and passive kind, and we are troubled if their self-love is as assertive as man's is permitted and expected to be. Not men alone, but women as well insist on this limitation . . .[2]

Trilling published that in 1957, nor was he wholly inaccurate for the time; thus had we been taught, in graduate school, to see ourselves. By 1976, when Ellen Moers would remark upon 'the disgrace of that paragraph', she would imply also the disgrace of women's earlier collusion in the belief that we did not exist as genuine moral destinies.[3] That was the change feminism brought about in the classroom. In 1951, when, still in the romantic mode, I earned my MA at Columbia, Trilling published *The Liberal Imagination*. In the preface to that collection of essays, he wrote the following sentences, amazing to us today: 'In the United States at this time liberalism is not only the dominant but even the sole intellectual tradition. For it is the plain fact that nowadays there are no conservative or reactionary ideas in general circulation.' He added that 'this does not mean, of course, that there is no impulse to conservatism or to reaction. Such impulses are certainly very strong, perhaps even stronger than some of us know.' But, he assures us, these conservative and reactionary impulses 'do not express themselves in ideas but only in action or in irritable mental gestures which seek to resemble ideas'.[4] He warned us that when a movement is bankrupt of ideas, we are terribly mistaken to assume it is at the end of its powers. He then refers us to the history of the last quarter of a century in Europe.

It is important to notice that while Trilling did not recognize his own ideas about women as conservative or reactionary, he understood very well the danger in which what he most treasured, the liberal imagination, stood. It is ironic, indeed almost comic, that the single movement – the Women's Movement – that first and most emphatically brought about the battle against conservative forces in the academy was the one movement he failed to recognize as 'liberal'.

To us women, back in those days of Trilling-like heroes in the academy, the revelation that we, too, were entitled to self-love, that we, too, had moral destinies and that, as students of literature, we could read, in texts and sub-texts by men and women, accounts of that female moral destiny, came upon us like a heavenly gift. It was only later, perhaps a decade later, that the realization that the masterpieces of Western culture are not the only, let alone the most consequential, literary accomplishments in the world, became palpable. Many feminists joined in that so-called multi-cultural campaign, but academic feminism in the United States was itself less concerned with reading different non-European texts than with finding new questions to ask of those texts we had read, with the passion James Atlas describes,[5] in the libraries that let us in. For myself, I am unalterably Euro-centred, even English-language-centred, and while I welcome into my field of knowledge works from other cultures, my life, my past, my present destiny, rest in the great works from Plato to today that I have read and loved and pondered in English. My job as a feminist – speaking only for myself – is to read the ancient and modern authors of the Western world, including, of course, women authors, and to ask new questions of them.

For, what are we feminists advocating in the classroom? That we too may claim there a moral destiny and the right to discuss the implications of that destiny in the classroom. Why is that so frightening a demand to those like James Atlas, who ask only to preserve the glories they remember from their student days? Is it feared that in asking questions of these great texts, we will somehow harm them? Literature is the most innocent of studies, for, unless censorship prevails, the text remains, ultimately unchanged by our interpretations, our questions, our theories. As to the argument that the major texts are being pushed aside by intruders hitherto unknown to the canon, my answer to that fear is twofold: first, that the canon, as an extensive Modern Language Association study recently demonstrated, is still what is mainly taught in college literature courses in the United States; second, that every body of literature requires the intrusion of new ideas and new texts. The English language is the richest in the world, we might recall, because unlike, for example, the French, it has always welcomed into its vocabulary words from other languages expressing nuances hitherto not present in English. A study of the Oxford Dictionary of the English language offers the amazing number of words used for the first time by Shakespeare, a great incorporator of hitherto alien expressions.

From Constance Jordan, a Renaissance scholar, I learn that the sixteenth-century French poet Louise Labé observed 'that to live a life that is never written is to have no past. Memory serves us ill: it gives us only the vaguest sense of where we have been and hence of what we have become.' Jordan goes on to notice that a Renaissance woman 'could claim the privileges of a Christian but she could not assume those of a citizen'.[6] We feminists wish to claim full citizenship in the academy, to live a life that is written and that continues to be written. We wish, moreover, to assert the privilege of expressing what we know, and questioning those who, like Trilling, presume to know with certainty what limitations for themselves women are supposed to insist upon.

The aim of feminism in the academy, as I understand it, is that women's point of view, women's sense of entitlement to a place in the cultural heritage, be understood and sympathetically included in the teachings of professors, men as well as women. Those men in the academy who observe with discomfort the teachings and writings of open-minded, feminist men may marvel, with Hamlet, that such a man could, in a fiction, in a dream of passion, suit his whole function to this liberal conceit. 'And all for nothing,' Hamlet cries, 'for Hecuba. What's Hecuba to him or he to Hecuba/That he should weep for her?' Alas, those who want to ban feminist advocacy from the classroom believe, with Hamlet, that only they, in their masculine hearts, have 'the motive and the cue for passion'.

We women who, like men, encountered Shakespeare and Milton and the Greeks (in translation) with all the fervency of youth, we also have our motives and our cues for passion, even as we find in the very works men cherish, questions too long unasked, of Penelope, Antigone, Andromache, Iphigenia. We need to remember that when Wayne Booth years ago recognized the insult to women in some of Rabelais's jokes and mockeries,[7] he did not suggest that we do not read Rabelais, but rather that we allow those injured and insulted to challenge the text, and that we read, not only Rabelais, but works by women as well, works which, in Constance Jordan's words, question the 'ideology, the doctrinal assumptions underlying our system of social thought and practice'.

We need to know, as Euripides understood, what Hecuba is to us, and we to Hecuba. I think of words written a century and a half ago by the young Margaret Fuller, a woman unmentioned in my college and graduate classes, whose name I scarcely knew, and whose agony I could not then have recognized as my own:

I feel within myself great power, and generosity, and tenderness; but it seemed to me as if they were all unrecognized, and as if it was impossible that they should be used in life. I was only one-and-twenty; the past was worthless, the future hopeless, yet I could not remember ever voluntarily to have done a wrong thing, and my aspiration seemed very high.[8]

My hope is that eventually feminism will need to advocate nothing special because the passions of women like Margaret Fuller, and all the young women whose frustrations she has named for them, will find themselves and their questions of the texts they read naturally and continually present in all the classrooms of the academic community. Yet that hope is hardly likely to be soon fulfilled. Columbia is back in the hands of the men whose primary loyalty is to Columbia College and each other. Even the new male professors brought in – and there have been, since the early 1980s, more than twice as many men as women hired – seem to climb up into the tree house and help the guys to tack on the sign: 'No girls allowed.' The year that I retired in protest, the department turned down for tenure a brilliant feminist woman in a field where we were short of staff (that place has yet to be filled), in favour of a white male member of the tree-house gang in a field where we already had five tenured professors. When, not long ago, I tried to persuade the department to hire one of the absolutely top feminists in the country (who would have been willing to come to Columbia, as many fearing the expense of apartments and schooling in New York City are not), I was voted down: she was too threatening as, I suppose, am I. Margaret Mead taught for years in Columbia's Anthropology Department but was for long not awarded tenure; when her fame made the offer of tenure imperative even to that misogynist department, she declined. She is supposed later to have said: 'I have been honoured everywhere but at Columbia.' I would have framed that and put it in the women's room at Columbia, if we had a women's room near the English Department big enough to hold it.

My own story of life at Columbia is both different from, and similar to, the experience of other feminist literary scholars. To me, roughly a decade and a half older than the first notable cohort of feminist academic women, their stories are both strange and achingly familiar. Strange because by the 1950s when most of them came of age, I was already married, having children (three, as it turned out, since the last two were twins) and organizing my life around them (no double parenting in those days, even from fathers who might have been willing: a woman hardly dared threaten that delicate, vital masculinity). There was the guilt of working, the rushing back and forth, the home-bound evenings (how could one be gone part of the day and the evening too?). By the time the 1960s came, indeed, the autumn before they came, I was working full-time as an instructor (a position since largely abolished), and while I clearly understood *The Feminine Mystique*, I was no longer in it. Indeed, in miraculously avoiding the suburbs, I passed from its major dangers. (Why do I say miraculously? Because the refusal to move out of the city was maintained with a resistance utterly inexplicable to my or my husband's family; I quite simply knew it would be the death of me. If a miracle can be defined as the individual strength to resist an overwhelming, universal convention, it was a miracle.) The 1950s were fearsome for me; Anne Snitow has evoked them well: '[Today] . . . forces are at work, half the time threatening us with loneliness, half the time promising us rich emotional lives if we will but stay home – a double punch combination designed to make the 1950s look, by contrast, safe.' The 1950s were not safe, not for me, anyway, and they don't become so with hindsight.

In 1957, I published 'The Character of Hamlet's Mother' in the *Shakespeare Quarterly*. It was my first publication and I mention it here because, like many of that first cohort of academic women to follow me, I chose Shakespeare and his time as my first area of concentration. We did so in large part, I think, because Shakespeare allowed, or seemed to allow, for infinitely varied interpretations that would not assault the sensibilities of the males who had already conquered the field. Few of us, of course, began by looking at the women in Shakespeare; that I was already looking at them in the 1950s suggests to me that I somehow understood the 'safety' of women in the 1950s to be more or less equivalent to their 'safety' in Shakespeare's tragedies. Maybe one needed to be simultaneously an academic and in the throes of 'a woman's traditional life' not to suppress the problems women faced in academia: except in childhood, some experiences are too palpable for suppression.

At any rate, I was in the 1950s fully of age, and found the women in my social life – there were, to all intents and purposes, none in academia – not only universally boring, having nothing to talk about but clothes, babies and parties, but also unwilling to admit that there were any serious pressures or problems in their lives. One of my most brilliant college friends said to me: you complain too much; you should be grateful for your three beautiful children. She eventually had three beautiful children, told me she couldn't bear talking to me any more, because I made her feel unfulfilled; her husband was weary of her repeated complaints of unfulfilment and knew them to be encouraged by me, or so he rightly guessed. A few years later she committed suicide; a terrible loss, and I shall never forgive myself for assenting to the silence she demanded from me. Alas, she was hardly unique in the 1960s for my, mostly non-academic, cohort. Those years are largely a blur, but I remember when I was teaching full-time at Brooklyn College, a man asked me what I did with my children while teaching: I told him I locked them in a closet. Or perhaps I only wanted to tell him that.

In the 1960s, much remained unchanged. Gayle Greene, a professor of English at Scripps College, describes, in a book she edited with Coppelia Kahn called *The Making of Feminist Literary Criticism*, her experience at Columbia's graduate school, which was identical to mine a decade earlier. Her dissertation on Shakespeare, who she felt validated her, turned out to be a self-directed project:

No one wanted to touch it . . . though [my sponsor] eventually did read and rubber-stamp it and set up a defense committee and smuggled me out the back door. It now strikes me as stubborn and perverse to have persisted in doing Shakespeare with everyone advising against it. Perhaps it had to do with Steven Marcus scaring me off George Eliot by naming every German philosopher she'd ever read and assuring me that I'd have to master all of them to write on her.[9]

That was the story of my dissertation too. I wrote on the Garnett family; no one cared, no one directed it, except that Jerome H. Buckley, before moving to Harvard, performed for me what Greene's adviser did for her: I was smuggled out the back door with a Ph.D. Two years later, when I was already teaching at Columbia, my dissertation was published. I didn't mention it to anyone at the university: there was no one who would have been remotely interested.

The 1970s and early 1980s are the times during which feminist literary criticism, in Greene's words, 'rose and burgeoned'. These were the years when my life and the lives of the women fifteen years younger than I coincided. Older than they, I was, I suspect, happier, if only by contrast. Suddenly the world, and above all the place of women in that world, righted itself and began to sing.

When I published *Toward a Recognition of Androgyny* in 1973, it was greeted by men as though I had been advocating S&M. But that was the year of Roe v. Wade, and Billy Jean King beating Bobby Riggs: anything seemed possible. *Ms Magazine* published a book called *The Decade of Women* on the 1970s; it seems to me now that, if in the 1950s I worried and seethed, in the 1970s I rejoiced. But something else was beginning to happen around me at Columbia, of which I have only in recent years become aware.

The astonishing fact I discovered a few years ago is that a great number of the women who would become the leading feminists of their generation passed through Columbia in either the English or French departments, and *Columbia kept not a single one of them.* They all, unlike me, who got a sufficiently early start to appear non-threatening, expended, again in Greene's words, 'enormous energy trying to get the attention of people who turn out not to have been looking, over what turns out not to have been the point', in an environment unbelievably hostile to what we were doing. I list their names here (and I may have missed some) with a grim, perhaps morbid sense of the idiocy of it all: Nina Auerbach, Carolyn Burke, Barbara Christian, Rachel Blau Duplessis (who provided most of this list), Kate Ellis, Judith Kegan Gardiner, Sandra Gilbert, Gayle Greene, Alice Jardine, Myra Jehlen,

Constance Jordan, Alice Kaplan, Kate Millett, Nancy Milford, Lillian Robinson, Naomi Schor, Catharine Stimpson, Susan Sulieman, Louise Yelin, each now an important professor or author or both. I was the only declared feminist who stayed, although I wasn't a declared feminist when I got tenure in 1966. It was reported to me, however, that Lionel Trilling had his suspicions, and the only reason I made it was because in the 1960s everyone made it who hadn't done something foolish, like publishing detective novels under one's own name or annoying the males in Columbia College. (I didn't annoy them because they hadn't really heard of me; women didn't teach in Columbia College until the year I got tenure. I've made up for it by annoying them unceasingly ever since.)

The price of being older than all those other feminists who came along was loneliness: the lack of female friendships. My friends from graduate school were men, and two of them are still, forty years later, among my closest friends. The 1970s and 1980s brought me women friends, all younger (the few academic women feminists my age are not in New York, and not, alas, often met up with). Their friendship has sustained me through bad and good times. Yet the isolation I endured, and it was extreme, went all unnoticed by me until a much later time when, like a woman leaving a battering marriage, I began to wonder at what I had accepted as 'normality'. Unlike a battered wife, however, I had my life elsewhere with a wholly other cast of characters, in another part of the city. The only lesson I ever learned from Marx was not to let your employer own your housing, and thus I escaped from the Columbia neighbourhood to a different world.

The first half of the 1980s, meanwhile, seemed like good times, by which I mean that the forces on our side were still making some progress; if we worried about 'political correctness', it was within the feminist community that we worried, not in fighting off the radical right. I don't know what the 1990s will ultimately be seen to have brought us, but, into the last half of them, I can say only that they don't look promising.

But what particular form did the backlash against feminism at

Columbia take? In addressing a forum on sexual harassment at a convention of the American Association of Law Schools, I tried to describe what I called another kind of sexual harassment, a kind of sexual harassment that most young women have not yet met. It is the only kind of sexual harassment that does not involve an inequality of power. Most sexual harassment exists because, in a hierarchical institution, the harasser has power over the harassed, but when you get to be my age – or even not quite my age – you have equal power with all of the men. In fact, you sometimes have more power and that scares them very much indeed. You then become terribly, unbearably threatening to the men around you who are not necessarily your age but are in your rank.

Toni Morrison has written of the secrets of male bonding and the demonizing of females who contradict males,[10] and that very much happens – primarily by the use of a device that our society always uses with ageing women. It is something all ageing women experience and something I have talked about often: invisibility. You stop being noticed. You are not, as we say in my world, any longer the object of male desire. (Not that being such an object earns you respect; one of the young, pretty women in my department who played up to the men, with success, I may add, since she, no feminist, was granted tenure, was referred to by many of them as the 'fuck bunny'.) Having lost your qualifications – such as they were – as a sex object, you must immediately be reduced to other stereotypes, and those stereotypes are usually of ageing women. A lot of words come to mind: frustrated, unhappy and so forth. I had thought that this equal power sexual harassment situation was unique to women until a gay male law professor on a panel with me at the convention of Law Schools came up with another analogy when we had dinner the night before our appearance. I do like other analogies because they make you feel that you are doing something essentially right. Law Professor Marc Fajer mentioned that one of the dangers that will await male homosexuals when they are openly allowed into the military, if they ever are, is that heterosexual men – let us assume of the same rank – will worry that they may be assaulted while taking showers.

Of course they are not going to be assaulted, that's a stereotype of gay men. But for the first time, those straight men are in the position of picturing themselves as victims, not absolutely in control of the situation nor at the top of the hierarchy, and that scares them mightily. Someone may be looking at *them*, they may become 'objects'. Clearly a successful woman in an academic department also threatens that male hierarchy.

How did it work particularly with me? In the first place, they didn't talk to me. I think not having them talk to you is better than having them talk to you in some of the ways they did in the past – but one is a social creature by nature. They don't talk to you and they don't include you in important committees, particularly when other women are being discussed. They find endless excuses for this careful manipulation, and making it work takes a lot of manipulation, believe me. One of my feminist colleagues was actually removed from the Faculty Senate by the ancient political manoeuvre of stuffing the ballot box; in the end, she was just too tired to go on fighting, and while no one could blame her, that is exactly the result they had hoped for. In another case, when a feminist was finally made chair of the department, all the men – with astonishingly few exceptions – never spoke to her, but spoke to the (male) vice-chairman instead. The illusion that talent and ability would be discerned and eventually celebrated took many years to desert me. Only recently did I come to realize that if they hated you, even for false and inadequate reasons, they could ignore your accomplishments with impunity. The general attitude towards feminists in my department was nicely exemplified by one of its chief movers and shakers: when asked by the *Columbia Spectator* to name the ten worst books in their opinion, this 'scholar' listed as his tenth choice 'Any book of poems by Adrienne Rich (all deserve inclusion).'

What exactly was the final male manoeuvre that made (or seemed to me to make) untenable my continued presence in the department? To be honest, I don't really believe that getting rid of me was their object: they almost certainly didn't believe that I, any more than they, would leave a prestige job with a good salary for a cause other than personal. But they were at the same time aware that if I did not have another feminist, male or female, in my field to work with me on dissertations and masters' essays I would be unable properly to serve my students. This was an end all the more devoutly to be wished, since a number of talented male students, interested in gender studies and in what they came to call 'queer theory', were also taking my classes. My field is modernism, particularly British modernism, but extending also to Europeans (Freud, Nietzsche, Ibsen, etc.) whose thought influenced the British writers. It was becoming increasingly clear to those not still mired in what seemed to me repetitive admiration for Joyce, Lawrence, Conrad and T. S. Eliot that the major preoccupation of these modernist writers was the fear of the growing social power of women and of women's voices.

An exceedingly talented woman was being considered by the department for tenure. She was fluent in French and German, a modernist, a comparatist and very highly regarded by students. She had directed more masters' essays than anyone else in the department, thus provoking envy and delaying her own work. Of course, this 'service' to students, always of prime importance to those wishing to promote an undistinguished male candidate, seemed only to count against this hard-working female. All the women in the department fought for this young woman's promotion, but I alone was in her field. Had she joined me, there would have been, or so the men thought, a highly threatening female centre of power. So, in the end, they defeated her, and promoted in her place a quite undistinguished male candidate in a field in which we already had five tenured people. There was, of course, more manipulation than merely the vote. The male candidate was given one of the most popular college courses to teach, so that his supporters could brag about how popular he was; the woman candidate was asked to teach a speciality course requiring languages, and was then jeered at for not attracting enough students; and so on. (I ought to mention here, parenthetically, that a woman surgeon at Columbia's medical school went through much the same machinations but triumphed in the end.

Her story, told by Elsa Walsh, was reprinted in the *Washington Post* and other newspapers, before its publication in a book called *Divided Lives*.[11] The endless lies, tricks and administrative intrigues were similar to those practised on the woman assistant professor in the English Department.)

I lost that fight, and recognized that while I was drawing graduate students to the department (and indeed, the president had mentioned me in a letter to an alumnus as evidence of Columbia's regard for women professors) I could not mentor them without a second reader for essays and dissertations; in my last year, I was actually helping students to sound less interested in gender in order to appeal to their male professors. The final shock, however, came for me not with my resignation but after it, with the exclusion of four excellent students of mine from the doctoral programme. The idea of injuring students as a way of taking revenge on feminism was appalling, and I decided to go public. Eventually, the four were taken into the programme. The rejected assistant professor, however, was a major loss to the department; they have since tried, unsuccessfully, to replace her.

When Anne Matthews wrote up my somewhat dramatic departure from Columbia's English department in *The New York Times Magazine* she noted that

Columbia's once stellar literature program is struggling; the department, as of last year, could boast only two superstars – the Middle East expert Edward Said, whose academic field is modern comparative literature, and Heilbrun. Whatever their public roles, their in-house prestige could be measured, Manhattan-style, in square footage. Said occupies a suite, complete with fax, computer system and two assistants; Heilbrun spent her tenure in a standard faculty office, licking her own stamps ... Though Heilbrun has been on or around the campus since the Truman Administration (when she was a graduate student), some senior male colleagues still seem unsure of her first name, referring to her as 'Carol', 'Karla' and 'Caroline'.

Matthews adds that some of my erstwhile colleagues retort that 'Heilbrun has a solvent, amiable husband and thus never needed to work at all.'

The backlash against feminism has now spread to the entire country. Women everywhere find it politic to avoid the title of feminist, which they rightly fear will bring down unreasoning wrath upon their heads. They may also notice that women damning other women as feminists have found the fastest route to media attention. What they fail to understand is that by refusing the title of feminist they reinforce the backlashers.

Feminists are now rarely, if ever, given awards, grants or prizes, unless they are not identified as such. One good example of misidentification is the 1995 Pulitzer Prize for biography, only the second biography of a woman by a woman to win the prize since it was established in 1917. Joan Hedrick's biography of Harriet Beecher Stowe is, in fact, a feminist biography, but could also be seen as an old-fashioned example of a well-established subject in American history. (The earlier Pulitzer for a biography of a woman by a woman went in 1986 to Elizabeth Frank's biography of Louise Bogan, the poetry reviewer for the *New Yorker*, and as womanhating and non-feminist a creature as ever was.)

Will the backlash against feminism in academia of the sort I encountered have a lasting deleterious effect? The effect might have been less were not the old boys cloning themselves, slipping into tenured positions young men who closely resemble them in their anti-feminist attitudes. There are many young male academics who are enlightened on gender, but they do not usually get ahead in English departments. At Harvard, for example, Henry Louis Gates was made head of a department of African American studies and given eight tenured positions to fill – this was, of course, wholly justified – while at the same time, only slightly more than 8 per cent of tenured professors at Harvard are women. Of these tenured women, sadly the most powerful is Professor Helen Vendler of Harvard's English Department, who has written diatribes against feminist criticism, in the process revealing her total ignorance of that subject. It is rumoured that she has a say about every woman hired at Harvard; the effect, in any case, is that not many feminists succeed there.

Still, feminism in the American academy as in the country

generally is, despite the highly organized and richly endowed opposition, unlikely to be altogether banished. The economic necessity for women to work in order to provide the two incomes needed for a family to remain solvent will not abate, and this will affect academia as well as other institutions. Also, whatever young women call themselves, and however mindlessly they may eschew the label 'feminist', they are becoming more aware of their numbers as students in all branches of learning, and therefore of their right to a voice. The naïvety with which I entered the field of literature will almost certainly never return. The disempowering grip of strict Freudian phallocentric attitudes towards women, unbelievably powerful in the US in the 1950s, has also loosened, making women's cooperation in their own secondary position in society less automatic. The rise of gay studies, 'queer theory' as it is fondly called by its proponents, must also have its effect on wider considerations of gender in literature.

Ultimately, however, the backlash against feminism will only fail when it is finally recognized how closely the source of that backlash in the United States, a heavily funded, widespread network of organizations calling itself the 'Christian Coalition', resembles the fascist movements in Europe in the 1930s and 1940s to which Trilling referred all those years ago. Among Hitler's earliest edicts were those against women's rights, particularly their rights over their own bodies and their own professional ambitions. The recognition of this backlash as embodying *not* ideas – Trilling was quite accurate – but actions or 'irritable mental gestures which seek to resemble ideas' must ultimately defeat it and the danger to the liberal imagination it represents.

My own belief, perhaps unduly optimistic due to my long obser- vation of academic cycles, is that feminism, whether or not it retains that name, cannot be expunged from the university. Not that promotion for feminist women is likely ever to be easy; sneers at women, for example, have again become excusable, as racial sneers have not. (A hint of this may be discerned in the detective novelist Robert Parker, a writer known for his feminism before the rest of the genre quite got it. But in his latest books, the belittling of women has surfaced: jokes about feminism occur, as do judgements of women wholly on their looks and sexual appeal, indicating that Parker, like so many, has joined in the backlash.) This sort of thing is characteristic of many male academics, but not all. However earnestly the frightened men in power clone themselves, there will always be some enlightened young men; more important still, there will be women in classes who may not call themselves feminists yet – college women are rarely radical, being more equal then than they will ever be again – but they are not apt to tolerate outright sexism, not having been brought up to it. They may have illusions about how easily their later lives will be lived, but they have a much lower threshold for tolerating sexist remarks and actions than their mothers had. An example of this, at least in the States, is that the right to abortion was won for young women by their mothers and grandmothers, and it is not a right they have been willing to see taken away from them without a fight. Similarly, they take for granted that as women they may, without the need for justification, occupy half the places in medical, law and business schools, among others; Ruth Bader Ginsburg, now on the Supreme Court, has related how, one of seven women in the Harvard Law School, she had to justify to the Dean her 'taking the place of a man'.

But this is not to sound sanguine. If the Republican right can make Americans believe that the major universities are under the influence of leftists, multiculturalists and feminists – and they have largely succeeded in this, despite all the evidence to the contrary – it becomes clear that the ability of the American people to see what lies behind simplistic interpretations of complex problems is feeble at best. If all the problems of American society can be, as is now the case, blamed on teenage mothers on welfare in the inner cities, it may take a few more years for the emptiness of right-wing rhetoric to reveal itself. Yet I continue to believe that, before too long, it will do so.

The Reagan and Bush years in the US, like the Thatcher years in England, have left universities and other cultural institutions impoverished, and their material situation is not likely soon to improve. What will change, however, is the public's propensity for assigning blame and grasping at wildly inappropriate solutions. In universities, as in marriage, conventional views may prevail for a time, but ultimately what are now everywhere in America called paradigm shifts will occur, and the conventional order will sooner or later be abandoned.

7

Homophobia and Hegemony: A Case of Psychoanalysis

JOANNA RYAN

'But what about the primal scene?'

I left the dinner party with the words of the somewhat dour but sincerely agonized analyst ringing in my ears. 'The primal scene' (of which more below) was by now a familiar locus around which anxieties seemed to crystallize when wrestling with the place of homosexuality within psychoanalysis. I had been trying to explain to her why it was so important to mount some kind of professional protest at the honouring of Professor Charles Socarides by an important psychoanalytic organization within the NHS, the Association of Psychoanalytic Psychotherapists (the APP). This protest and the reaction to it within the profession produced many wider discussions about psychoanalysis and homosexuality and the nature and extent of homophobia in some aspects of the theories and practices of psychoanalysis. In this chapter I shall outline the terms of these discussions, the significance of which relates not only to issues within psychoanalysis and its cultural location, but also to the backlash politics of the Thatcher years.

Psychoanalysis is by no means a unified discipline, consisting as it does of many different schools of thought, and also of both radical and conservative tendencies. Throughout the history of psychoanalysis there have been many points of contestation between different forms of radicalism and conservatism. The work of feminist psychoanalytic writers of the last two decades is one such example, in which critiques and reformulations of psychoanalytic ideas about women have been put forward. This has led to a rich plurality of new psychoanalytically informed understandings about sexual difference.

In the case of homosexuality there has been until recently little discussion within the profession of prevailing orthodox theories. Despite Freud's categorization, in *Three Essays on the Theory of Sexuality*,[1] of homosexuality as an inversion (of the sexual object), rather than a perversion, subsequent psychoanalytic writings have for the most part seen homosexuality as a form of perversion. Freud's ideas about homosexuality, male and female, contain many different strands, as Kenneth Lewes elaborates for male homosexuality,[2] and other writers have for lesbianism. Freud's relative liberalism, his caution in generalizing, his consideration of the possibility that homosexuality was not a symptom in itself, and his acknowledgement of the important contributions many homosexual individuals have made to society, was largely superseded by much more pathologizing, sometimes attacking, and conformist theories of homosexuality. As we describe in *Wild Desires and Mistaken Identities*,[3] the socially conservative, very limited and sometimes homophobic views to be found in some modern psychoanalytic writing have mostly gone unchallenged. To critique such views, from both a clinical and a theoretical viewpoint, is not as is sometimes thought to indulge in 'psychoanalysis bashing'. It is rather a necessary first step in harnessing the methods, values, insights, and potential of psychoanalysis for the contribution they can make towards evolving less prejudicial and more adequate understandings of the complexity and diversity of homosexuality now.

At a time when psychoanalysis and psychotherapy generally receive much adverse and badly informed comment in the media, it is problematic, in putting forward such a critique, if this is perceived as adding to the chorus of negative voices. Historically psychoanalysis has often been an embattled profession, having to counter much external hostility, and this has frequently impaired the possibilities for internal debate about points of difference and disagreement. But rather than keeping a defensive silence, it is, I would argue, more fruitful to find a way of acknowledging and speaking out about what is held to be wrong within the profession, for example, the adherence to the more orthodox theories and practices of psychoanalysis concerning homosexuality, in order that this can become a point of positive growth for psychoanalysis.

Socarides, well known for his extensive work on psychotherapy and psychoanalysis with gay men and lesbians, represents some of the most conservative and orthodox thinking in this area. He adheres in various forms to the notion of the necessary pathology of homosexuality, maintaining there are no homosexuals free of psychopathology. His major concern, refined in various ways, is with homosexuality as a result of serious pre-Oedipal disturbance in relation to the mother. He is also one of the leading advocates of the notion of a therapeutic 'cure' for homosexuality.[4] One of his claims is that homosexuals who say they are not suffering from their homosexuality are deluding themselves. Furthermore he has never attempted to disguise his vehemently anti-homosexual views,[5] which are widely available and documented in a scholarly way by Lewes.[6]

It seemed shocking, therefore, that an association of professionals within the NHS should confer some respectability and legitimation on Socarides by inviting him to give their prestigious annual lecture (in April 1995). There seemed little chance of a serious discussion in which dissenting psychoanalytic views on homosexuality could be aired since the 'discussant' for the lecture was Dr Ismond Rosen. Rosen is editor of one of the main textbooks on sexual deviation.[7] In this, homosexuality is uncompromisingly seen as a form of perversion. His own theories differ only slightly from those of Socarides. And further, he argued on British television some years previously in favour of Clause 28 of the Local Government Act of 1988 (of which more below), thereby placing himself squarely in the public domain in relation to gay and lesbian politics.

The organizers of this APP lecture were taken aback by the extent of the reaction to their honouring of Socarides. This reaction included articles in the national media underscoring the extent of professional division on this subject,[8] and also the circulation of a Letter of Concern, expressing serious dismay at the implications of the invitation to Socarides, and raising related issues concerning possibly discriminatory attitudes and practices within the profession.[9] We may perhaps be surprised at their seeming naïvety as to how their invitation to Socarides would be construed, and wonder how such naïvety is possible from positions of considerable professional and institutional power. Or else we can wonder what it is about psychoanalysis that has allowed the seeming persistence of attitudes and theories such as Socarides's within the psychoanalytic establishment.

The possibilities for dissent, dialogue or difference in relation to homosexuality are worryingly limited within the psychoanalytic profession. There are many individual practitioners who do not see homosexuality as necessarily a symptom of underlying disturbance, and who would endorse the possibility of gay men and lesbians as practising psychotherapists and psychoanalysts. However, this is largely a silent, unreported and until recently undiscussed point of view, that has not contributed as it should to the development of psychoanalytic thought on this subject. There are very few case histories involving homosexuality that present other than orthodox points of view, and little theorizing that challenges the dominant positions which are largely taught in the training organizations. This state of affairs can be described as hegemonic. Such hegemony has been disturbingly confirmed by the many psychotherapists who said they would like to sign the letter but did not dare do so from fear of the professional consequences. The degree of outrage expressed by yet other professionals about the protest has been considerable – the instigators of the letter have been accused amongst other things of 'damaging psychoanalysis'. The damaging effects of psychoanalysis on the lives of many gay and lesbian individuals in legitimating and supporting anti-homosexual ideas and practices disappears in this concern to protect the profession.

The wider context of this is the recent history in Britain of legislation about homosexuality, which illustrates the various forms of backlash against both the liberalizing legislation of the 1960s and the many changes in lesbian and gay lifestyles that have taken place. Anna Marie Smith[10] usefully applies the notion of hegemony to an understanding of these anti-homosexual aspects of Thatcherite politics of Britain in the 1980s. She puts forward an understanding of hegemony in which articulations of ideas become hegemonic not through popularity but through the normalization of the notion that there is no alternative; hegemonic articulations become established as the rules which bestow coherence and intelligibility. Smith argues that the demonization of queerness in the latter part of that decade was central to the legitimation of Thatcherism, part of a new right tradition of fostering and attacking an 'enemy within'.

The last decade has indeed seen an unprecedented amount of anti-homosexual legislation or attempts at such legislation, much of it concerning family issues. Clause 28 prohibits local authorities from funding activities that 'promote' the acceptability of homosexuality, which is named as a 'pretended' family relationship. There followed restrictions on the access of lesbians and single women to donor insemination, in the Human Fertilization and Embryology Act, 1990. A nearly successful attempt was made to curtail the rights of lesbians and gay men to be foster parents (under guidance regulations for the Children Act, 1989). Clause 25 of the Criminal Justice Bill increased the severity of penalties for various sexual acts in public, mainly acts for which gay men particularly have been or are likely to be prosecuted (e.g. gross indecency, soliciting). The illegality of consensual SM sex between adults in private was also established, following the Operation Spanner case, in a ruling which is widely considered to affect gay men particularly.

This spate of legislation could be seen as a backlash against the undoubted gains in the possibilities for lesbian and gay lifestyles since the 1960s, part of the onslaught on the so-called permissiveness that the right likes to lay at the door of the left. It is undoubtedly a central part of the right's campaign for 'family values'. To talk about backlash, however, is to remain within the terms of a discourse of suppression and liberation, and also contributes to a notion of gay victimology. Rather, the Thatcherite attack was an attempt to ensure the hegemony of heterosexuality by legislating that lesbian and gay families were only a pretence – an extraordinarily imperialistic move which also underscores the importance of language to power. Not only were certain activities (for example financial support for lesbian and gay groups, sex education that could be construed as endorsing homosexuality) rendered illegal, but the very terms of description of homosexual relationships were enshrined in legislation.

Through such legislation the 'family' is deemed to exclude lesbian parenting or what Smith calls 'dangerous queerness'. She argues that lesbian mothering, along with the figure of the black lesbian, became symbolic of what was regarded in 'official' discourse as unacceptable homosexuality, to be contrasted with respectable, untroubling homosexuality.[11] This attempt to differentiate between homosexuality which does not in any way disrupt or threaten the prevailing social order, which is in effect totally closeted, and that which is regarded as threatening or excessive, because it is open or assertive, she sees as a tactic to hide the anti-homosexual nature of the attack on various forms of lesbian and gay relationships. The fantastical nature of this construction of the 'family' (like that of the 'nation' in racist discourse), in the face of the lived experience of lesbian (and gay) parenting, is revealed by the violence and absurdity of describing these relationships as 'pretended'. Smith also underlines how this representation of lesbian reproductive activity as dangerous is part of a wider attack on women's rights to control their own bodies and create their own forms of non-patriarchal family relationships.

Clause 28 attracted massive protest. It is still (at the date of writing) law, and there are many recorded instances of local authorities using it to justify the withdrawal of funding and the curtailment of sex education. Although the protests[12] did not change the law, it is generally agreed that this ostensibly repressive move has been 'productive' in Foucault's sense, in that it generated enormous amounts of discussion, publicity and understanding of lesbian families. Generally speaking, the last twenty years have seen a sea-change in the possibilities for lesbians as regards having children – lesbian families in all their staggering variety have become much more of a recognized phenomenon, much more of a practical and subjective possibility for many women. Romans,[13] for example, in her survey of lesbian motherhood describes the changes that have taken place from a position of 'almost silent apology to a positive and confident assertion that lesbian motherhood [is] a valid, alternative lifestyle in which to raise children'. 'Lesbian' no longer has to equal childless as it used to in popular, scientific and also lesbian imagination. Apart from the possibilities opened up by donor insemination (either self-insemination or through a clinic), lesbian mothers in previously heterosexual relationships have somewhat better chances of keeping custody of their children than used to be the case. Lesbian (and gay) fostering and adoption has also become more of an established practice, despite the often vocal opposition to it.

This briefly sketched background is the context in which the seeming alignment of some sections of contemporary psychoanalysis with homophobic views and practices takes on a special significance. The APP's invitation to Socarides to give their annual lecture, combined with the protest against this, has brought much of this into the open and created an unprecedented amount of discussion within the profession. Although deplorable, it has, like Clause 28, been 'productive'. What this has also underlined, however, is the hegemonic status of the main psychoanalytic theories about homosexuality, which persists despite the divergent views and practices of many individual practitioners. In *Wild Desires and Mistaken Identities*[14] we describe the paucity of dissenting or alternative positions within psychoanalysis, and the marginalized status of oppositional voices – something we attempt to address by both a critique and a reformulation of the issues.

In some of its theories and concepts psychoanalysis bears an uncomfortable resemblance to right-wing discourse. The depiction of lesbian and gay families as 'pretended' in Clause 28 uncomfortably echoes one leading psychoanalyst's descriptions of lesbians as having 'fictive' identities. She, Joyce McDougall, sees lesbians as maintaining 'the *illusion* of being the true sexual partner to another woman'[15] (my italics). For McDougall, 'true' sexual desire can only occur between a man and a woman: in perversion, there is a denial of the difference between the sexes, and also that this difference is the cause or condition of sexual desire. Another analyst, Janine Chasseguet-Smirgel, argues that homosexual creativity in art is 'pseudo-creativity'.[16] Such statements occur in the context of the modern psychoanalytic consignment of homosexuality to the category of perversion, something that is at the basis of many psychoanalytic ideas about gender and sexuality.

Homophobia in a wider context has many possible origins, but most socio-psychological studies suggest that it correlates with generally authoritarian attitudes and with very traditional and rigidly held views about gender roles for men and women.[17] The kind of psychoanalytic theories that most support the notion of homosexuality as perversion are those in which, amongst other things, homosexuality is seen as either linked to or stemming from a supposed disorder in gender identity, i.e. in the assumedly right or natural order of things in relation to masculinity and femininity. For example, Socarides sees male homosexuals as having 'faulty' gender identities,[18] and McDougall cites a 'deviation' in gender identity as typical of her lesbian patients.[19]

This extremely common psychoanalytic conflation between sexual orientation and gender identity issues can be criticized on clinical grounds, as we do in *Wild Desires and Mistaken Identities*. Its significance also lies in the naturalism or biologism concerning men and women that it often supports, and its conformity to unquestioned social norms. It is just this conflation, seen for example in the assumption that a male homosexual must be feminine in character, that Freud argued so strongly against at the beginning of *Three Essays on the Theory of Sexuality*. He did however later substantially depart from this position,[20] in describing his female homosexual patient as taking up a masculine attitude. Later psychoanalytic writers developed this ascription of masculinity much further into disorders of gender identity, with Freud's earlier views being altogether dropped.

The Letter of Concern, which my dinner-party analyst refused to sign, also drew attention to possible discriminatory practices in admission to training on the part of some psychoanalytic organizations. This question has been aired in print before now,[21] but not received any considered discussion, other than a blank denial from the organizations in question. Freud's letter to Jones in 1921, cited by Lewes,[22] in which he opposes the exclusion of candidates from psychoanalytic trainings on grounds of homosexuality, has become an obscure footnote in history, contradicted by discriminatory practices in many countries. The concern about discrimination turns round the question of whether the criteria for admission to training as an analyst or psychotherapist specifically or by implication exclude gay men and lesbians. This is especially so in the case of those organizations whose explicit criteria specify perversion as a ground for non-acceptance, given that many psychoanalytic theories include homosexuality as amongst the perversions.

Although my dinner-party analyst certainly did not support any such discrimination, she did spontaneously reveal some common psychoanalytic anxieties and prejudices about homosexuality that stultify and rigidify thought on this subject. She was very worried, she said, by a lesbian patient of hers who was pregnant with a baby conceived by donor insemination (DI). How would the baby manage without any father and being conceived without sexual intercourse having taken place? I glossed over the fact that she had moved from discussing with me the theories and position of the Institute of Psycho-Analysis, and the extreme difficulty that she freely acknowledged about getting any discussion about homosexuality going there (it was, she said, like a Freemasonry), to effectively telling me what disturbing things lesbians do. This was to become a familiar form of argument (if we can call it that): look how pathological they really are. Lesbian motherhood, especially via DI, was the favourite form of this, speaking perhaps to age-old social anxieties about who is seen as fit to reproduce, and the licence that so many people feel they have to make judgements about this. The other strong contender for the look-how-disturbed-they-really-are argument, which my discussant also mentioned, are the homosexual patients seen at the HIV and AIDS groups at the Tavistock Clinic, about whom several papers have been written by the analysts concerned.[23] These patients seem to have become frighteningly emblematic for the disturbances allegedly associated with homosexuality, in that they were frequently cited to us in discussions arising from the Socarides invitation.

Moral panics about who is fit to reproduce are familiar to anyone versed in the history of sexuality; immigrants, mentally handicapped people, the supposedly degenerate working class, have all been targeted as threats to either the purity of the race or the social order – as single mothers and lesbian mothers now are. What is problematic for our purposes is when this kind of concern creeps into the practice of psychoanalysis. The rapid and usually unacknowledged move from discussion of the meaning for the patient when DI is involved to an over-anxious and excessive concern about the actual baby was a recurrent phenomenon of these debates, echoing what little there is in the psychoanalytic literature on the subject. Thus the eminent Kleinian psychoanalyst Hanna Segal: 'Two lesbians adopting a baby ... what the hell is going to happen to this boy [sic] when he reaches adolescence?'[24]; and John Padel, referring to the process of identification of the self with aspects of the parents, 'Perhaps the difficulty in making such an identification should be a strong reason against the bringing up of a child by a lesbian couple.'[25]

As part of the ensuing discussion around Socarides, other psychotherapists have also spontaneously come up with anxieties about their lesbian patients who have or intend to have babies. 'Surely,' another therapist, also very concerned about the procreative activities of her lesbian patient, assured me, 'the symbolic meaning of lesbian relationships is that they are infertile?' This particular form of crude biologism, in which the heterosexual basis of reproduction is made into one of the criteria of psychic maturity and health, has often come from Kleinian quarters.

Why does an analytic stance become subsumed to other considerations when trained analysts are faced by lesbian motherhood? It seems that in these cases the phantasy of the analyst replaces or displaces that of the patient. A particularly ignorant form of developmental psychology takes over from psychoanalysis. Ironically, actual developmental psychology studies of children brought up by lesbians have repeatedly failed to find any important differences let alone deleterious effects,[26] when compared to other children. Thus in a comprehensive review of existing studies, which covered a wide range of characteristics and groups, very few differences were found, and none repeatedly. Strikingly, no disturbances of gender identity were reported despite the confident assertions of some analysts, not in fact based on any clinical evidence to this effect. This corroborates an earlier English study[27] by Golombek, Spencer and Rutter, which specifically looked at aspects of gender identity, sex-role behaviour and (where appropriate) sexual orientation in the children. Again no differences were found.

It is, of course, very significant that gender identity is what is focused on in this way because, as we have seen, the conflation of gender identity with sexual orientation lies at the heart of so many psychoanalytic theories where homosexuality is rendered as a perversion. Furthermore, one of the few psychoanalytic studies to look at dread of homosexuality[28] found that such fears in heterosexual male patients are closely related to the felt threat homosexual impulses pose to their status as men, that is their masculinity or gender identity.

Many of the most anxious responses to homosexuality thus appear to contain a barely dressed-up naturalism of the crudest kind, and it does seem that this lies at the basis of at least some psychoanalytic homophobia. The notion that there is an essential complementarity of the genders, and that full psychic maturity is to be found only in such a complementary union is a common one. The idea of complementarity in relation to gender exerts a strong hold on the psychoanalytic imagination, even where this is not attributed to biology. Like all complementarities it does rest on a basic and unquestioned binarism of thought, which, as we have argued in *Wild Desires and Mistaken Identities*, underlies the privileging of heterosexuality.

The ideological status of such naturalism and binarism is never considered by its adherents; this just is 'reality' and lesbians and others are perverse in their denial of this reality, they do not know the 'truth'. Thus Segal: 'I think that there is some reality sense and some innate idea about the parental couple and creative sexuality which is attacked by homosexuality.'[29]

The role and function of such biologistic ideas in supporting homophobic attitudes and practices is thus apparent.

One of the accusations hurled at us, the organizers of the Letter of Concern, was that we were 'standing psychoanalysis on its head'. It was also maintained that Socarides's ideas were not so discredited in the psychoanalytic world.[30] This notion, that some fundamental order of things is being disrupted, is also to be found in one of Socarides's pronouncements,[31] that to support or advocate homosexuality rather than heterosexuality is 'to turn the world upside down'. Another analyst, Hildebrand, in his account of working with a dying AIDS patient, finds it necessary to assert the heterosexual normality of his own life (young children, riding, swimming, enjoying life), as if this was a highly necessary prop, something none of his patients would have access to, but one under threat from contact with such patients. It is, he says, 'difficult for us to maintain our inner standards when they [homosexual AIDS patients] come to us with their existential problems'.[32]

What is felt to be so threatened? Recently a Tory minister spoke in positive tones about the richness and diversity of gay and lesbian lifestyles[33] and against the notion of homosexuality as any kind of illness. Why does an influential group of analysts cling to the notion of homosexuality as a perversion? And why do the many more liberal-minded practitioners, who do not actually subscribe to this view, feel so unable to speak out, even in the face of the flagrant institutional support for someone as extremely homophobic as Socarides?

Let us return to the dinner-party analyst. What she was asserting with such conviction was the unquestionable status of the primal scene, thereby demonstrating a form of fundamentalism in her thought. What is the nature of her (and many other analysts') belief in this? Primal phantasies, according to Laplanche and Pontalis,[34] are 'typical' phantasy structures, '. . . which psychoanalysis reveals to be responsible for the organization of phantasy life, regardless of the personal experiences of different subjects'.

The examples they, following Freud, give of such structures are interuterine existence, primal scene, castration and seduction. The primal scene is that of sexual intercourse between the parents which, it is held, the child either observes, infers or phantasizes, and which the child generally interprets as an act of violence on the part of the father. In the Kleinian version the phantasy of the 'combined parental figure' is one in which the parents, or rather their sexual organs, are locked together in permanent intercourse.[35] The infant is conceived of as wishing to attack this couple as well as endowing them with violence towards each other.

Laplanche and Pontalis note Freud's emphasis on the universality of these phantasies, 'the constant sameness' that characterizes these phantasies. This he attributed to some element of phylogenetic inheritance. Others, especially Kleinian writers, refer to unconscious phantasies having an 'innate form', and the infant as possessing innate knowledge (cf. Segal, above).

Laplanche and Pontalis underline how such primal phantasies provide a representation and a seeming solution to what may be a major enigma for the child. In the case of the primal scene this is the child's own origins. The exploration of anyone's anxieties, phantasies and ideas of how they came about and what this means for the person concerned is often an important concern in psychoanalytic work. However, this does not mean that there is therefore one answer to the enigma of origins (heterosexual intercourse, on either the Freudian or Kleinian model) that either will or should be found in the analysand's phantasies, though of course some version of this may well be quite common. It is rather that one answer is found within psychoanalytic theory, as to what must be the content of such phantasies, and this is made normative and universal. A particularly problematic version of this is found in the

Kleinian account of homosexuality, which undoubtedly has been and still is a major influence on British psychoanalytic thinking about homosexuality.

In such thinking biological phenomena are unquestioningly made into psychic and social reality. This is a familiar form of conservatism, and something which all 'waves' of feminism have had to contend with, in different historical periods. A preoccupation with the allegedly universal and supposedly innately known primal scene seems to lead to the neglect of the meaning that the putative lesbian mother attributes to her baby's conception both for herself and the child. The imposition of this schema means that the diversity and richness of experience, especially in more unusual forms of parenting, are seldom heard and inadequately understood.

What would cause psychoanalytically trained people to drop their careful psychoanalytic thinking in favour of such a crude and concrete dogmatism? What kinds of anxiety are provoked by the thought of women reproducing without men? Of children being brought up in lesbian milieux/families? It is precisely psychoanalysis that might be able to provide useful insights here, although so far it has scarcely done so. What is also needed is more reflectiveness on the part of psychoanalysts as to the embeddedness of their theories within aspects of the prevailing culture. If such reflection is missing, and if there is little understanding of the anxieties and defences surrounding homosexuality, then it is likely that distancing or attacking responses will ensue.

A frequent accusation made against the Letter of Concern was that it was 'too political'. This has also been used as the justification by most of the professional journals approached for refusing to publish it, along with the signatures. It is instructive to ponder on what 'too political' signifies. In the mouths of those criticizing us it appears to mean too partisan, not purely concerned with clinical issues (the proper domain, by implication), polarizing, attacking and controversial.

In this context the criticism that the letter was an attempt to limit freedom of speech is interesting. Firstly, of course, it was not true, in that we actually called for more debate not less.[36] Secondly, it assumes a level playing field to exist within psychoanalytic discourse as regards the expression of dissenting views, which it most certainly does not. What about the freedom of speech of those too frightened to sign the letter? Thirdly, the worry about freedom of speech seems to take over from the issues themselves – what people actually think about homosexuality in a professional context, and perhaps disguises views that people fear will be unpopular. It also protects against the knowledge of what damage can be done by the legitimation of homophobic views, and indeed has been done within the history of psychoanalysis in relation to many gay and lesbian patients. In such a way it is a defensive and diffusing tactic.

The accusation of 'too political' also carries with it the unargued assumption that psychoanalysis is or ought to be a politics-free zone. Of course there is a certain kind of autonomy and specificity to clinical work: that is not what I am concerned with here. It is rather the ruling out of court of all the many questions of power and knowledge, of professional issues of patronage and access to training and other opportunities, surrounding psychoanalytic discourse that is so concerning, as is the dismissal of any overtly political intervention. The Foucauldian notion of a politics of truth is light-years away from Kleinian notions of truth, knowledge and reality. It is here that the embeddedness of so much of psychoanalysis purely within its own discipline and its extraordinary cultural insularity, especially in this country, are so frustrating.

We are faced with the challenge of understanding the intertwining of different epistemological and political positions implicit in psychoanalytical theories. It is only through such a path that we can evolve a psychoanalysis that is better suited to understanding the vicissitudes, conflicts and creativity of homosexuality now, and that might also be helpful in providing an analysis of the kinds of extreme homophobia that at times hold sway in our society.

8

(Anti)feminism after Communism

PEGGY WATSON

Introduction

In some respects, what has been seen as a resurgence of anti-feminism in the West – the threat to welfare rights, the ideological reassertion of family-based feminine identity and the explicit rejection of feminism in some quarters – appears similar to, if less extreme than, what has also been experienced in Eastern Europe since 1989. Yet Western feminists have tended to describe the reorganization of gender and the de-grading of feminine identity after communism as a specifically East European phenomenon, explicable almost exclusively in terms of the experience of communism. In view of the marked parallels between the two sets of experiences, this is surprising. What I set out to do in this chapter is to suggest a way of viewing these 'Eastern' and 'Western' experiences as related, and at the same time historically specific phenomena. In this way we can see what is at stake for women and feminists – East and West – in these two similar sets of events.

One way of pointing up the historical specificity of the post-communist experience is by considering the extent to which the rise of masculinism there can be labelled 'anti-feminism' at all – given the fact that what women have been 'losing' was not, strictly speaking, a feminist gain in the first place.[1] We need, at the very least, the social presence of feminism and feminists, as well as a valid notion of feminist-driven social change and female emancipation, before the de-grading of feminine identity can be legitimately considered to constitute anti-feminism. This is not a trivial issue. For framing much of the polarizing discourse of transition in Eastern Europe is the assumption that political identities, which, in fact, are historically specific, pre-exist democratization rather than being formed through it. It is precisely this universalizing assumption which underpins the view of democracy as offering 'freedom' for the expression of pre-existing political identities, including feminist and nationalist identity which, it is argued, communism has simply 'suppressed'.

One part of my argument, therefore, is to highlight the refusal by Eastern European women of Western feminism. For this is what can be more legitimately counted as anti-feminism in Eastern Europe. How are we to interpret and explain this phenomenon? In particular, how are we to understand this (anti)feminism in the light of the universal rise of masculinism which has accompanied it? Retaining the distinction between 'Eastern' (anti)feminism on the one hand and 'Western' anti-feminism on the other, I argue that what is at stake in the democratization of Eastern Europe is not, as is commonly implied, the elimination of anti-feminism, but rather its creation – a process which encompasses the rise of both masculinist and feminist political identity.

The rise of (anti)feminism in Eastern Europe depended, on the one hand, on fixed ideas of gender difference and the prior *naturalization of ideas of gender difference* under communism – through the fixed opposition of a family- and household-based 'society' to a prerogative 'state'. On the other, it involves the *politicization of this difference* through the implementation of universal rights of citizenship and the creation of liberal civil society. That is to say, the introduction of democratic citizenship rights, including property rights, endows with new political meaning those social differences, such as gender or nationality, which are capable of making abstract rights concrete.[2] It is democratization itself which allows gender the opportunity to become a politically exclusionary/inclusionary social characteristic, and an important principle for the patterning of precisely the social/political power under which communism had been eradicated.

In conceptualizing the transformation of Eastern Europe in this way, I am also engaging critically with those feminist accounts which are typically constructed in terms of an opposition between the 'legacy of communism' on the one hand, and feminism/ civil society/democracy on the other, with 'transition' entailing an evolutionary progression from one to the other. Within this latter discourse, 'obstacles to democracy', 'anti-feminism' or the 'failure' to achieve a 'genuine' civil society are most frequently understood in terms of the persistence of the legacy of communism (for example, as a consequence of nationalism), while the 'crisis of Western feminism', for example, is typically repressed.[3] What this discourse does in the context of East–West interchange, in effect, is to put beyond question the universalism of democratic citizenship, which in other contexts feminists have identified as 'a lie'.[4] In this way it preserves a linear view of feminist history and democratic change, and thereby serves to mystify Western 'backlash'.

By way of contrast, I argue that the 'facts' of transition to liberal democracy in the former Soviet Bloc undermine the evolutionary view of democratization which is deeply rooted in the West, where political citizenship has been conceptualized in terms of the accretion of rights on top of, and as a counterweight to, pre-existing political inequalities. After communism, democratization has, *in itself*, a politically polarizing effect, involving the institutionalization of political exclusion as much as political inclusion. Democracy after communism polarizes because it replaces a communist system where political citizenship was universal both in a (positive) abstract and (negative) concrete sense with a system of democratic political citizenship, which is universal in abstract terms, but within which the concrete rights of some are formed at the expense of the rights of others. The political exclusion of women as distinct to men – their reconfiguration as a 'minority' grouping – is a precondition of feminism in Eastern Europe; it is a process which is not an obstacle to, but is rather constitutive of the democratization of Eastern Europe. In the West 'backlash' is a name some have given to intimations of this built-in democratic exclusion.

(Anti)feminism in Eastern Europe

Eastern European (anti)feminism has arisen very largely in the context of the post-communist encounter between Eastern European women on the one hand, and Western feminists/feminism on the other, although the reasons for it are not wholly contained within that encounter. It has, in effect, been significantly evoked by a specific form of 'transnational feminist practice'.[5] '[I]n all East European countries, feminism is still something of a dirty word,' wrote Maria Adamik shortly after the downfall of communism.[6] This (anti)feminism has proved to be deep-seated, since by and large it persists in the face of the undoubted losses democratization has brought to many women. For many Western observers, keen to forge links with the East, the strength of Eastern European resistance to the idea of feminism has been unexpected.[7]

'I was one of those Western feminists rushing in with shining eyes to Eastern and Central European countries . . .'[8] wrote one investigator – who was to discover to her surprise that even among those she had thought would be most intensely interested in their new democratic freedoms – ex-dissidents and their children – feminism was a universal non-issue. Gender was 'denied as having any relevance when collective political identity is at stake. These women want to change society; they care for the protection of the environment or worry about social inequalities between the northern and the southern societies, but not one brings forth gender divisions as having something to do with what is to be acted upon.'[9] Many feminists have thus been led to ask, as Barbara Einhorn did: 'Why does one encounter such an antipathy to feminism? . . . In the upheaval of transition in East-Central Europe . . . women stand to lose those social (welfare) and employment rights which they did enjoy under state socialism, without in the short run appearing to gain much in exchange. This makes the non-emergence of a mass women's movement appear as yet another paradox.'[10]

Insofar as Western feminist discourse could not reconcile an obvious loss of rights with an almost universal repudiation of the idea of feminism, it constructed the 'absence of feminism' in post-communist Europe as a historical anomaly, a 'paradox'. East European (anti)feminism, in turn, represents a refusal to acquiesce in that construction. Indeed, East European (anti)feminism has been as clear a sign as any that early claims suggesting that 1989 had brought with it a 'unification of language'[11] had been mistaken. Former GDR citizens 'still speak German . . . but we are unable to make ourselves understood', wrote Barbel Böhley.[12] West German feminists perceive East German women as 'backward' with respect to Western feminism, and as having 'failed to appreciate' their new freedom, while East German women resent West Germans theorizing about them, instead of reflecting on blind spots in their own thinking.[13] And while some East European feminist intellectuals express the view that feminism is prevented by 'a low level of understanding' there,[14] others find Western feminist certainties misplaced: 'We object to some of the Western feminists' insensitive conduct towards us: as those who "already know everything" they class our arguments and counter-arguments among "teething troubles" we will soon get over. This sometimes reminds us of the attitudes of apparatchiks or of those imparting political indoctrination.'[15]

Democratization as a Loss of Rights

The democratization of Eastern Europe has been tantamount to a selective political empowerment of (some) men, and the question of women's rights has been secondary to the establishment of stable political and economic hierarchy. Almost universally,[16] the institutionalization of the new political order was heralded by a questioning of existing rights to abortion. In this respect, the post-communist governments – in the first flush of democracy – did not greatly differ from those authoritarian ones of which

Joan Scott has written that an 'assertion of power or strength was given form as a policy about women'.[17] 'It is rather telling,' wrote one Hungarian author, 'that one of the first big discussions of the newly elected [Hungarian] parliament took place about a draft law to ban abortion. It is rather intriguing that in the middle of a deep economic crisis, political chaos and social insecurity, when the very foundations of society are to be re-shaped, abortion has become a primary question in almost all post-socialist countries.'[18] In Poland, one of the architects of an early anti-abortion bill told of the 'harpies' demonstrating outside the Senate Building and shouting 'Keep away from our bellies!' – 'But we will nationalize those bellies!' (*Uspołecznimy te brzuchy!*) he exclaimed.[19]

As the parliaments acquired a measure of real social power, so women were excluded from them. Although men swept into the democratic parliaments in force, their claim to rule was nevertheless a fragile one: it could not be readily justified in terms of the superior experience, skills or qualifications of men, since the procedures of democracy were new, and women had been at least the educational equals of men since the 1960s.[20] Nor, at the outset, was political power founded on private property. Radical claims of gender difference were the sole basis for the legitimacy of the rule of men, and constituted an explicit justification of the exclusion of women from power in Eastern Europe. One Polish representative on the Council of Europe said, for example, that 'it is impossible to speak of discrimination against women. Nature gave them a different role to that of men. The ideal must still be the woman–mother, for whom pregnancy is a blessing.'[21] In Russia, a leading perestroika politician expressed a similar view: 'If we think of humanity as one big family, then women in this system are responsible for stability and continuity, whereas men are responsible for taking risks, moving forward, experimenting . . . Women can never play a primary or even an equal role in politics.'[22]

With economic reform and the introduction of a competitive labour market, women have also become particularly vulnerable to low-grade employment and unemployment. 'If there were equal opportunities legislation, women wouldn't get any jobs,' said Jacek Kuroń, a former Minister of Labour and candidate for the Polish presidency.[23] Tatiana Klimenkova has described Russian news-papers in recent years as being full of articles whose 'aim has been to create in women a feeling of being second-class citizens. According to these notions, working women should feel guilty about working, and ashamed of taking any interest in their work, since this interest betrays an "active" – i.e. unfeminine attitude to life.'[24] Women have also become increasingly vulnerable to sexual harassment and exploitation in the workplace. 'A young man has bought this place,' said a Kraków shop assistant. 'And because he owns it, he thinks he can do what he wants with the women here.'[25] Among the new owners, women are poorly represented, particularly in larger firms. Fong and Paull have chosen to explain this in purely rational terms: it is, they say, because women 'have fewer accumulated assets which can be used as collateral or start-up capital required by banks. Women also comprise a very small number of the members of newly created business associations. Finally, the executive training programmes in the new business schools are dominated by men, partly because of admissions criteria which emphasize previous managerial experience, which women rarely have.'[26] At the same time, market ideology and fiscal crisis have meant that centrally administered social rights have been severely eroded, while privatization has seen to it that enterprises too have shed this aspect of their previous responsibilities. 'The idea of social spending on housing, nurseries, holiday places for workers, has been buried. We are now a normal industry,' said Krzysztof Piotrowski, director of the Szczecin shipyard, in a Chan-nel 4 report on a 'Polish success story'.[27]

'Us' and 'Them'

How, then, is one to account for this pattern of change, this seeming 'regression' in the former Soviet Bloc? Is 'communism' still in some way preventing what we expected to be the benefits of democratization? And how, in any case, would we imagine a process of transition whereby the East became more like the West? The way one answers these questions very much depends on the way in which the difference/similarities between East and West are conceptualized. For example, some Western scholars have been concerned to develop 'models' of communist society – that is to say, there have been efforts to conceptualize communist 'difference' in wholly self-contained, communist terms. In the face of such attempts, Chris Hann has argued strongly against theories of a 'great divide' between East and West, objecting to what he sees as the way in which much Western academic work has portrayed Eastern Europe as the 'second world', completely different from the civilized West. 'It is only the academic analysts who have been forced into schizophrenia, for the main thing that is unique about Eastern Europe is the effort which has gone into discrediting socialism there,' he writes.[28]

However, to recognize objective similarities between East and West, as Hann does, should not push us into the position of rejecting all difference between the two. Democratic citizenship, or the comprehensive lack of it, may not be tantamount to the presence of agency or its absence – but that does not mean that democracy itself counts for nothing. In the same way, the sheer diversity of social practice under communism should not prevent us from recognizing that the political meaning of those diverse practices becomes reconfigured with the re-shaping of political community – the redefinition of the terms of co-existence – which democratization brings. There are important differences between life under communism and democracy which need to be grasped if we are to understand what is at stake in the democratization of Eastern Europe, particularly if we are to understand what is at stake for women in this regard. These differences are to be found not in material discontinuities between East and West, or the absolute difference of daily activities in Eastern Europe under communism, but in terms of the political context within which specific practices/identities interrelate and acquire a superordinate sense. What is basically at issue are overarching principles for the organization of social/political power. 'Gender' is a prime category for capturing the differences in question, and it is for this reason also that the restructuring of gender is crucially involved in the democratization of the former Soviet Bloc.

Rather than obliterate these differences, the point is that they cannot be grasped simply through close inspection of one side (Eastern Europe) only. The difference lies between the two: the West, as much as the East, has to be included in the conceptual frame within which these differences are to be understood. The question is not, or should not be, the Western-centred one of: 'How are they different from us?' but rather the question which needs answering is: 'How are we different from each other?' It is an understanding that calls for self-inspection on the part of ourselves in the West. If we leave the West out, and seek to account for 'difference' in exclusively Eastern European terms, then we make a powerful statement about the West in any case, by default. This is well illustrated by the (six) reports about Polish women, which appeared in the British press between 1980 and 1988.[29] According to the picture presented in these articles, Polish women, in the early 1980s were leading quite different lives from their Western counterparts. 'It seems astonishing,' wrote the *Sunday Times*. 'Women in Poland are still expected to fill an eight-hour day and then go home to their other roles as wife and mother.'[30] The implicit message here is one about the civilized West, where women do not have to put up with such blatant exploitation any longer.

The end of communism in Eastern Europe and the Soviet Union has profound implications for the identity and self-understanding of the West – the 'free world', which has for the last fifty years been partially constituted by, and defined in opposition to, the 'captive' Soviet Bloc. The 'vindication' of the West does not simply lie in the 'defeat of communism' in 1989, but is continuously constructed in the interpretation of transformation in Eastern Europe. In retaining 'the "us" and "them" paradigm that stems from modernist modes of description and representation',[31] the discourse of transition reflects and embodies global power asymmetries – and serves systematically to polarize symbolic advantage in favour of the West. The intellectual construction of the transformation of Eastern Europe, then, is at the same time frequently a process whereby the West becomes deproblematized as it is 're-invented'.[32] I see this as an important factor behind the 'neo-modern' turn in social theory which Jeffrey Alexander[33] has identified as taking hold in the wake of the events of 1989. Feminism sustains, rather than challenges, this trend insofar as the feminist construction of East European 'paradox' is resolved in wholly East European terms, that is when it identifies the rise of masculinism – the loss of rights for women and radicalized definitions of gender – as a (specifically East European) 'anti-feminism', and then looks for the 'cause' of these losses in the 'legacy of communism'.

'Nationalism Versus Citizenship' in Eastern Europe?

'Nationalism,' it has been written, 'is the name intellectuals and publics are now increasingly giving to the negative antimonies of civil society . . . nationalism is now routinely portrayed as the successor to communism,'[34] and the feminist literature on democratic transition confirms this view. In the conclusion to her book on gender in Eastern Europe, Barbara Einhorn, for example, writes that:

Active citizenship and the revival of civil society was what the upheavals of 1989 seemed to promise for the former state socialist countries of East Central Europe. Yet since then, women's rights appear to have been eroded . . . The family and the nation are being posited as central in the search for identity and for new ethical and moral values. Yet while market-oriented democratic theories stress individual autonomy, national pressures subordinate women yet again to a collectivity which denies them participatory citizenship and democratic control. Woman, even when represented as Nation, is in fact the quintessential Other of national-ist discourse . . . in this too, there is more continuity with the state socialist period than at first meets the eye.[35]

Consider, too, the way in which Katherine Verdery draws a line of contrast between the ethno-national nation on one side, and the citizen nation on the other. Noting the patriarchal parallels between the two, she at the same time sees in ethno-nationalism an 'unsettling commonality' which unites practically all of the countries of the former Soviet Bloc – even though in other respects they are becoming increasingly diverse.[36] It is precisely ethno-nationalism which Verdery holds responsible for the fact that the return to democratic politics is proving to be 'misogynist' in all of the Eastern Bloc – even though the direct reasons for this misogyny are strikingly varied. Thus, in Poland and Croatia the reasons are attributed to the resurgence of the Roman Catholic Church; in the former GDR, the reason is unification with West Germany, while in Hungary the reasons are less clear.[37] For Verdery, there is a direct and unproblematic link between ethno-nationalism, communism and 'anti-feminism': 'Because Communist parties all across Eastern Europe mostly toed the Soviet internationalist line in public, national sentiment became a form of anti-communism. This resistant aura to nationalism makes it an obvious means of reversing the damage Communists did to the nation they suppressed. To the extent that women are seen as having benefited from socialism or as having had the socialist state as their ally, feminism becomes socialist and can be attacked as anti-national.'[38]

It is not the presence of nationalist discourse in post-communist politics which is at issue here. Nor is it the fact that this is a highly gendered discourse which has been invoked for purposes of exclusion. Indeed, the work of a number of feminist scholars has documented the workings of such discourse in the post-communist context in some detail.[39] It is also right, I think, to point to the way the experience of communism acted to preserve an idea of nation,[40] which was often defined in opposition to the state. Within the context of a rejected 'prerogative state',[41] social consciousness was overwhelmingly shaped in terms of a binary opposition between 'state' on the one hand, and 'society' on the other.[42] This opposition did not imply that all of society was engaged in political activity against the state; rather, it was the framework within which political identity was defined. It explains why, for example, Stefan

Nowak,[43] in his landmark study, found that Poles identified with family and nation – but with no other intermediate institution/idea pertaining to the public sphere. The omnicompetent state was held responsible for all social ills, and by the same token, the family-based gender identities and national identities of 'society' were naturalized and essentialized. Importantly and less frequently stressed is the fact that under communism, these identities were politically cohesive and inclusive. That is one reason why women's so-called 'double burden' under communism was typically viewed as a state, rather than a gender, problem.[44] It also goes some way to explaining why traditional gender identity served as a vehicle for social transformation in Eastern Europe, rather than being the object of desired change.[45]

The difficulty with this account, rather, is that it pits nationalism and democracy against each other: normative (theoretical) democracy pulls one way, and nationalism the other. This 'nationalism versus citizenship' account of the reorganization of gender identity in Eastern Europe lies in its 'them and us' approach and all that this implies in terms of the underlying one-sided assumptions it makes. These assumptions carry great force and are capable of overriding many of the fundamental empirical 'facts' of transition (as well as what we, as feminists, already know about democracy in the West). The nationalism/citizenship or communism/democracy polarity produces an account of democratic transition whereby Eastern Europe is at odds only with itself and its own past – against a background of, and facilitated by, a neutral democratic 'freedom'. The inert quality of democracy[46] in this account is frequently conveyed through the physically illegitimate metaphor of civil society as an *absolute* 'political space', devoid of power relations or the capacity to itself shape or be shaped by specific political identities.[47] The implicit division of conceptual labour within this paradigm, then, is that democracy offers a blank opportunity for self-expression, while communism is the catch-all for the 'causes' of observed 'counter-democratic' trends. In this way, a gravity-defying discourse is constructed whereby what is empirically present under democracy in Eastern Europe (a nationalism which *divides citizens from each other* politically) is accounted for in terms of the experience of communism – where this kind of nationalism was, in the main, empirically absent. Under communism, the idea of nation was not, in general, *politically* divisive, even across national difference, but rather *held citizens together vis-à-vis* a commonly repudiated state. For similar reasons, feminism itself acquires a virtual reality in this discourse, insofar as the rise of masculinism and anti-women rhetoric/policy is called 'anti-feminist' in the empirical absence of feminism itself. Meanwhile, the possibility is suppressed that democratization itself engages and mobilizes difference in the construction of historically specific political identities. In this way, a universalizing concept of feminism and of women, and an evolutionary view of feminist/democratic change, are preserved from the deeper implications of feminist refusal and the rise of masculinism in Eastern Europe. The discursive consequences are conservative:

One of several ironies here is that Western policy-makers accustomed to thinking of nationalism, with its irrational 'tribal' passions, as not in keeping with a modern Western political economy are suddenly finding that the best promoters of the westernizing, anti-communist values they hope to foster are local nationalists. Western liberalism has always found ethno-nationalism suspect, for it restricts the 'demos' of democratic participation to the members of the chosen people, excluding the ethnic 'others' from full citizenship. This challenge to the notion of universal citizenship, which liberal political theory would place at the heart of democratic politics, is now lodging itself at the centre of Eastern European 'democracy'.[48]

This passage, I think, shows how easy it is, within this paradigm, to construct a text which reads as though 'local nationalists' and 'western policy-makers' are almost different breeds: the one, irrational and 'democratic'; the other, by sheer force of contrast, rational, reasonable and 'truly' democratic. The Western policy-makers which would come within feminist sights, were one to pursue the 'causes' of neo-liberal backlash against feminism here in the West, can thus effectively be 'laundered' through juxtaposition with the East. Within the discourse of change in Eastern

Europe, in effect, the exposure of one sets of 'myths', that of nationalism (in the former Soviet Bloc), reaffirms another, that of the universalism of democratic citizenship (in the West). Alertness to the role of 'selective forgetting' in the former mythology[49] is achieved at the expense of 'theoretical amnesia' with respect to the latter.[50] Again, this involves an intellectual process which is highly selective in its approach to the 'facts'. It is salutary to recall, for example, just how 'democratic' Western policy-makers have been with regard to the management of change in Eastern Europe. A number of authors have in other contexts been at pains to point out how striking have been the similarities between Western-driven 'transition' and communist-imposed social transformation in the former Soviet Bloc, where 'the free market' is now associated with the 'vanishing invisible hand'.[51] As Gowan puts it:

... the liberal principle that ends should govern means has been opera-tionally rejected within ST [Shock Therapy] in favour of a more 'dialecti-cal' approach: the existing social, legal and political institutions are likely to be resistant to ST, but ST is the only, or best, path to truly democratic, legal and civil institutions, so we must negate the existing institutions from above and outside in order to realize true democracy and civil society ... This ... has been at the very heart of the operational priorities of ST: to subordinate the will of electorates and parliaments to the overriding priority of rapid systemic transformation to capitalism, down-grading constitutional development, social and political consensus-building, and respect for economic and social solidarity.[52]

The task for feminist theory, then, is to provide a conceptualization of change in Eastern Europe which avoids the Manichaean con-frontation between democracy and its 'enemies' – for this kind of opposition leads, ultimately, to a position which is both conservat-ive and anti-feminist.

Democracy as the Institutionalization of Exclusion

Underlying the construction of 'obstacles' to democracy/civil society/feminism in Eastern Europe, as I have argued, is a compel-ling narrative of evolutionary change. It is a narrative which has been shaped by events themselves. For in a heroic wave which swept the region in 1989, the countries of the former Soviet Bloc became free. Although the shedding of communism was not yet a 'transition to democracy', it was powerful and dramatic enough in itself to lend a triumphant meaning to the democratic idea. It was an idea which had, in one view, brought about the 'end of history'.[53] And although few now accept Fukuyama's thesis, nevertheless there remains an underlying conviction that, were it not for all the barriers, the democratization of the former Soviet Bloc would mean joining a path leading in the same direction as other paths to democracy, both historically in the West, as well as in other more recent 'transitions'. The ability to express feminism, in this view, would simply be one more democratic benefit to be gained along the way.

However, to assume this kind of analogy between democracy after communism, and other transitions to democracy, would be a mistake. Indeed, in some respects quite opposite processes of change are involved. That is because in other democratic transitions what is involved is an attempt to reduce the extent to which political inclusion depends on social difference. In South Africa, for example, democratization means lessening the extent to which social difference – colour – determines political identity – the way in which a person belongs within the political community, and the civil/political rights they enjoy in concrete, everyday terms. Democratization in such a situation aims to achieve the *depoliticization of difference*. Precisely the opposite is the case after communism. That is because under communism everyone in 'society' was excluded from political power in equal measure: the state assumed all prerogative in the public sphere, and society became a 'private society'. The monopoly achieved by the 'prerogative state' over the public sphere corresponded to the comprehensive curtailment of any real rights of political, and to some extent also civil, citizenship. This is usually what is referred to when it is said that under communism there was 'no civil society'. Insofar as new rights of citizenship in post-communism are dependent for their realization on social resources, democratization and civil society in Eastern

Europe may be said to entail the mobilization of the very differences which under communism had been a matter of political irrelevance. Democratization in Eastern Europe involves the *politicization of difference*. What is important to note is that under communism, *both* abstract and concrete rights of political/civil citizenship were universal: all of society enjoyed theoretical rights and at the same time was equally deprived of these rights in everyday life. That is not the same as saying that everyone was equal under state socialism; they were not. What I mean is that political/ civil citizenship in both its normative, positive, abstract sense, and its actual, everyday, negative sense, was not a function of social difference. Whatever the effect in daily life of social factors such as gender, level of wealth, ethnicity or age, in terms of political identity, participation and voice, they were of no consequence.

By way of contrast, the political and civil rights of democratic citizenship represent universal capacities or opportunities, some of which (the right to vote) are more genuinely universal than others.[54] 'A property right (for example) is not a right to possess property, but a right to acquire it *if you can*, and to protect it *if you can get it*'[55] [emphasis added]. Similarly, the right to 'free speech' is not a legally guaranteed equal right to voice, but a conditional capacity which is dependent on the outcome of the complex interplay of a variety of social factors. Consider, for example, the gap noted by Heinen[56] between the outlook of the unemployed in Poland, and the confident national and international press accounts of 'successful' economic transition in that country. (This gap in fact currently separates the national/international press and a 'successful' minority from the rest of the population.) Or consider again, the way in which Solidarity 80 Union representatives were informally but effectively banned by management from expressing their views to the press during the high-profile privatization of the Szczecin Shipyard.[57]

With democratization, gender takes on a new and specifically political meaning, because it begins to matter with respect to how individuals come to be differentially included within the new political community created by democratic citizenship. Traditional ideas of gender difference reinforced under communism are integral to the realization of the new rights of citizenship, and it is this new fusion of the social with the political that produces the 'male subject' or 'political man'. In this sense, democratization in Eastern Europe *is* the construction of a 'man's world'. It is important to be clear about what is at stake for 'women' in these changes. It has recently been written, for example, that under communism, 'the felt absence of collective political voice' was part of the powerlessness 'directly evident in the experience of *women's* subordination by collective . . . male power'[58] [emphasis added]. The argument I am making here is that precisely the opposite is true: the felt absence of collective political voice, or powerlessness, is just what is *not* part of the 'subordination of *women*' under communism, since voicelessness/powerlessness under communism is a genuine universal. It is only with democratization that 'absence of political voice' and 'powerlessness' can become meaningful aspects of the 'subordination of women', as what is there to be voiced also changes. That is because within liberal democracy, citizens are excluded *relative to each other* in a way that was impossible under communism. It is democratization itself which brings a new, essentially divisive, political force to gender relations. It is within the context of the universal political emancipation offered by Western-type democracy, then – the creation of a specific political community – that women acquire the 'minority identity' which is the prerequisite of feminism. Within this context too, differences among women acquire political significance. Ethnic strife and divisive nationalism are also understandable in part as a consequence of democratic citizenship. For under appropriate historical circumstances, ethnicity can be invoked as the key difference by means of which access to the benefits of citizenship is to be defined. The paradox of democracy after communism is that, in radically redefining what is politically at stake for social differences, democracy itself *mobilizes* those self-same differences which subvert its universal ideal. It is this which crucially underlies the rise of masculinism and the appearance of divisive nationalism in Eastern Europe. Democratization after communism itself requires that the institutionalization of political inclusion go hand in hand with the manufacture of political exclusion. The democratization of the nation-state in this context – the creation of the 'citizen-state' – means the active hierarchization of citizenship.

Conclusion

The 'paradox' of Eastern European (anti)feminism can be sustained only as long as we, as Western feminists, do not also subject ourselves to scrutiny as we observe the transformation of Eastern Europe. This does not just mean acknowledging that feminism is characterized by multiple contestations and differences in itself, and then entering into East–West interchange anyway, on the grounds that any feminism is always better than none. It means that we need to respect the post-communist experience for what it can tell us about ourselves. Crucially, it means recognizing that the rise of feminism in Eastern Europe is in itself a deeply ambivalent development. For the rise of masculinism and the appearance of masculinist nationalism – mobilized by democratization – do not prevent feminism in Eastern Europe, but are rather (ultimately) constitutive of it. It is only with the rise of feminism that pro-masculinism can in turn become anti-feminism – where backlash is essentially a signal of inherent contestation over political identity, fought out over shifting social terrains. Under communism, the widely expressed dissatisfaction with women's so-called 'double burden' did not give rise to feminist political identity, but was rather associated with its repudiation. The paradox which we have sought to abject from ourselves is that the emergence of feminist identity in Eastern Europe is predicated on the political redefinition of women as 'second-class citizens' which is precisely what the universal emancipation of Western-type democracy brings.

9

'Damned if You Do and Damned if You Don't': Psychological and Social Constraints on Motherhood in Contemporary Europe

PATRIZIA ROMITO

Introduction

This chapter aims to discuss the difficult and often contradictory status of mothers in Europe – the real and symbolic attacks inflicted upon them, and the forces underlying this situation, including the roles played by women themselves, both as individuals and as organized groups.

Though oppressed, women are not necessarily passive: they defend themselves by counter-attacking, organizing and proposing. Moreover, 'women' is not a homogeneous category: they/we differ from each other in many respects and may disagree with each other on numerous issues, including the meaning and status of motherhood.

In developing my argument, I shall first briefly consider some conflicting feminist ideas on motherhood as they have developed in industrialized countries in the last twenty years. I shall then analyse two different topics – free access to contraception and abortion, and the situation of employed mothers[1] – taking my arguments mostly from the Italian situation.

As it is fashionable to stress these days, what I write is not independent of who I am: my knowledge, too, is located knowledge. I am a white, middle-aged feminist researcher; I am heterosexual, and without children by choice. Also relevant to the content of this chapter is the fact that I live in Italy. Like Ailbhe Smyth,[2] I feel myself to be a peripheral feminist. Not only is Italy outside the English-speaking intellectual world, but also Trieste, the north-eastern town where I live, only a few kilometres from Slovenia, is on the edge of the Italian intellectual world.

There may be some advantages in looking at the attacks on mothers from this position. Italy is probably one of the most contradictory countries in the world in this respect. It is a country where 90 per cent of the population say they are Catholic,[3] and co-exist with a Pope violently opposed to contraception, but where the women seem to be resisting motherhood: the birth rate in Italy is among the lowest in Europe and in the world.[4] If we take the generation of women who are now around forty, one in five is childless; in northern Italy, the proportion is one in four.[5] This is a country famous for its archetype of Mediterranean motherhood (*la mamma italiana*), but where there have been increasing reports in recent years of live newborns left in public places, or even thrown into dustbins.[6] Curiously enough, the strongest reactions to this have come from anti-abortion movements and right-wing political parties. In one northern town, the Italian pro-life movement has reintroduced the '*ruota degli esposti*' (a kind of revolving hatch in the wall of a convent where babies can be left). The Equal Opportunities Committee of the National Alliance (the ex-fascist party) has proposed a free helpline which mothers who want to abandon their babies anonymously can call. Alessandra Mussolini, a leader of the National Alliance, has suggested calling this 'Sweet Cradle'. Italy is a country that is also known for its traditional ideas and practices concerning men's behaviour and virility,[7] but it is also one where the Equality Law of 1977 extended to employed fathers most of the rights of employed mothers.[8] And, on top of everything, Italy is the country where statues of the Madonna shed tears of blood. In April 1995, before the regional elections opposing the virulently anti-communist coalition of Berlusconi to the 'centro-sinistra' coalition,[9] a small plaster figure of the Madonna started to weep bloody tears in Civitavecchia, near Rome. Analysis revealed that the blood was human, with a male DNA, but this has still not prevented enthusiasts from claiming a miracle. (The Madonna seems to be rather popular lately outside Italy too: US pilot Scott O'Grady, whose F-16 was shot down over Bosnia and who spent several days without food before being rescued, said he had visions of her during that time.)

Feminists and Motherhood

Since the 1970s, women (many, but not all, of whom would call themselves feminists) have developed and sustained conflicting ideas about motherhood. As Letherby put it, describing the English-speaking world:

In the early days of the Women's Liberation Movement, the emphasis was on challenging the myth that motherhood was women's inevitable destiny . . . and the Women's Movement provided a space for women to voice the negative aspects of mothering . . . Many feminists felt that this was alienating to women who want children, and one reaction to this was the development of a strand idealizing motherhood . . . Ruddick (1980), for instance, stressed that the experience that all women share is their capacity to mother – which makes them closer to nature, of higher morality, more peace-loving and caring than men.[10]

It is not always clear whether these alleged qualities are attributed to the actual state of being a mother or to some 'essential' female characteristics. In any case, this tendency to exalt motherhood has been criticized by other feminists.[11]

In Italy we have witnessed a similar development. It was difficult for the women's movement of the 1970s and early 1980s to come to terms with the issue of motherhood. As Passerini[12] has pointed out, many Italian feminists experienced a profound rebellion against traditional ideas of motherhood, but this hostility towards motherhood did not receive proper theoretical attention, and it created painful conflicts between women who had children and those who had not. An opposite trend developed at the end of the eighties. La libreria delle donne (the Women's Bookshop) in Milan, set up by intellectual and professional women, produced a local version of the *pensiero della differenza sessuale* (thinking of sexual difference), which stressed the need for a 'symbolic mother' – an authoritative woman acting as a mediator for other less powerful ones. Linked to the idea of a powerful mother is the concept of *affidamento* (literally, 'entrusting') – a 'psycho-political' link in which the less powerful woman puts all her trust in the more powerful one, perhaps running little errands in exchange for an enhancement of her 'feminine identity'.[13] The legitimacy given to power differences among women (and at times to power abuse), along with the obscure, almost esoteric language of the Milan group, was opposed by many Italian feminists.[14] But these theories were given credit within the men's world, probably because, unlike other feminist tendencies, they were not designed to challenge men's power.[15]

A more influential version of the *differenza* has been developed by women of the PCI (the Italian Communist Party), which in 1991 became the PDS (the Democratic Party of the Left). PCI/PDS women have never considered themselves as 'feminists': they passed from an 'emancipationist' position to 'sexual difference' thinking without acknowledging the idea of women's oppression. They 'adopted' the French Lacanian psychoanalyst and philosopher Luce Irigaray in the 1980s. During conferences held in Italy from 1986 to 1989, Irigaray graced us with her ideas about 'sexual difference', and one of the most important of these was that any national constitution should include rights which are 'different according to the two sexes and appropriate to women'.[16] For instance, women should be guaranteed the right 'to virginity, to free motherhood, to the privileged tutelage of children, and to the care of their home';[17] 'men are war-making, traditionally carnivorous, sometimes cannibals . . . only women can help men to find their own limits, because women do not belong to the patriarchal community'.[18] In Irigaray's opinion, the mother–daughter relationship should become the model for all relationships.[19]

Another important step in the conceptualization of motherhood was a conference organized by the women of the PDS in Rome in 1992. It was entitled 'The Time of Motherhood' and was an uncritical celebration of motherhood, placed at the centre of the party's political programme. According to a popular psychoanalyst, Silvia Vegetti Finzi, '. . . female identity always contains an essential maternal component . . . as a consequence, women should enter the political world as mothers; this will represent the dawning of their future political power'. Along with these conceptualizations comes a reconsideration of the abortion issue, in which the 'rights of the embryo and the foetus' should be considered too.[20] All this sparked off an angry debate among feminists, many of whom were extremely critical.[21] The conclusions reached at the conference were all too consistent with the pro-family stance re-emerging in the country generally. Around the same time, a number of regional governments in Italy passed Family Laws to be applied locally, which encouraged marriage and child-production by means of financial incentives and housing benefits, and offered women small amounts of money to stay at home and care for a child or a disabled person. Since Berlusconi's right-wing government in 1993, moreover, we even have a Minister for the Family.[22]

The result of these trends is to restrict women's identity to the family and motherhood. As Delphy asked: 'But who needed feminists to do that?'[23]

Contraception and Abortion

Is it possible to speak about the 'choice of motherhood', at least in industrialized countries? According to Oakley et al., '. . . the concept of "choice" is something of a red herring in a society that places such a high value on children, marriage and the family, and in which motherhood is still perceived by many as the primary female role'.[24] Ten years later, Letherby stressed that 'In Western society, all women live their lives against a background of personal and cultural assumptions that all women are or want to be mothers.'[25] The pressures to consider motherhood as central to female identity exist even within feminist circles: women who do not have children often feel compelled to justify their decision and prove they can still be maternal, receptive, peaceful and so on.[26] The idea of 'choice' is misleading in other ways. In difficult social circumstances, many women and men may feel prevented from having the children they desire. Moreover, babies do not always arrive on demand, even when wanted.

Despite the limitations of the concept of choice, however, the possibility of separating sexuality from fertility, and of securing free access to contraception and safe abortion, is of crucial importance for heterosexual women. Without these basic resources, any discussion of 'choice' in relation to motherhood is irrelevant.

The sale of contraceptives was illegal and abortion was prohibited in Italy until 1978: according to the Fascist Penal Code (still in force), they were crimes against the race. Although reliable data are lacking, it has been estimated that around 2 million illegal abortions took place every year, and thousands of women died as a consequence. Then, under pressure from the Women's Movement and progressive political groups, the Italian parliament approved Law 194, which permitted abortion in certain circumstances in the first ninety days of pregnancy and, in special cases, even later. The law was the result of a compromise: the issue of abortion was placed within the context of a discourse on the 'social value and social protection of motherhood'.[27] Although it is the woman who actually decides, she has to discuss her choice with a doctor; abortions may only be performed in public hospitals. In other words, abortion has not been decriminalized, and reproductive freedom has not been established and guaranteed. In circumstances other than those described above, abortion is still illegal. Moreover, health workers can declare themselves 'conscientious objectors', and thus avoid having to do abortions at all.

The backlash against Law 194 was immediate, and has never really ceased. The first attempt to abolish the law led to a national referendum in 1981, and despite an intimidating display of moral authority from the Catholic Church, a large majority of Italians (67 per cent) voted in favour of maintaining the law. Regardless of this initial success, by the end of the 1980s around 60 per cent of gynaecologists were objectors; in some hospitals, all the personnel objected, including the porters.[28] The current Pope, Karol Wojtyla, has always claimed that abortion and contraception are horrible crimes, and these opinions are reiterated in the most recent papal encyclical, *Evangelium Vitae* (March 1995): abortion is murder, and contraception destroys conjugal love and is a kind of murder too; Christians everywhere should object to laws permitting abortion.[29] The Italian pro-life movement launched a campaign to give legal status to the embryo, and a high-placed cardinal officially invited Catholic pharmacists to refuse to sell contraceptives, condoms in particular.[30] The same trend can be observed in other countries. In France, in 1990, the president of the National Union of Christian Europe organized a pilgrimage to Auschwitz, '. . . to make Europeans realize that a far worse genocide is taking place . . . with RU 486 replacing the Cyclon B gas used in the camps as a human pesticide'. According to some anti-abortionist groups, the French abortion law is the result of a 'Jewish plot against the Aryan race'.[31] In the new state of Croatia, the rightwing government is trying to impose a law making abortion possible only in the first ten weeks of pregnancy, and after the woman has consulted a doctor, a social worker and the parish priest.[32]

All this may appear grotesque, but we should bear in mind that doctors performing legal abortions have been murdered by Catholic activists in the USA in the name of the same principles,[33] and that contraception and abortion are now almost impossible to obtain in Poland.[34] Anti-abortion policies in the USA have forced international agencies to reduce drastically funds allocated for termination, and often for contraceptives too, in developing countries, where it has been estimated that at least 200,000 women die each year from the effects of clandestine abortion.[35]

Along with the ideological attacks on the abortion law in Italy, we are now witnessing a substantial reduction in those very health services (called Family Counselling Clinics) whose job is to prevent abortion by providing information on reproductive matters and free contraception. Due to cuts in health spending, the number of these clinics, which is already insufficient, will be further reduced. Again, similar trends can be seen in other countries. In France, the government has slashed spending on the once-glorious Family Planning System.[36] In the Netherlands, which has the lowest abortion rates in the world, the Minister of Health has proposed that the pill should no longer be regarded as a basic health need and distributed free of charge. Health experts predict a dramatic increase in the abortion rate should this measure be passed.[37]

Meanwhile, male leaders of the Italian left have seized every opportunity to flirt with their colleagues on the Catholic right on issues such as 'natural' contraceptives, foetal rights, women's responsibility or irresponsibility and so on, and are obviously eager to come to a gentleman's agreement on such matters, perhaps using abortion as a cheap and handy bargaining counter.[38] As noted earlier, they have been joined by many female members of the PDS, some of whom are now saying that women are 'wrong' for not 'safeguarding foetal life'.[39]

Among other Italian women, attitudes and behaviour with respect to these issues have been diverse and sometimes contradictory. Many female health professionals have continued to work in difficult conditions, doing their best to help their clients to obtain information, contraception or termination. Feminists have reacted strongly on a few specific occasions, when the abortion law has come under direct attack. In June 1995, for instance, hundreds of thousands of women of all ages and from all over Italy gathered in Rome for a feminist demonstration in defence of the principle of 'self-determination' and the abortion law. Many women from the PDS stayed away, or joined in rather half-heartedly, and the women from the Women's Bookshop failed to participate too, albeit for different reasons. What has been lacking, however, has been some sustained reflection on the issue of abortion, along with a continuous monitoring of how the law has been implemented.[40]

By way of contrast, it is interesting to note that much more energy has been invested over the same period in the subject of childbirth, with theorizing, conferences, books and ever-increasing activity on the part of groups involved in home births, water births, sweet births and so on. The pay-off has been rather poor: a few women have succeeded in giving birth in a more satisfactory way, but obstetricians have accepted only superficial reforms in birth management in hospitals, and by now Italy has the highest Caesarean section rate in Europe (22.4 per cent), and the third highest in the world, after the USA and Brazil.[41] The rate has doubled since 1980, when the childbirth movement was most active.[42] In the meantime, women were having abortions (when they could get them, despite the objectors) in often humiliating conditions, with service-providers making them feel guilty and putting them in the same room as new mothers, or in the worst rooms in the hospital. In this context, it is hardly surprising that a 1995 survey shows that 20 per cent of Italian women of reproductive age are not even aware that abortion is legal.[43] For these reasons, some women end up opting for an illegal abortion in the private sector, often performed by a doctor with another job in a public hospital where he is officially an objector.[44] It has been estimated that, since Law 194 was passed in 1978, around 100,000 to 150,000 illegal abortions have been performed every year, and women still die from them.[45] Again, a similar trend exists in France, where around 5,000 women per year have to go to the Netherlands to get an abortion.[46]

As we have seen, the ideas of many influential Italian women on abortion have become more similar to those of the Catholic right. In the last few years, almost every article on the subject written by 'progressive' women and published in a national newspaper has begun with the sentence: 'Abortion is the most tragic thing which can happen to a woman.' In fact, this statement is simply not true, for all women are different: an abortion may be a tragedy for one, but not for another. Besides, what if we were to draw up a list of all the possible tragedies which may happen to a woman and put them in order of importance? After analysing the relevant literature, Patricia Lunneborg, a North American feminist and psychologist, concludes that the principal feeling most women have after an abortion is relief; long-term negative psychological effects are rare, and many women actually feel better – with an enhanced sense of control, maturity and self-esteem.[47] Lunneborg also remarks how astonished many authors seem to be by such good adjustment after a termination. One of the most astonished is Everett Koop, former US Surgeon General, who was asked by President Reagan in 1989 to review the scientific literat-

ure on the issue. Koop, an adamant anti-abortionist, was forced
to conclude that post-abortion psychological problems were min-
uscule from a public health perspective; by contrast, pregnancies,
wanted or unwanted, that come to term have well-documented
adverse mental health effects.[48] Postnatal depression, for example,
affects between 7 per cent and 35 per cent of new mothers.[49]
Other data show similar findings for women's physical health. In
the US, the overall death rate for women having a legal abortion
(including those at twenty-one weeks or more) is 0.6 per 100,000,
eleven times lower than the 6.6 deaths per 100,000 for women
undergoing childbirth.[50]

It is wise to remember the links between women's free reproductive choices and babies' health and well-being. In New York
State, a liberalized abortion law came into force in 1970, and its
effects on the outcome of pregnancies were studied in six different
maternity hospitals. Spontaneous abortion fell by 20 per cent; the
proportion of very small babies (500–1,000 g.) fell by 36 per cent;
the proportion of abandoned babies fell by 56 per cent.[51] By way
of contrast, other data show that the children of mothers who are
denied an abortion may have problems with their psycho-social
development.[52]

It is not my intention here to praise abortion, in opposition to
the uncritical exaltation of motherhood. Obviously, abortion
should be avoided whenever possible. But the resurgence of an
extremist right and of a violent, anti-women fundamentalism
involving all the principal religions forces us to make the right to
a free, safe and legal abortion for women all over the world one
of the main objectives on the feminist agenda. It is an objective
that will be very hard to obtain, but whether we like it or not,
and despite the fact that all of us have other projects and interests,
we will have to struggle hard for it in the coming years. Nor is it
a question of ignoring the feelings of those women who suffer
after a termination. But this tendency to consider abortion as 'a
tragedy for all women' is misleading as well as unfounded, because
it implies that the alleged tragedy is inevitable, and is linked to
the very fact of interrupting the sacred reproductive process, rather

than to the many adverse circumstances which may surround an abortion – the indifference and/or violence of the man; the loneliness of the woman; the guilt-inducing attitudes of health professionals; and the dreariness of the bureaucratic health care process. The problem is that, despite twenty-five years of the new feminism, motherhood still retains its sacred aura. Mothers still do not dare to admit how burdensome the constraints and difficulties of their condition can be. Voluntarily childless (or childfree) women feel uneasy about admitting they are happy without children. Women who have had an abortion are ashamed to tell the truth if their principal reactions have been relief and a sense of release. This kind of censorship may help to explain why, when new mothers are interviewed about their feelings of sadness, unhappiness or depression some months after the birth, some of them give the following reasons: 'hormones', 'lack of iron' and even 'classic post-partum depression'.[53] This is a real victory for bio-reductionist psychiatry, and a real backlash against mothers, for 'post-partum depression' has been shown to be linked instead to the very variables shaping motherhood in a society characterized by gender, class and race inequalities – an unsupportive partner, dissatisfaction with perinatal care, economic and housing difficulties, unemployment and being a migrant woman.[54]

Serious debate about the political and psychological aspects of sexuality and contraception has been rare. Are we really so sure that by now all the problems have been solved in our part of the world? It is the HIV/AIDS epidemic, and not feminist pressure groups, which has reawakened interest in these issues. The results of a British study of young women's sexual behaviour revealed that many felt unsure about their identity and worth, and about the legitimacy of their feelings and desires. For these reasons, they were unable satisfactorily to negotiate sexual encounters with their male partners, and often ended up accepting unprotected penetrative sex, for instance, when they did not want penetration and would at least have preferred to use a condom.[55] But the sexuality–contraception issue has been neglected in feminist circles, too. Two recent articles by French feminists seemingly take it for granted that the pill is a good contraceptive choice, while the condom is either a bad one or no choice at all.[56] On the contrary: it is absurd to suppress a physiological process by chemical means in order to make male penetration and ejaculation possible, and even more absurd, given that many heterosexual women do not particularly like penetration.[57] The point here is not to decide whether one contraceptive is more politically correct than another. But feminists do seem to have become rather reluctant to discuss their ideas and experiences regarding sexuality, contraception and abortion, as well as motherhood. The uncomfortable fact is, that with the second millennium only a couple of years away, these subjects are still largely taboo.

The Attacks on Working Mothers

According to recent data, 42 per cent of Italian mothers with a child under nine are employed, most of them full time; 15 per cent say they are unemployed; the others are presumed to be full-time housewives. The corresponding figures for Italian fathers are 95 per cent and 3 per cent respectively.[58] The proportion of employed mothers is higher in northern and central Italy, where 54 per cent of those with a child under three are in paid work.[59] In Europe as a whole, the proportion of mothers with a child aged nine or younger who are employed is higher (51 per cent) and that of mothers who are unemployed is slightly lower (13 per cent), but more women work part time.[60] Another feature of women's employment in Italy, which is shared with France and with other Mediterranean countries, is that the birth of the first or second child does not mean that mothers leave their jobs, and women's activity rates do not vary much with the number of children.[61]

In one longitudinal study carried out in Trieste,[62] 141 first-time mothers who had all had paid employment during pregnancy were interviewed when their baby was fifteen months old. At this time, 84 per cent still had paid work. Women with a higher educational level, those with a qualified job during pregnancy and those employed in the public sector were significantly more likely to still have a job than those with only compulsory education, with a less qualified job, and either employed in the private sector or self-employed. Among the twenty-two non-employed mothers (16 per cent), a third said they preferred to stay home with the baby; a third had lost their jobs during or after the pregnancy; and a third had been forced to give up their jobs for other reasons (the employer had refused to accept part-time work; the crèche was too expensive, and so on). All in all, it seems that Italian mothers with a qualified, secure and fairly well-paid job in the regular labour market tend to keep it after the birth of their first child, and only a small minority of new mothers (around 6 per cent) prefer to stop work at this time. This is confirmed by the preliminary results of another study of 820 mothers in the north-east of Italy, who were interviewed a few days after giving birth. Seventy-eight per cent had a paid job during pregnancy; the activity rate was significantly higher among more educated women. Among non-employed women, 45 per cent were in this situation because they had lost a previous job; only 21 per cent said they had actually chosen to stay home with the child. When their baby was twelve months old, 483 mothers – 66 per cent of the whole sample – were in paid work. This included 76 per cent of those who had been employed during the pregnancy.[63]

These results suggest that having paid work is an important part of most Italian women's identity, and that this is not called into question when a baby arrives. Doing paid work, raising the child, coping with the housework, and in most cases with wife-work too, is made possible by legislation to protect the rights of working mothers. This is extended to all employed women, regardless of seniority and of the number of hours worked weekly. During the post-partum period, three months' mandatory maternity leave is provided for, with the woman receiving at least 80 per cent of normal earnings; a further six months' leave, paid only in part, can be taken by the mother or the father, before the baby's first birthday. Either of the parents has the right to work two hours less every day until the baby is a year old without any loss of salary; and either can be absent from work when a child aged three or younger is sick.[64]

The situation of working mothers in Great Britain would seem to be far more difficult. Here 'traditional images of motherhood are enduring, pervasive and incompatible with paid employment'[65] and maternity rights are accessible only to a limited number of women.[66] Child-care facilities are among the poorest in Europe, since publicly funded services offer places to only 2 per cent of children under three and only 35 per cent of three- to five-year-olds.[67] Compared to other countries, fewer women in Britain resume work after childbirth. In 1988, only 45 per cent of mothers who were employed during pregnancy had a job nine months after childbirth, more than half of these part time.[68] Women with young children who go out to work are often made to feel they are not good mothers.[69]

Italy is far from being a working mother's paradise, although the situation is easier than in other countries. The problem is that a mother's right to regular employment is continuously under attack. Firstly, although Italian law prohibits the dismissal of a pregnant woman, employers still find ways around the law, usually by making prospective female employees promise in writing that they will resign if they become pregnant.[70] For those mothers who manage to keep their job, life can be made difficult by the shortage of day care and after-school facilities. In Italy, publicly funded services offer a place to 5 per cent of children under the age of three and to 85 per cent of three- to six-year-olds. School for older children finishes at one o'clock, and after-school facilities are rare.[71] Regional disparities are wide. Even in Emilia-Romagna, which has been ruled by a Communist local government for the last fifty years, and where the day-care services are among the best in the world, with attendance by 20 per cent of under-threes, access is still denied to at least 2,000 'stand-by' children every year.[72] In the face of these shortcomings, the extended family is called to the rescue, and the second most common form of child-care in Italy (after their mothers) for babies whose parents are employed is grandparents (mostly grandmothers). Among the 483 employed mothers interviewed in the north-east of Italy twelve months after the birth, 63 per cent left the child with the grandparents during their working day.[73] The idea that under-threes should be cared for within the family is so deep-rooted in Italian culture that parents wanting to put their baby in a publicly funded crèche have to sign a form stating that the grandparents are not available, because they are either dead or seriously ill (the fact that grandparents might not want to take on the job of looking after the baby, or may not be in a position to because of other responsibilities, is not considered a good enough reason).

As in other industrialized countries, material attacks on employed mothers accompany ideological attacks. As Susan Faludi[74] has cogently argued, we are witnessing a war against women, and this includes a campaign against their right to have a paid job or a career. The media play a central role in this undeclared war. In January 1993, Italian newspapers gave a great deal of coverage to some 'scientific results' presented by an Italian doctor at an international meeting on female contraception. According to his study, having a career entails stress, and this is linked in turn to fertility problems: the women most at risk are women doctors and journalists, especially those working in television. The newspaper headlines ranged from, 'A Career is Bad for the Stork'[75] to, 'Too Much Stress. Sterility Risk for Female TV Reporters'.[76] Sadly, women journalists and left-wing newspapers seemed to accept this news just as uncritically as the others. The message is overwhelmingly that having a good job or a career is dangerous for women's reproductive health. In May 1993, a Swiss French newspaper published a long article entitled 'Stress and Pregnancy: What Risks?'[77] The author, a certain 'Docteur 33', explained how career women, and especially those with a 'frail narcissism', who are incapable of abandoning their 'impossible plans', run a high risk of having a pre-term baby, thereby jeopardizing the health of the next generation and making themselves responsible for the excessive spending on health care. The author concludes by advising women to take cavemen as a model for the division of work between men and women. It should be borne in mind that Swiss laws concerning the protection of pregnant workers are far behind those of other European countries. This particular article appeared in a Geneva newspaper, in the very city where the World Health Organization and the International Labour Organization have their headquarters. Yet there were no letters of complaint.

Once again, empirical results show a different picture. Since 1970, research data from different countries have shown that full-time housewives have more pre-term babies than employed women; this relationship holds even when controlling for socio-demographic factors and for chronic health conditions.[78] Among employed women, those most at risk for perinatal problems are manual and less-qualified workers and those exposed to chemical substances, and certainly not 'career' women.[79] Nor is paid work detrimental to the health of mothers of young children: on the contrary, in many situations they fare better than full-time housewives.[80]

A relatively new ideological contribution to the backlash against working mothers is represented by the discourse of La Lèche League International, a pro-breast-feeding and pro-family organiz-ation, founded in the USA in the 1950s and present in many industrialized countries. In Italy, the League's counsellors have considerable influence. They are all mothers themselves, and usu-ally work in collaboration with home-birth groups, but also have direct access to new mothers. In their handbook,[81] they take it for granted that a mother's job represents a threat to the baby's health, to breast-feeding and to the mother–child relationship. It is assumed that all mothers, if they could choose, would prefer to stop work and stay at home full-time, suckling their babies and toddlers for years. It is also taken for granted that all the housework and caring for other family members is the breast-feeding woman's responsibility. The handbook provides a series of useful tips on how to carry out all these different tasks smoothly and with a radiant smile. According to La Lèche League, if mothers really must work for money, it is better to choose a part-time, home-based job, for instance child-minding (never mind if this kind of work is badly paid and without benefits). If mothers really must work outside the home, they can train the baby to sleep during the day, so that they can spend as much time as possible with the little one and breast-feed as much as possible at night.[82]

Scientific data do not confirm these prejudices. In a thorough review of the literature, Van Esterik and Grenier[83] conclude that the association between maternal employment and the decline of breast-feeding worldwide, which has been so widely publicized by many paediatricians, is a belief unsupported by empirical evidence. They quote several studies showing that where maternity rights are well-implemented, employed mothers are more likely to initiate breast-feeding and to continue it for a long time. A recent Italian study confirms these results. In this employed mothers breast-fed significantly longer than full-time housewives, even after controlling for relevant socio-demographic variables.[84] The fact that employed women in the US tend to breast-feed for a shorter time is more likely to be a reflection of the negative effects of substandard maternity rights, rather than of the incompatibility of paid work with maternal responsibilities, including breast-feeding.[85]

A similar picture is evident in research concerned with the consequences of mothers' paid work on child development. In the wake of John Bowlby's theories, psychologists, psychiatrists and paediatricians have spent years looking for negative outcomes, but without success.[86] In the words of Moore et al.: 'It is significant how few negative effects have been documented, given the diligence with which they have been pursued.'[87] What results have shown, instead, is some positive effects of maternal employment and of day care on children's social and psychological development.[88] Although 'Bowlbyism' seems to be less influential in Italy than in other countries, many professionals involved in child-care activities still believe that employed mothers are 'selfish' and that day care is bad for youngsters. In Trieste, for example, there was a violent clash a few years ago between female day-care workers and employed parents: many parents had signed a petition asking for day-care services to be continued during the summer instead of closing for the usual two months, as most people only have a month's holiday. The day-care workers strongly defended their 'right' to enjoy long holidays, because they were mothers and their children needed them, stressing that day care was 'not necessary, not useful and not pleasant' for a child, apparently oblivious to the fact that they were devaluing their own work and skills in the process.[89]

While the rights of some employed mothers are ignored, others benefit from privileges. Women employed in the public sector generally do best; their working conditions are generally better: they have shorter working hours, longer holidays, sick leave, better reimbursement during maternity leave and no risk of being sacked. Research results show that women working in the public sector stay at home much longer on full pay, both during pregnancy and after the birth, than women employed in the private sector.[90] In one study,[91] a number of public-sector pregnant women cheerfully admitted when interviewed that they had obtained a 'false' sick note from their doctor, even though their job was not tiring or dangerous and they had no health problem. It should be said that many of these women tended to do more housework as soon as they were home full time, and ended up feeling more tired than when they were at work. Moreover, until 1990, women employed in the public sector, if they were married or had children, could retire on full pension after only fifteen years' work: five years before their male colleagues and many years before private-sector employees. This could be seen as one way of recognizing part of the unpaid work employed women do within the family, and it was consistent with pro-family values and politics. It also created different categories of working women: the public-sector employees, who can switch easily to full-time motherhood and housewifery, and still get paid with the taxpayer's money; and the private-sector ones, who have a struggle to cope with all their different jobs/roles, and often spend a sizeable chunk of their salary on child care and domestic help. Then there are the women who have failed to find a steady job, and who end up in the totally unprotected illegal labour market, and/or in unpaid, involuntary full-time motherhood and housewifery. Protective legislation thus reveals the conflicting ideology surrounding the role of women in Italy, a paradox present in the country's Constitution (1948), which states that every citizen has a right to employment, but also that working conditions must allow women to carry out their 'essential family duties'. It will come as no surprise that this is the article of the Constitution which seems to be taken most seriously: all the relevant data show that Italian women do most, if not all of the domestic and caring work, whether they are employed or not.

The meagre contribution of Italian men to housework and child care[92] is another aspect of the backlash against women in general, and employed mothers in particular. These are the disheartening results emerging from interviews with 483 working mothers carried out when their babies were twelve months old:[93] 92 per cent of the women did all or most of the washing, 80 per cent the ironing, 77 per cent the cooking and 64 per cent the cleaning. The shopping was more likely to be shared, with 'only' 51 per cent of women doing most or all of it. The male partners of full-time housewives do even less. Men's participation in housework actually decreases between the pregnancy and one year post-partum.[94] Since a number of studies from different countries show the same trends (men do less after the birth than during pregnancy and their participation decreases as the number of children increases), we can only surmise that this strange behaviour is not exclusive to Italian males.[95] A battle would seem to have been lost, for most men stubbornly refuse to collaborate, despite the manifest discontent shown by many women. Among the mothers mentioned above, 52 per cent said they would like more male participation; and 48 per cent said this situation created conflicts for the couple. Qualitative studies help to shed more light on this issue. Married or cohabiting women are faced with the discordance between the dominant cultural model of the 'modern' couple, in which the man participates or at least 'helps', and an often grim reality in which he does almost nothing. Feeling responsible for the situation, they try to preserve their self-esteem and keep the peace, finding excuses for the man and concluding that everything is fine.[96]

The reluctance, or downright refusal, of men to cooperate has negative effects on women: it robs them of their free time; it makes them more tired; and it may decrease their self-esteem. Not surprisingly, empirical data have shown an association between low male participation in housework and child care and depressive symptoms in mothers, regardless of employment status.[97] In an attempt to address these problems, the women of the PCI/PDS prepared a new law in the late 1980s called the Law on Women's Time, which was never formally discussed in parliament. It was widely debated within women's circles, however, and has influenced the cultural debate on these issues. It consisted of a set of measures to make it easier to combine paid work with family life. It envisaged the possibility of parental leave (twelve months to be taken before the child is eleven) or family leave (six weeks every two years), paid at an equivalent of half the average national wage; an unemployed parent caring for a child would have the right to a 'parent's salary' for a twelve-month period; working hours would be reduced for all workers; and more flexible hours would be introduced in schools, shops and offices.[98] No mention was made of day-care and after-school services.

The PCI/PDS proposal was interesting because it tried to humanize adult working life without discriminating between women and men, or between the employed and the non-employed. As soon as it got to the discussion stage, though, the idea of a parent's salary was shelved, along with that of shorter working hours: there would have been no chance of obtaining the necessary funding to pay parents, and reducing the working week would have been a mammoth task in itself. If passed, the remaining measures were also likely to pose problems. As with maternity rights, parental and family leave would have been more difficult to obtain in the private sector. In the absence of a cultural revolution, or coercive measures (or both), it is doubtful that men would have queued up to obtain leave. According to a survey carried out in Trieste, only one in ten of fathers qualifying for 'extended post-partum leave' actually makes use of it.[99] But despite its ambitious aims, at the heart of the proposal lay traditional values concerning women's role within the family. As the women of the PCI put it in the preface to the proposal, 'We [women] demand to be helped to reconcile our different roles.'[100] Many women read the message, but were not taken in. One working mother said in a public debate: 'If all this is meant to give me more time to do the shopping, no thanks.'

The situation is similar in France. Part-time work is presented more and more insistently as the magic formula enabling women to reconcile paid and unpaid work.[101] But a part-time job is often a very bad deal: wages are usually very low, and a career is highly unlikely. To make matters worse, whenever a woman shifts from full-time to part-time work, the man's contribution to family work drops sharply.[102] As Delphy[103] points out, even when part-time work is 'chosen', this is a forced choice, the result of two contradictory tendencies: women's desire to work and the fact that nothing has changed in domestic task-sharing or in working conditions and professional careers. Both women's paid work and their domestic work consequently become less socially visible.

Another bad deal in France is parental leave after the birth, which can last for three years and is only reimbursed (at a very low level) after the second child. Recent data show that this often leads to loss of employment, because it can be difficult for mothers to be reinstated after such a long absence.[104] In Great Britain, where part-time work is already widespread among mothers, downward job mobility is common after childbirth, and is often a direct consequence of going back to work on a part-time basis.[105] In addition, there are the financial penalties attached to leaving the labour market for an extended period. It has been estimated that lost earnings due to childbirth amount to more than half of a typical woman's future potential earnings from the age of twenty-five onwards.[106]

Should we consider all these different options – part-time work, extended parental and family leave – as strategies intended to lead mothers gently back into the cosy world of the family? The answer is yes. For many mothers struggling with a badly paid full-time job, a shortage of good-quality, affordable day care and an unco-operative partner,[107] parental leave or part-time work may seem like a good solution – the very lifeline which saves them from drowning. In fact, these are measures which rationalize the exploitation of the work mothers do both inside and outside the family.

It is notable that, despite this pervasive pro-family culture, many Italian mothers continue to say that they enjoy their jobs, need more child-care services and are unhappy when unemployed. For example, 45 per cent of employed women interviewed in the north-east of Italy[108] said that they had been 'fairly' or 'very' happy to go back to work after the birth; 44 per cent reported mixed feelings (happy to be back at work, but sad or worried about the baby); and only 11 per cent said they had been 'fairly' or 'very' unhappy. When they were asked what kind of social measures might be helpful for mothers or families with young children, the most frequently chosen category of answers (32 per cent) con-cerned day-care services, which they thought should be more numerous, of better quality, cheaper and more flexible. The chance to work part time came second (22 per cent). The third most frequently chosen answer (11 per cent) cited extended maternity leave (more than one answer was possible). The non-employed mothers gave a more scattered range of answers: the most fre-quently chosen was a system of allowances for mothers or families with young children (16 per cent). Then came part-time work (11 per cent) and child-care services (8 per cent). Some mothers wanted a safe place to leave the baby for a few hours (6 per cent); and others expressed the need to join a group with other mothers or parents (7 per cent). Interestingly enough, the same small proportion in both groups (4 per cent) proposed an increase in men's salaries which would enable mothers to stay home full time.

Another unwarranted belief is that job loss and a return to unpaid, domestic work has little impact on women's well-being. Recent studies show that being made redundant is associated with depression in women workers as well as men, and the negative effects of job loss are not attenuated by the fact of having a secure marital relationship and being the mother of a pre-school child.[109] Results from an Italian qualitative study confirm these findings. The mothers interviewed reported that when they had lost their jobs, the reaction of other family members (husbands, children, mothers, mothers-in-law) had often been positive: back home at last and fully at our disposal, a cause for celebration! But despite these pressures upon mothers to declare that they were happy, most women reported feeling miserable.[110]

These results should be read in the context of recent Italian unemployment statistics. In 1993, unemployment rates were 15.9 per cent among women and 8.5 per cent among men. In the fifteen to twenty-four age range, 38.8 per cent of women were unemployed; in the twenty-five to thirty-four age range, 17.8 per cent; and in the thirty-five to fifty-four age range, 7.1 per cent.[111] Official statistics tend to underestimate female unemployment, and there are probably even more women and mothers who would like a job.

Conclusion

In contemporary Italy, the choice of motherhood is still unquestioned; becoming a mother is still seen as essential to being recognized as a real, mature woman; enormous symbolic value is still attributed to motherhood. These ideologies obviously inform current values and practices concerning all women, be they mothers or not. In the context of a Mediterranean cultural legacy, various forces and traditions have come together to develop and sustain these ideas: the continuing influence of the Catholic Church; the presence of a new right on the political scene which includes the former Fascist Party; the increasingly traditional, pro-family attitudes and policies of progressive political parties such as the PDS and, more recently, the fashionable 'thinking of sexual difference', emphasizing women's allegedly essential difference, extolling the potency of mothers, and diffusing an idea of motherhood as 'redemptive'.

In this context, acknowledging the difficulties and constraints of motherhood, let alone its darkest sides, is problematic, and trying to change the situation is not easy. It is extremely difficult unambiguously to defend women's right to free, safe abortion, and even more difficult to demand that the conditions in which women have abortions should be improved, so that it may become as positive an experience as possible. It is difficult to struggle for the right to do paid work, because social organization, social policies and men's behaviour are all consistent with the idea that a mother's priority is her family. It is difficult to ask for more child-care services of a higher quality rather than, for example, an extension to maternity leave, since the very existence of child-care facilities endorses the idea of mother–child separation and of mothers leading an autonomous life. It is also very difficult to understand and explain mothers' depression, for why ever should women be depressed if having a child is the fulfilment of a woman's life? It is almost impossible to come to terms with the all too frequent tragedies of mothers who kill their children. The newspapers say these women have been really upset since the birth; sometimes they have already had a nervous breakdown. But they had wanted their child so much and had been such wonderful, devoted mothers until the tragedy that only a fit of insanity could explain what happened. And what about the mothers who throw away their newborn babies? Only extreme poverty and ignorance could explain that. Motherhood is always a marvellous experience, except for those who fail the test.

In short, the idealization of motherhood would seem not to be in the best interests of real mothers. As Oakley has put it: '. . . in a patriarchal, family-oriented culture . . . women come to motherhood with quite unrealistic expectations . . . this idealization can be counted as a form of "transmitted deprivation". Women are deprived of the chance to understand not only the benefits but also the hazards that motherhood will pose to their own identities and lifestyles.'[112]

There are feminists in Italy, but they have been rather noncommittal on the issue of motherhood. In any case, they have difficulty gaining access to the media, which tend to give space only to specific currents, such as that of 'the difference'. Despite this, it is clear that many ordinary Italian women are silently opposing these pressures and attacks: the birth rate, statistics about mothers' participation in the labour market and the unemployment figures all indicate an obstinate resistance. In a sense, women who kill their own children are enacting a terrible, extreme form of resistance too. They may not be numerous, but this is no excuse for forgetting about them, because they are a clear indictment of a society in which both having children and not having them can be just too difficult.

I conclude with a wish for the future. I should like to contribute to a society that gives worth and legitimacy to the choice of not having children, on the one hand, and is able to assure all mothers decent conditions in which to raise their children enjoyably, on the other. I should like to live in a country where not everyone has to have a child, but where everyone feels deeply responsible and ready to care for the children already with us.[113]

10

Dangerous Design: Asian Women and the New Landscapes of Fashion

PARMINDER BHACHU

We need to develop a new feminist cultural politics that will centrally include the agenda of women of colour. This will recover the voices of British Black and Asian women, which have emerged from landscapes that are very different from those underpinning hegemonic feminisms;[1] these reflect neither the complexities of Black and Asian women's lives, nor their diverse class, economic and cultural locations.[2] The new kind of feminism must be inclusive and elastic enough to occupy the global and local cultural landscapes of diaspora Asian women, and to embrace their agency – their active role in creating, generating and engaging with their cultural base.

While white women's agency has been written about and celebrated, the agency of women of colour has so far been largely ignored by mainstream feminists, who have tended to reduce their cultural and symbolic economies to fit into the mould of victimology. In the early 1980s, soon after I had finished a Ph.D. on the property rights of British Asian women, a white British feminist invited me to contribute a paper to a seminar series. She said she was interested in my work on the wedding economy of a multiple migrant group in Britain, especially on the changes in its dowry system from India, from their two migrations in the early part of the twentieth century to the late 1970s. These movements were from India to East Africa to Britain. In my paper, I emphasized the active and transformative role of these women in interpreting these cultural systems, and the fact that this old and traditional property system had been reinterpreted dynamically and continuously on the British scene by these wage-earning brides, through their command over cash. But this is not what the feminist who had invited me expected to hear: I think she wanted to hear about the control exercised by patriarchal agencies on women as property, and women's property as manipulated by men. In such a picture, women are seen as powerless passive objects of exchange, as pawns in the games of acquiring social prestige and with no control over their destinies. They can only manoeuvre an arena for themselves once they have acquired seniority as grandmothers, when they exercise control over the household through their sons.

In 1990, I was asked to present a talk to an audience that was roughly similar. I spoke about the multiplicities of British Asian women's local, regional and subcultural locations and their diverse class positions, which had existed since the eighteenth century. I referred to the impact of this diversity in determining their consumption styles, cultural locations and their varied interpretations of the wedding economy. I pointed to the *transformative* role of British Asian women in the construction of their identities and the local diasporic spaces they occupied. I talked about their emergent cultural spaces and their simultaneous position in the local, national and global arenas, in which they reconstituted and created cultural forms and images. These diasporean aesthetics were and are as much part of their ethnic cultural base as they are of their socialization to particular local, regional and class cultures in Britain. But my audience responded by interrogating me about the so-called pathologies of British Asian cultural systems and about their casualties, and about the problems Asian women have with their arranged marriages and their orthodox parents, who were described as being out of touch with contemporary mores. It was as if they were saying, 'How dare you *not* talk about the problems faced by migrant and settler Asians in Britain?' I explained that I did not want to engage with these overworked themes of cultural pathology and victimology, and that I was fed up with this focus on the casualties of a system, as if they represented the whole fabric of these settler communities.

In my research at the time, I was documenting case studies of women who were *not* just passive participants in cultural systems that were imposed on them by patriarchal agencies. I could not relate to these simplistic models, which were (and still are) vigilantly regulated by certain feminist gatekeepers. This is not to say that no arenas can be constructed positively in terms of the victimology agenda: much valuable work has been done on the domestic violence suffered by British Asian women; on their low-status economic position within European economic hierarchies; on their problems within the system of arranged marriages and kinship; on their difficulties with immigration laws and authorities; on the lack of attention to their health needs; on the racism underpinning some aspects of local government policy and provisions; on oppressive employment conditions; and on racist immigration legislation. Moreover, the lives of Asian women are affected by the issues of economics, class and region that abound for women everywhere, regardless of ethnicity. But there are many cultural dynamics that simply cannot be captured by the victimology framework, which were and are producing complex cultural textures.

In this chapter, I present an argument for the agency of British Asian women. In relation to the various strands of the white feminist movement and the current backlash against it, my argument is that the multiplicity of women's agencies and 'feminisms' was never adequately represented in 'the' feminist movement. Consequently, the present moment of backlash does not relate to the cultural position of many groups of women. While acknowledging that diaspora Asian women are not free from obstacles, my discussion does not focus on this but, rather, on the strategies they have developed to innovate new cultural forms. They have used global commodities and consumer products to create new local interpretations of cultural identity, and these patterns emerge from their sophisticated command of the symbolic and political economies in which they are located.[3] These novel patterns are as reflective of the local codes of their subclass and subcultures as they are of the transnational spaces to which they belong.

My argument is not made through any kind of ideological rhetoric, but through a specific analysis of current fashion that is sensitive to the cultural frameworks of diaspora Asian women and recognizes the bottom-up power that is wielded by women as consumers. In particular, I am going to explore the commoditization processes involved in the production of the *salwaar-kameez*. This outfit, which is sometimes referred to as the Punjabi suit or the *salwaar-kameez*, is made in all sorts of fabric and comprises a long tunic, loose and often baggy trousers, and a long scarf called *dupatta* or *chuni*: the top often has a slit down each side, the trousers may have a cuff at the ankle, and the scarf is between two and three metres long.

Culture and Consumption

Salwaar-kameez suits, which are important in the wedding economy, are a powerfully coded attire, both politically and culturally.[4] They have become a garment of high fashion globally and reflect fashion geographies – both those that are local to the Indian scene, and those that are generated by Asian women in the diaspora. They represent a multiplicity of movements and sites of production, as well as specificity of cultural identities and fashion trajectories. The malleability powers of *salwaar-kameez* suits in their 1990s form are immense, in their projection of various identities and in negotiating new consumption and cultural styles and new ethnicities. Notions of multiple 'Britishness' are inscribed in the interpretation of the suits, thus contesting British sartorial hegemonies.

These suits represent mainstream consumer expressions that can be found throughout the socio-economic strata of Britain, much like British Indian food – which has been dubbed 'the currification of Britain'. *Euronews*, the main news programme of Zee TV, the Asian Cable Channel, reported in 1996 that 15 per cent of the British population chose curry as their favourite meal, surpassing roast beef at 12 per cent and Chinese food at 11 per cent; the 'average British person' ate curry once a week.[5] The *Daily Star* ran an article in the same year on the Queen's Indian food choices and favourite restaurant, which was illustrated by a computer-generated picture of the Queen with a turban on her head; the headline of the article was, 'It ain't arf Hot Ma'am: Queen Orders Two Tikkaways a Week.'[6] Popular Indian cuisine includes the recent balti movement, which has led to the easy availability of balties (a cooking utensil much like a wok) in most household goods stores on the high street. Some of these trends are facilitated through the cable shopping network, QVC. Furthermore, there is a mushrooming market for a whole variety of ready-made Indian sauces to be cooked with meats and vegetables, which have been promoted on British television in a series of advertisements, with Asian actors playing working-class Indians with strong regional accents, especially those of Scotland and Northern England. Asian fruit juices, too, which are perceived to be exotic, are in increasing demand. All these products are available at exclusive shops like Harrods and also at most major high-street supermarkets, like Marks & Spencer and Sainsbury's.

The impact of Indian cuisine on British food consumption is one of many examples of Asian influence, along with music, dance and language styles, labour relations and political styles.[7] Like *sal-waar-kameez* outfits, these cultural products have multiple sites of production, but are also locally produced. They have a social and cultural life that emerges from specific places, migration histories, and local political and symbolic economies. For example, the music of Apache Indian in Britain has the specificity of a young Punjabi man raised in multi-ethnic working-class Birmingham in the British Midlands. His music topped both the reggae and bhangra charts in 1991, the year in which he was also voted Best Newcomer at the British Reggae Industry Awards. He has played to packed stadia in India and is famous and controversial in the international South Asian diaspora, whilst at the same time being authenticated by African Caribbean diasporic communities. Apache is thirty-year-old Steven Kapur, whose Hindu parents migrated from Jalandhar district of Punjab, which has produced the majority of

Punjabi migrants internationally since the late twentieth century.[8] In both simple and complex ways, trends like these are reflected in community organizations and clothes, in the interpretation of public and private spaces, and in the interpretation of home and interior decorations, where women are the central interpreters of these cultural styles and consumer expressions. These niches have moved beyond so-called ethnic boundaries to the British mainstream and are being interpreted, in a variety of complex ways, as one facet of the 'Asianization' of the West.

These cultural processes are not restricted to middle-class bourgeois women, who can afford to patronize exclusive *salwaar-kameez* retail outlets, but apply to a whole range of socio-economic groups. A further point to be emphasized here about class markers and class-specificity is that Asian women in Britain come from complex and complicated class locations. It is also a mistake to assume that all transnationally located women belong to an élite: in the 1990s, transnationalism is no longer an exclusive phenomenon, but spreads across a range of class groups that regularly cross national boundaries and diasporic spaces, from blue-collar workers to corporate executives. I myself inhabit these multiply located and transnational spaces, which inform the observations presented in this chapter. I was born in Tanzania, lived in Uganda and Kenya until I was fourteen years of age, then migrated with my parents to South London in Britain in 1968; in 1990, I moved to the USA, where I have started life as a migrant in two different places, Los Angeles and Massachusetts.

Some of the processes that are commoditizing the wedding economy, of which the *salwaar-kameez* suits are a large component, include the boutiques selling ready-to-wear clothes, which have sprung up all over London and the Midlands and the other major centres of the Asian population in Britain. These shops are mostly found in areas where there is a high concentration of British Asians, but they are also found in the main shopping areas of London, like Mayfair, Baker Street and Knightsbridge. The ready-to-wear outfits sold by these shops cost anything from £30–100 to £200–5,000 for designer suits. The Asian women involved, who are wedding service providers, also feed many other diaspora clothes markets. Some of these entrepreneurs are locally born or raised, while others are from India and have excellent connections to Indian goods and services. White British designers have also entered as prominent interpreters of consumption trends among British Asians. These include designers like Zandra Rhodes, who was especially popular among Asian women in the 1980s and whose designer suits and saris were sold in high-status Indian clothing stores in London. A relative newcomer to this scene is British designer Catherine Walker, who designed Jemima Goldsmith's dress for her wedding reception in 1995 and also Princess Diana's attire for her visit to Pakistan in 1996. Equally, there are locally produced clothes designed by young British Asians trained in Britain, mostly young women in their late twenties and early thirties.

A global cultural and consumer flow, which was unexpected in its impact but very important in determining wedding consumption for the large metropolitan centres of the Asian diaspora (London, New York, Los Angeles, Sydney), is the ready availability of designer clothes flown to London and other metropolitan and provincial cities. These consumer flows, which have a strong local impact, include designers trained in Europe and the USA, as well as those based in Bombay, Delhi, Lahore and Karachi. This personnel consists mostly of women, though there are a number of important male players, whose mail-order catalogues have led to the steady accessibility of their clothes for mass market consumption. This is not a class-specific phenomenon, restricted to the upper-class transnational élite. These are processes that are to be found in every class and subcultural group and are influential in producing many new versions of 'Europeanness' and 'Asianness' in the late twentieth century.

Global markets are determining the fashion styles of these suits, with cross-flows of information between the major international cities and design centres: cutting instructions, shapes, embroideries, and *chuni/dupatta* styles are swiftly transferred across the world via fax machines. The styles and the fully stitched garments are then rapidly inserted into the various diaspora markets via courier services (many of which have recently expanded in order to deal with this rapidly increasing clothes traffic). In many cases, the suit designs are rapidly copied for domestically stitched suits by women seamstresses and a few male tailors, who operate out of their homes in all the major British cities. These locally made garments are available through the postal services, which means they are penetrating the market as never before, facilitated by extended kinship and friendship groups. Frequent travel to India and Pakistan by diaspora Asians further extends the cross-flows of the latest fashion designs and information about them. Women-led retail niches – the high-status designer boutiques in Mayfair, Wembley and Knightsbridge, as well as those in Southall, Hounslow, East Ham, Romford, and the many market stalls – have mushroomed. A whole range of women-led marketing initiatives has produced a plethora of commercial enterprises run by women entrepreneurs who act as designers, redistributive agents in these economies, tailors, embroiderers and professional service providers.

Contesting British Sartorial Hegemonies

Salwaar-kameez suits are inscriptions of ethnic pride and are a highly political piece of clothing. After the army action at the golden temple in Amritsar in 1984, for example, many Sikh women in India and in the diaspora stopped wearing the sari, because they considered it to be a 'Hindu' dress form, representative of the Congress Government that initiated the army action. Instead, they assertively donned the *salwaar-kameez* suit, a gesture similar to that of Sikh men who adopted turbans, some coloured orange (which is the colour of martyrs and martyrdom). In so doing, they made a powerful political statement against the actions of the Delhi-based Congress Government. Following the pogroms against the Sikhs after the assassination of Prime Minister Indira Gandhi by her two Sikh bodyguards, some women are still not wearing the sari. Their wearing of the *salwaar-kameez* suit makes a powerful statement both about their rejection of the Indian action and also as a reflection of 'ethnic pride' in their British 'ethnicity'.

These highly politicized scenarios have quite different implications from the adoption of the *salwaar-kameez* by key media stars and other wealthy women in the mid-1990s. These include upper-middle-class women like Princess Diana, who wore three different *salwaar-kameez* outfits (in pink, creamy pink and light turquoise blue) for her controversial and unofficial trip to Pakistan in February 1996, which was widely covered by the media; the *Daily Express* ran an article on 'A Touch of Eastern Cool: How to Follow Diana's Example and Spice Your Summer Wardrobe'.[9] This article also published advice by Koo Stark regarding how to wear the *salwaar-kameez* and information about some of the up-market retail outlets which sell them. This was followed in April by a slot on a programme called *Off the Peg*, on Cable News Channel One for London, which showed how to wear a *salwaar-kameez* through a demonstration by a Black British model. In the previous year, *Woman's Hour* on Radio 4 had produced a programme on these outfits.

Other leading ladies who have worn *salwaar-kameez* suits include Lady Helen Windsor, the daughter of the Duke and Duchess of Kent, who in the summer of 1994 appeared in one both at the wedding of Lady Sarah Armstrong-Jones, Princess Margaret's daughter, and at the wedding of her best friend Arabella Cobbold, at which she was matron of honour. Lady Helen's outfits were bought from Egg, the highly innovative Knightsbridge shop that was opened in early 1994 under a glare of media attention. Egg is the joint commercial venture of style 'supremo' Maureen Doherty and Asha Sarabhai, a Girton graduate who is a designer of textiles and clothes and has produced an exhibition of her work at the Victoria and Albert Museum in London; she has a cult following that includes serious aesthetes like the painters Frank Stella and Robert Rauschenberg, the writer Gita Mehta, and Issey Miyake. Her career in textiles began in 1975, when she married a man from a respected and wealthy Indian textile dynasty; its headquarters are located at Ahmedabad, north of Bombay, where the plan for Egg was hatched. A full-length evening coat from Egg, cut like a kimono and finished to couture standard, costs

£700, while a natural indigo cotton tunic costs £40; the clothes are made to last and, even, to improve with age.[10] This shop has created a very interesting new space, reflecting an aspect of Britishness that is being negotiated in the 1990s by both British Asian women and by their many white peers in different British contexts.

Jemima Goldsmith, the daughter of one of the wealthiest men in Britain, wore a *salwaar-kameez* at her much-publicized wedding to Imran Khan, the famous Pakistani cricketer. Emma Thompson, the Oscar-winning British actress, wore a *salwaar-kameez* suit (in black and white) for the international promotion in early 1995 of the film *Junior*, in which she starred with Arnold Schwarzenegger. Benazir Bhutto, Pakistan's Prime Minister, is another *salwaar-kameez*-suited woman. Her carefully studied and striking style, designed for media consumption, often involves wearing a jacket on top of her suit with a white *chuni* to cover her head. Prime Minister Bhutto's consistent wearing of the white *chuni* clarifies her facial features for presentation to the media; and in addition, it befits her political position and appeals to her supporters. She has been instrumental in familiarizing the international public with this form of dress: the two suits she wore at the ceremonies at which she was sworn in as Prime Minister were widely copied for months afterwards, both in Pakistan and elsewhere in the diaspora. These copies became high fashion, and were more in demand from Pakistani and overseas tailors than any other outfits.

Of course, there are many multi-directional cross-flows. There are Asian women who have adopted the Lady Helen Windsor style of interpreting their *salwaar-kameez* outfits, precisely because they share a similar class niche or emulate the 'Sloany' style presented in *Vogue* and *Harpers Bazaar*, and by its famous Super Sloane icon, Princess Diana. Similarly, during 1994 and 1995, many metropolitan Asian women wore the top half of the *salwaar-kameez* with a full body stocking and with Doc Marten or thick platform shoes, which were a prominent feature of popular dress at the time. Mohicanized and punkized *salwaar-kameez* outfits have also been worn by Asian women in the last decade. The whole gamut of current styles in vogue – from punky and funky to grunge to baggy hip-hop – can be seen in the interpretation of the *salwaar-kameez* by diaspora women. This has localized the consumption and interpretation of the outfit, even though there are many standardized garments available in all the main markets of the global diaspora.

The presence and influential cultural agency of Asian women in various British niches has fundamentally shifted the European cultural textures of all Europeans. The activities of these cultural entrepreneurs have created new spaces, generating new European landscapes and ethnicities[11] and new European consumer styles and material economies. The negotiations involved are facets of the ethnicization and 'Asianization' of some of the most Anglo-Saxon of British circuits, just as it is a facet of the 'Englishization' and 'Anglo-Saxonization' of the British 'Asianness' of British Asian women. This represents potent new forms of 'Europeanness' in the late twentieth century. These mutually influential and sartorial interpretations are the subversive outcomes of the shared cultural geographies of British women in the 1990s, regardless of their class and ethnic locations.

The styles of these suits also reflect the shared commodity context that produced Egg and other path-breaking commercial ventures, such as the two shops called Rivaaz in Knightsbridge and Wembley. These were pioneered by Gita Sarin, a designer and entrepreneur who has collaborated with leading Parisian designers and who was the first to produce a clothes mail-order catalogue of *salwaar-kameez* suits, ten years ago. She has relied for her success on rapid communications networks: her designs, patterns and stitching instructions are faxed to India, where the garments are manufactured, which means that her designed clothes are available in London within a very short space of time. Chiffons is the name of two designer boutiques that were started in East London and Birmingham by Babi and Nina, two young Punjabi sisters who were British born and raised. Creations in Southall, a wholesaling and retailing outlet in West London, is the brainchild of Mala Rastogi, a dynamic entrepreneur, who organized a major fashion show of *salwaar-kameezes* in 1996 at London's Grosvenor House Hotel. Another upmarket enterprise, which opened in 1996, is Ritu in Mayfair: this was created by Ritu Kumar, the famous Indian 'revivalist' designer of beautifully embroidered *salwaar-kameezes*, who has innovatively revived many embroidery and craft traditions and has also produced designs for Indian celebrities. These are just some of the new spaces being produced by Asian women's entrepreneurship and by the cultural brokerage of the partnerships forged by British Asian women and by other transnational Asian women.

Towards an Inclusive Feminism

The interpretation of 1990s *salwaar-kameez* suits reflects a whole taxonomy of fashion style and a multiplicity of identities and cultural class locations: both those that are local to the Indian scene, and those that determine the styles of Asian women in transnational diasporas. The suits are fundamentally reflective of the stitching and suturing of the many terrains and textures in which Asian women are situated. The crafting of their lives and locations is a continuously negotiated process, tempered by all the strictures and freedoms faced by women in general, all over the world.

I have focused on Asian women's creative suturing of ruptured systems in order to negate the narrow conceptualization of Asian women as victims which is produced from some white feminist circuits of knowledge production. These include publishing houses and prestigious feminist journals, essentially controlled by powerful white middle-class feminists. This effective silencing is a result, I think, of the threat presented to them by British-raised, highly articulate and very commanding Asian women, who have entered the world of academics as knowledge producers and who question hegemonic conceptual models. In the multiplex fields of the media, too, British-raised image-makers, film directors, artists and other producers of culture create quite different images of Asian women. One example is Gurinder Chadha, the first British Asian woman to direct a movie feature, the internationally and critically acclaimed *Bhaji on the Beach*, and the first to direct a BBC drama.[12] Not only does Chadha have a dynamic style of interpreting the image of British Asian women through the medium of film, but she also presents a powerful personal image that interprets the *salwaar-kameez* in a fusion style. Her publicity material shows her dressed in Union Jack socks, Doc Marten shoes, a long embroidered Indian skirt, a long *chuni* tied on one side, a leather jacket, and leading a bulldog on a leash – a media-savvy interpretation of fashion, strongly influenced by the *salwaar-kameez* and reflecting her British Punjabi/Asian identities. Chadha collaborated on the story of *Bhaji on the Beach* with the actress and writer Meera Syal, whose recent semi-autobiographical novel *Anita and Me* (1996) refers to her childhood in the Midlands as a second-generation immigrant of Punjabi parents. She has been portrayed 'as very funny in an English kind of way' in her attempts at 'exploding stereotypes' about British Asian families.[13]

I do not suggest that Asian women are free of the frame imposed on *all women* by capitalist producers and patriarchal hierarchies, but I want to argue that existing conceptual frameworks need to be revised and new contemporary vocabularies need to be devised. These would provide a means of capturing and framing the experiences and lives of Asian women, as dynamic and innovative negotiators of the multiple new cultural geographies of the late twentieth century. The recent history of the *salwaar-kameez* raises broad questions about the kind of inclusive feminist future we should build in a globalized twenty-first century – one that is multi-textured, multi-ethnic and transnationalized,[14] yet still highly localized. In this way we shall be able to recover and include the submerged voices of Asian women, dynamic and innovative negotiators of the many new cultural textures of the late twentieth century.

II
Feminism, Fatherhood and the Family in Britain

JULIET MITCHELL AND JACK GOODY[1]

The Child Support Agency (CSA), established by the British Government in 1991, aroused a number of violent protests, which included street demonstrations, 5 November carnivals outside the Commons, threats to its officials and to their children, tyres slashed, excrement posted through doors. Although there was anger at the Poll Tax a few years earlier, there was something different about the violence directed towards the Agency. The tactics were often personalized and reminiscent of anti-vivisection lobbies, of anti-abortion campaigns or of racial struggles; it was as though life or death issues were at stake. Staff received threats from clients and morale was lowered.[2] Some attacks were violent, others threatening, causing employees to become afraid of disclosing their identity in public. The Agency's first director, Ros Hepplewhite, was branded as 'guilty of the torture of innocents', her employees as 'SS members'.

Given that the Act had wide cross-party support, the reaction was largely unexpected. This chapter seeks to explore the particular reasons for these objections and how they reflected wider changes in social relations. For both the Child Support Act itself and the protest against it raise complex questions about the position of women, of men and the backlash against feminism as well as about the nature of the contemporary family. Does the Act represent a realistic appraisal of changing family patterns, thus recognizing the future, or is it another instance of a back-to-basics family policy, trying to preserve permanent heterosexual unions and parental responsibility? The protests show that the Act pits men against women but also, because of changes in social patterns of family relationships, women against women. The protest against the Act is both overtly and extremely anti-feminist, but it is also feminist. Misogynist men's groups cooperate with some feminist women's groups in joint opposition. Right and left meet. These are strange bedfellows. Thus the feminist Campaign Against the Child Support Act (CACSA) argues that the capitalist state should pay all mothers to nurture and rear its future workers. In the same spirit, the late Lord Houghton of Sowerby told the House of Lords: 'It is intolerable that we should pursue in this way the old-fashioned idea that fathers and breadwinners are responsible for the upkeep of their children.'[3]

Both the Act and the protest against it are rife with contradictions. Thus according to CACSA's claims, the Act is hitting just those groups, Blacks, immigrants, the unemployed, those on 'benefit', which the 'average' Tory voter is supposed to have hoped it would pursue. But the irony is that in fact it was the middle-class absent father who was the first to be outraged, because it was he who was asked to pay far more than he ever imagined. So CACSA is perforce fighting on the same side as the privileged males, who themselves feel victimized by the Act, but who CACSA claims are treated more favourably relative to the poorer employed and unemployed.

The Act (on which the Agency was based) had the aim of getting absent parents (in 90 per cent of cases these are fathers) to contribute sums appropriate to their income for the maintenance of their children.[4] It introduced an administrative arrangement for the assessment, collection and enforcement of maintenance for children on a uniform basis, a strict 'formula' that assessed the means and some specified needs both of the absent parent and of the parent with care. As the principle was that *all* parents should support their children, absent parents who were unemployed or on benefit had to contribute a portion of what they received.[5]

The organization being set up was a new one with extensive powers to enquire into people's personal lives on a vast scale. In the words of one commentator, 'For the first time the state becomes the regulator of financial relationships between private individuals when they are not in receipt of benefits.'[6] Of course, the courts could already do this. But groups that protest against the Act and the Agency see the courts as independent and hence as not representing offensive government interference. More importantly, courts could be ignored.

The previous judicial-based system of the courts produced great variation in the demands made on the absent parents, many of which were very low compared with any realistic costs. The government tried and failed to get court awards increased. In 1990 the average maintenance being paid by an absent parent in the UK, when it was paid at all, was £18 per week for a child up to eighteen. In that year the National Foster Care Association recommended payments of £34.02 per week for children under five. Since some 70 per cent of absent parents made no formal contribution to the maintenance of their children, the carers (usually women) often had to rely wholly on benefits.[7]

Even these low sums often remain unpaid. In recent years there has been an increasing failure of absent parents (that is, predominantly fathers) to support their children or even to see a reason for supporting them, an active and explicit rejection of responsibility sometimes representing in itself an act of violence against the children as well as against the parent left in charge, usually the mother.[8] Enforcement by the courts themselves proved almost impossible and was very costly. Maintenance orders were widely ignored and well described as 'legal fictions'. The Child Support Act was thus a response to a situation which had reached crisis point. As such it could be seen to be paradoxical. It recognized shifting patterns of family life and of child care, the enormous rise in lone-parent families, but by enforcing two-parent responsibility it could be thought to be trying to be a rock in the flood waters of social change; if absent parents were going to have to pay there might be less incentive to separate in the first place. It is often argued that the CSA is a confused piece of legislation. In fact it is a very clear bit of legislation trying to sort out and clarify very muddied waters. The response to it highlights the confusion of the circumstances rather than of the Act.

The focus of this chapter is an attempt to analyse the protest, but as the protest has increasingly seemed to us to be a reflection of the underlying confusion we have isolated four factors of the changing situation that would seem to be major contributors to present conditions. These are dominant rather than exclusive factors. They are:

1) the growth in divorce, leading to lone parenthood and composite serial families;[9]
2) the rise in single motherhood;
3) the shift from largely paternal to largely maternal custody (now called residence);
4) the change in women's sexual rights and socio-economic position.

These factors are not all new. Frequent divorce was found in Rome and the Near East; single mothers (and cohabiting couples) were common in eighteenth-century England and Holland. Like divorce, dominantly maternal custody and relatively equal sexual rights (to dissolve a marriage, for example) seem new to European patterns, although some moves in this direction were made by early Protestant groups.[10] However, in the current situation these factors have to be read against the overridingly important background of women's potential economic independence through their ever-growing participation in the paid work-force and the contributions of the state. The Act and the protest against it both seem to us to be responses to these critical changes.

The Protest

The Act was not easy to administer. There were no local precedents; procedures and organization had to be worked out from scratch. Many of the staff were inexperienced and found the resistance and abuse difficult to deal with. Parents did not always co-operate. One of the problems lay with self-employed parents, who can more easily conceal their real earnings. So far the CSA has proved largely impotent in the face of this particular problem.[11]

The protestors fall roughly into three main categories. First, absent fathers who object to paying maintenance or higher maintenance than they want to; they are supported by some women, largely second wives, with new children to maintain. Second, there are a wide range of women's interest groups who argue that the Act has worsened the situation of lone mothers. Third, there are those who see the CSA as indicative of a wider crisis of the family in which fathers are being scapegoated and cast out in the cold. The public demonstrations of the first and third groups were mostly led by men, but the rallies often appeared as mass family affairs.

The first group of protestors claim that if they paid the amounts demanded by the Agency they could not support their new families. One father, Robert Gibbens from Southampton, is reported to have said that he had reached a settlement with his ex-wife of £216 a month, but the Agency had demanded that he pay an extra £200. 'They ignored the fact that I was supporting step-children.'[12] His stepchildren should in theory have been the responsibility of their father, just as his own should have been entitled to a full share of his income. However, this complaint was so widespread because of the structure of composite families that it produced one of the main changes in the operations of the agency, which was introduced as a result of the report of the Commons' Social Security Committee in November 1994. The allowance made to absent parents for the new families they had procreated or acquired through marriage was increased, stepchildren were taken into account. When this change occurred the mass public protest that was largely produced by second families virtually faded away. The opposition of the other groups continues.

The second group of protestors consists of lone mothers, one in ten of whom refuse to cooperate with the Agency. Marion

Davis, an information officer of One Plus, claimed that lone mothers affected by the Act suffered from depression sometimes leading to suicide, from mental breakdown and more generally from a neglect of human potential. The government, she maintains, saw them as a threat to economic and social stability, while the Act affected a number adversely because those who get maintenance just above the level of income support may lose free school meals, milk tokens and health benefits. Some women, the same group suggested, had to take low-paid or illegal jobs rather than deal with the Agency which involves them with the ex-partners they are afraid of. In fact, allowance was already made by the Act for the fear of the ex-partner which provides a valid reason for non-cooperation.

Some lone mothers have issued a call to absent fathers to join them in getting rid of 'the requirement to cooperate' and in rejecting maintenance altogether. The most far-reaching and articulate exponent of this position is CACSA, an explicitly feminist group which draws its strength from women on income support and lower- or unwaged fathers and is in alliance with the men's 'Payday' group. CACSA takes up a political programme started in the 1960s by some feminists as the campaign for 'Wages for Housework'.[13]

At the centre of CACSA's position is the argument that child-rearing is work and work should be paid. It condemns the Child Support Act because it 'denies that mothers are entitled to State benefits for the work of raising children'. These children are the future workers of the capitalist system; capitalism pays for work, housework and child care should be paid for. CACSA claims to speak particularly on behalf of women on benefits, as well as low-paid or unwaged men and impoverished second families. It points to discrepancies in the treatment of social classes within the Act; the Act and even more its amendment does not take as high a percentage of earnings of wealthy absent parents as it does of less wealthy ones. CACSA has a strong feminist thrust, but its protest is more on behalf of an underprivileged social class than it is of women in general.

In nearly all cases women who were already receiving mainten-ance from the absent parent have had the sum considerably increased, but the Act has given nothing additional to women already on income support, possibly less if they were also receiving extra gifts from partners who were now having to support them through the formula.

The third category opposes the Act from the diametrically opposite position from that of CACSA and the organizations representing lone mothers. Like the first category, it consists largely of men, but ones who see the Act as part of a wider conspiracy. The groups in this category include Dads After Divorce, the UK Men's Movement, Families Need Fathers, Children and Male Parents Society, Parental Equality, Parents Forever (The Shared Parenting and Joint Custody Support Group), Men in Crisis Help-line, Family Law Action Group, and others, some of which are affiliated to the International Men's Movement and, in the specific context of this legislation, to Network Against the Child Support Act.[14] In the shadow of the Act and of the Lord Chancellor's proposals for divorce on unilateral demand, a number of 'pro-family' men's organizations met in Cheltenham in April 1994 'to establish a programme of initiatives to combat Government policies that are destroying the traditional structure through the marginaliz-ation of the male role'. The first of these initiatives by the Chelten-ham Group was a conference on Restoring Marriage by Recognizing Men, which was supported by Christian groups as well as by intellectuals of the right and left such as Patricia Morgan and Norman Dennis. Their protest is against the changing marital situation, which reduces the father's role by facilitating women's economic independence, women's capacity to initiate divorce and which generally allocates care to the mother when a split occurs.

The Act is condemned by these men's groups as part of a more general attack on legal marriage which removes all moral consider-ations from divorce law. The CSA has a formula that takes no account of the guilty party; 'absent men have to pay whatever their wives may have done'.[15] The Act dissolves the distinction between marriage and cohabitation, and eases 'the administration of financial support for a mother and her children', thus making separation easier. This protest group represents the better-off, is well-financed and vocal, and is associated with men's groups in the USA. The group is small in numbers, but is an articulate exponent of a virulent backlash against feminism and against all women who are not 'attached' to men.

International Comparisons

Problems similar to those that brought the Act and the Agency into being have arisen in all major 'developed' countries. Divorce rates have climbed dramatically over the last thirty years; so too have the numbers of never-married mothers. A high proportion of lone parents everywhere has been in receipt of state benefits which originally had been designed to aid a limited number of families in need, such as those headed by widows. In all these countries the funds required by the government for child support have increased rapidly. In all advanced nations measures have been taken to try and enforce parental responsibility. But while most countries are facing similar situations, their responses have differed. It was the New Zealand and Australian legislations that were used as models for the British Act, but there were differences. In 1979 a new scheme was introduced in New Zealand and the administration itself became responsible, not only for assessing the level of absent-parent support (by means of a formula) and for effecting its collection, but also, unlike in Britain, the same agency made direct welfare payments. In Australia parents receiving benefit payments are allocated part of the contribution made by the absent parent or non-custodial parent, whereas in Britain the Treasury takes all.

The general problem in the United States is similar, with 75 per cent of absent parents failing to contribute. The absolute numbers of one-parent families have increased rapidly. In 1970, 8,265,500 children were living with one parent; in the 1980 census the figure was 12,163,000 – an increase of nearly 50 per cent in ten years. It is estimated that one out of every two children born today in the US will spend time in a single-parent household before reaching the age of eighteen. At the same time only 59 per cent of women who pursued child support awards received them (according to a 1984 source) and only 49 per cent of these got the full amount. In the early 1970s the US child support system was described as lying 'in shambles' and later as 'one of the greatest social problems of the 1980s'.[16] New legislation was introduced to enforce the payment of orders, although these were still made by the courts. That attempt at enforcement was originally seen by the *Washington Post* in 1974 as 'an unwarranted intrusion of the federal government [into personal lives]', but four years later the paper had changed its tune: 'About one million parents who otherwise would pay nothing are now making payments.'[17] Commenting on this situation, Krause writes of 'enormous progress' made in alleviating a serious social problem.

In the United States the protests against enforcement have been largely from men's groups, some of which were connected with a broader backlash against women and feminism. In some European countries changing legislation has been spread over a longer period than in the UK and seems to have been received in a less contestatory fashion. France already had more effective procedures for collecting maintenance through the courts, which could debit salaries; the state paid the parent with care and then made itself responsible for collecting from the absent parent. In Sweden absent parents are required to support their children, but in cases of hardship the government offers favourable loans, a system that is found largely acceptable. All in all the arrangements made in other European countries have been received in a better light than in the UK and other English-speaking countries, so that they have not formed the basis of major protests either by male or by female groups. That may be due to differing cultural traditions of opposition but some of the European schemes seem to have created fewer problems because, in Denmark, Germany, France and Belgium, they are based on 'advanced child support' in which the government first pays the parent with care and then attempts to claim back from the absent parent.[18] The UK provides no such advance and hence does much less to alleviate the hardships of the parent with care. That situation may account for part of the greater level of protest in this country.

The Changing Family

What light do these protests against the Agency throw on the changing nature of domestic life? With single motherhood and divorce or separation, fatherhood becomes a more marginalized role with regard to 'first' children. In 90 per cent of cases custody or care remains in the hands of the mother. In England some 40 per cent of absent fathers no longer see their children after the first two years.[19] It has been said of the US that divorced men are now more likely to meet their car payments than their child support obligation.[20] This situation is being recognized as a crisis and Vice President Al Gore has called for 'a nationwide father-to-father movement' to reconnect fathers with their children.

Family historians like Stone, Laslett, MacFarlane and others have traced what they see as the emergence of the so-called isolated nuclear family, what Stone calls the 'affective' family, which is marked by especially close relations between husband and wife and between parents and children. This family form is now perceived as under threat. In fact this schema romanticizes the past and sees as an endpoint, a culmination or triumph, what is in any case only a particular point in the continuing development of domestic arrangements. Kin networks are obviously becoming more complex; their basic unit is certainly becoming smaller as the number of households containing one child (or even one person) has increased dramatically.[21] But neither the rise in cohabitation nor the vast increase in divorce really establishes the decline or end of marriage. Most cohabitation in England and France leads to marriage, and as a living arrangement is analogous to a pre-marital sexual relationship: both pre-marital sexuality and shared residence now seem to be the norm. If cohabitation leads to marriage, so too does divorce lead to second or third marriages. In any case, 70 per cent of children at age sixteen live with, or have always lived with, their own parents. Western Europe is not a 'Society without Fathers', nor is the US 'Fatherless America'. Apocalyptic messages have always been uttered by those unhappy with present arrangements. Domestic groups have ever been subject to change, taking a variety of forms, although the majority turn around heterosexual coupling, procreation and some sharing or exchange of labour and property, however residual this may be.

There have, however, been a number of dramatic changes since the Second World War. While it is easily possible to exaggerate the role of fathers in the past, the present has gone further in dissociating men from a proportion of families. That obviously affects the whole family. Women bring up children alone for part of their lives, not only having to bear all the practical demands of domestic maintenance and child care but all the inevitable anxieties as well. Shared care between non-married or divorced parents is rarely a practical alternative, although step-parenthood may serve in part to redress the balance. Hostile relations between the partners may lead to the mother making access difficult (and vice versa), hence further reducing the father's role and his willingness to contribute. The research carried out by Simpson and others (1995) stresses the difficulties men have in keeping in touch with their first children. Such men may make good fathers in their second or third families and thus provide the examples of what Burgess (forthcoming) calls the 'new father'. It is first families, not the family *per se* that are in crisis.

The smaller family and longevity may be background factors that have put the *first* family in jeopardy. In the mid nineteenth century a woman spent on average fifteen years of her life in pregnancy and lactation; her average life-span was roughly forty-five years. Today the average time spent in pregnancy and nursing is less than four and a half years and the woman's average life-expectancy is well into the seventies. There is a lot of life left over after the establishment of a family. The first wife and mother has her one-parent family, the first father/husband is not only 'free' but at a loose end domestically unless he forms a second family. If he forms a second family, access to the first inevitably becomes not only more difficult but also less necessary – for him. On the other hand, men who do not form second families can feel very deprived of contact with the children they have supported and cared for and loved.

The virulent opposition by absent parents to paying for their children links maintenance and access. Without access, how can a father feel or act as a parent? Equally naturally women would prefer that the children should not be supported rather than that they should be abused. The responsibility for procreating is all too easily forgotten, and seen from a child's perspective that absence of primary responsibility can extend to a mother taking no responsibility for the child having a father and the father taking no responsibility for the mother he, at least in some sense, chose for his offspring.

The problem of maintenance has been dramatically increased by the rapid growth in the number of divorces and of all lone parents. In England and Wales, the annual divorce rate has risen more than sixfold since 1961.[22] Divorce was responsible for a considerable part of the increase of lone parents during the twenty-year period 1971 to 1991, with the number of divorced mothers rising from 120,000 to 420,000. The rise in single (that is, never married) mothers was of roughly the same order, from 90,000 to 430,000, while the numbers of separated mothers started the period higher than the divorced (170,000) but only rose to 240,000, while widowed ones dropped 30 per cent. Lone fathers increased from 70,000 to 100,000 over the same period, a quarter of whom were widowers (see Table 1, on p. 214). Lone-parent families in Great Britain comprised 5.7 per cent of the total number of families with children in 1961, 8.0 per cent ten years later, 13.0 per cent after twenty years and 19.0 in 1991.[23] The latest figures show that in 1992 there were 1.4 million lone parents, with the largest increase being in single mothers, who now account for nearly 40 per cent of the total.[24] Anti-feminist men's groups have used this increase to promote an image of a nation of women pushing men to the margins – both in the home and the work-place. In fact most single mothers do not remain without heterosexual partners for long, while some degree of cohabitation may be concealed under the single (and the lone) category. The division into 'divorced' and 'separated' obscures the fact that the largest group of lone parents are women who have been left by or have evicted men, many of whom have formed second partnerships and possibly second families.

As we have seen, there is nothing unique about this situation; similar figures exist for Germany and Australia. It is transcultural, at least in so-called advanced societies. During the 1980s the numbers of lone-parent families in European countries increased by between 25 and 50 per cent, representing 17.3 per cent of families with children; the figures are especially high in Norway, Finland, Britain, Belgium and Austria, significantly less so in the Mediterranean countries. The same is true of single-person households, whose numbers have risen from 22 to 27 per cent of all British households in ten years, reflecting in part the changing age-distribution; both the old and the young display a greater tendency to live alone, though such households are still rare in the south.[25] Other European countries such as France, Netherlands and Belgium started with higher rates of lone parenthood than Great Britain and ended the period with lower ones. The one country with different figures of lone-parent families was the United States which started in 1970 with 12.3 per cent and had reached 22.9 per cent in 1988. As the most 'advanced' of the capitalist countries, the United States tends to be used as a predictive model for the future in other countries.

The change in the paternal role implies corresponding changes in the situation for mothers and for children, for the increase in cohabitation and divorce may indicate the direction of longer-term trends. Though a recent national opinion poll indicates that 60 per cent of children of lone-parent families think two-parent families are preferable and 70 per cent believe marriage should be forever, it is surely interesting that 40 per cent and 30 per cent, respectively, do not.[26] These are significant figures given that such children are nearly always economically and most often economically and socially disadvantaged. Likewise the fact that 30 per cent of sixteen-year-olds are still living at home but not with their own two parents is again significant.

As the recent protest against proposed legislation that aimed to give the same rights and protection to cohabitees as to the married suggests, whether followed by marriage or not, cohabitation is on the way to becoming a socially and even legally recognized domestic relationship.[27] This pattern would seem to cut across the social classes, whereas earlier common-law marriage was characteristic of the poorer classes, who were less likely to be concerned with legal rights whether married or not.

The ratio of cohabitation to marriage doubled over the decade from 1979 to 1989 but this does not necessarily indicate an altogether new development.[28] It has been estimated that in the eighteenth century 50 per cent of all marriages were 'common law', that is, they had union not legality as their basis.[29] In other words what is new is not the cohabitation but its social class composition.

Lone parenthood has always been one possibility among others. In the past it has most often been brought about by the death of the partner (usually the father, as men tend to marry later and die earlier) and by fathers abandoning families. Between 1750 and 1850 pre-marital childbirth and single motherhood rose among the working class.[30] What is new today is the increase in lone parenthood (motherhood) as a result of divorce. Changes in family structure affect not only the stability of the conjugal family, and hence the long-term views and prospects of the participants, but also wider kin relations. Male and female partners tend to make a decisive break not only between themselves but with their respective affines. While the senior generation can break off relations, that cannot be the case for children, who remain attached to fathers and grandparents despite the conjugal split and the possible lack of contact. That difference sets up contradictory attitudes to relatives on the part of parents and children; what are temporary affines to the former are permanent kin to the latter. It is important to remember that while men and women may have ex-wives or ex-husbands, no child has an ex-father or ex-mother.

So the situation for children is also new. For the last 1,500

Table 1 (after Burghes 1994)

NUMBER OF LONE-PARENT FAMILIES BY TYPE

Great Britain (in thousands)

Family type	1971	1976	1986	1991*
Lone mothers				
single	90	130	230	430
separated	170	185	190	240
divorced	120	230	410	420
widowed	120	115	80	80
All mothers	500	660	910	1170
All fathers	70	90	100	100
All lone parents	570	750	1010	1270

*provisional

Source: Haskey, J. (1991) 'Estimated numbers and demographic characteristics of one-parent families in Great Britain', Population Trends, No. 65, Haskey, J. (1993) 'Trends in the numbers of one-parent families in Great Britain', Population Trends No. 71 and House of Commons Hansard, 2 December 1992. The definition of lone parenthood excludes cohabiting couples.

years, divorce in European countries has usually been impossible, separation has occurred, but the main loss of parents has been through death. The child might then grow up with a step-parent leading to more complex family structures.[31] In cases of divorce and remarriage there is a similar trend, as described by Judith Stacey in her study of the reconstituted family in Silicon Valley. Nevertheless, the difference between loss by divorce and by death remains of great significance.

The situation is crucial to understanding the protest against the Child Support Act, since it is often the second families that are objecting to increased payments to the first. One major problem is that our society has been unprepared for the serial coupling that has overtaken it. The increase in divorce in a society that has been dominated by small conjugal households has radical consequences. In the south of Europe such domestic events are less frequent and can be absorbed in the larger households and networks of kin. In the north one is left with separated parents, some with children, living in small or solitary households (but not independent of all kin networks, reduced as these may be). Just as the elderly can now just about live alone with state support or with private savings (without having to make an implicit contract for maintenance with their children), so too lone parents can just about exist without being thrown back on their natal families or continuing their conjugal ones. That is, there is a reduced personal (and familial) accountability for divorce and, specifically, for starting a second family. As part of new courting behaviour, adultery is now an almost necessary prelude to serial partnerships for women (a major change since the last century) as well as for men and its quasi-acceptability at a social level contributes notionally and actually to the greater impermanence of marital ties.

The Child Support Act claimed to put children first – so does much of the protest against it. In fact, we have been struck by how little the literature of both sides (for and against the Act) really considers the perspective of the child. There is work on objective effects of divorce but little attempt is made to grasp the child's subjective experience. Clearly, parental separation changes children's whole lives. But objective effects have to be reassessed. For instance, statistics on the decline in success at school following divorce must now be seen in the context of similar underperformance in children from conflictual marriages.[32]

The child's experience will vary but must always be part of the picture. One child from a conflictual marriage, looking back, commented that the day his father left was the best day of his life; another that, although an adult and parent herself, she had never recovered from her father's desertion.[33] Separating parents tend to forget or have never realized that, however much they insist it is the spouse not the child who is deserted, this is never so from the child's point of view. An older child may understand the adults' situation, but in reality she or he *has* been abandoned by one parent. The pain of this desertion is compounded when the absent parent fails financially to support or even to visit the child. Many absent parents do not like visiting the old home – forgetting that the child may not like to visit the new. No one takes into account the fact that when the state supports first families and the father takes care of the second, from the point of view of the child this difference 'illegitimizes' the first children and 'legitimizes' the second.

Second families come to be seen to represent the positive values of family life while first families may be seen as unseemly single-women-and-child units; the woman who has the man, and the child who has the resident father, always tend to be more highly valued. The weight of convention and social approval has thus – ironically – shifted to the second family, at least in terms of rhetoric and imagery.

Lone parenthood has to be seen in conjunction with the large increase in employed women and in particular employed mothers and the social expectation of women working.[34] Increasingly it is expected that a woman herself does not need financial support – she can get a job. But the time available for the parent with care to earn a living is probably half that of the absent parent. This situation is understood in the 10 per cent of cases where the parent with care is the father, but not when it is a mother.

Two aspects, serial marriage due to divorce and the maternal care and custody of children, have not featured in any significant way in the Western European system of kinship before this century. Both go a long way to explaining the setting-up of the CSA and the diverse protests against it. Divorce is now at an all-time high and showing little tendency to decline, although lately it has levelled off. Rates of divorce accelerated during and immediately after the Second World War, then declined and started to rise rapidly in the 1960s, so that there has been a sixfold increase over the last twenty-four years. This is not, however, the simple incremental process that it appears to be at first sight.

Feminist groups, particularly in the US, battled for women's rights to divorce throughout the last two-thirds of the nineteenth century. They helped to change the nature as well as the prevalence of divorce. What is new is the equalizing of the grounds for divorce for men and women. In the eighteenth century divorce in England necessitated an appeal to parliament, when a man had to accuse another of seducing his wife; her rights were very much more limited. In England the Divorce and Matrimonial Causes Act of 1857 improved married women's rights to divorce. Women were legally allowed to divorce in that Act,[35] but the grounds were unequal, for example, for the husband the adultery of the wife, for the wife the incestuous adultery of the husband. That changed after the First World War when the Sex Disqualification (Removal) Act of 1919 'sought to establish equality in law between the sexes'. Today the number of women initiating a divorce has superseded the number of men, with women bringing 73 per cent of the cases. This is probably due to women's growing economic independence, even though the divorce laws were actually liberalized at a time when many women returned to the home. What we are witnessing with this practice of women divorcing is that for the first time in European history, women have equal sexual rights to men. These women are the target for attack by much of the protest from the men's groups. However, a number of these divorces are brought by women because they will no longer tolerate male abuse or adultery. So that the double standard would still seem to exist for many men. Men do not see themselves as deserting the family if they are the ones having affairs, but never the less perceive women as attacking hearth and home should they do so. Very often the men's groups blame women for throwing them out of the house and breaking up the family when the women regard the man's infidelity or abusive behaviour as unacceptable.

However, it is not divorce in itself that has dramatically changed the situation in domestic relationships, but the combination with the mother's custody of children. In most societies, except some matrilineal ones, the custody of children remains with the father; indeed patrilineal systems depend upon the continuation of father and son bonds for residence and for descent in the same lineage or clan. In the case of divorce or separation a woman might take her infants with her but they would almost certainly return as children to their fathers. The man's identity was bound up with the existence of co-resident sons.

Maternal custody is a phenomenon that developed in the nineteenth century. If a woman in the eighteenth century left the marital home, she 'lost' the children. The father's paternal role was reinforced, the mother's maternal one diminished. The first move towards changing the situation whereby men had automatic custody of the children of a marriage came in 1839 with the Infant Custody Bill. That Act permitted the Lord Chancellor to hear a petition of the mother of any infant who was in the sole custody of the father and to make an order for access. If the infants were under seven, the mother could be given custody until they reached that age.[36] However, no mother who had committed adultery was entitled to benefit from the Act.

The situation was further clarified in an Act of 1925 which specifically followed on the Sex Discrimination (Removal) Act of 1919, the preamble of which stated: 'and it is expedient that this principle [to establish equality in law between the sexes] should obtain with respect to the guardianship of infants'. In making such arrangements, no account was to be taken of the claims of the father or mother; 'the court . . . shall regard the welfare of the infant as the first and paramount consideration'. Section 3 of the Act provided for a maintenance payment by the father to the mother, the amount of which the court decided, taking into account the means of the father.[37]

Although equal rights to petition for custody were only finally realized in 1925, nevertheless judicial decisions had gone increasingly in favour of the mother during the nineteenth century, partly as the result of women's agitation but also because of the general insistence on the role of motherhood, which, beginning in the 1830s, came to be increasingly stressed in the context of factory work and the employment of women. One of the consequences of stressing the woman's domestic role, including the maternal aspects, was to see her as the 'natural' carer in the case of the dissolution of marriage, the male role having been to work and provide for the family. But the result was that men were distanced from their children when the couple split (as the woman had earlier been), making it easier to avoid providing for them. Women formed the majority of adult recipients of support from the new Poor Law of 1834 and many of today's arguments about lone mothers on benefit were already in place 160 years ago. Problems about custody do not seem to be on the minds of the majority of fathers, although access is. Between 1850 and 1950 a shared consensus developed that the child's interests were best served by being cared for by the mother and was accepted by-and-large by women and men alike. It came to seem 'natural'.

The cult of motherhood reached its apotheosis with the second Industrial Revolution which tended to upgrade men's pay with the family wage and further to exclude women and children from the workplace and to lead to a more radical division of labour between man the breadwinner and woman the carer, the home-maker. Mothering – raising rather than producing children – was seen as a full-time vocation, indeed as women's 'highest calling', with fathers being marginalized from the domestic scene through their absence at 'work'.[38] Of course, many women continued in paid work but their contributions became less visible because of the emphasis on child-rearing.

The same process involved a revaluation of the role of children. Formal education, often encouraged by the mother, became critical in determining children's future. Their contribution to the domestic economy diminished, many of the costs of upbringing increased, and the numbers of children in a family fell. Children are of course emotionally important even when they are economically non-productive for individual families in advanced industrial countries.[39]

By the turn of the century the position of women had become more complex: valued at home as the home became valuable mainly as the place for child-rearing but, increasingly, for the urban lower-middle and upper working class, also as property; taking part in external employment where they were underpaid compared to men and were often seen to be acting in sharp contradiction to their domestic role. So the position of women shifted between idealization and denigration. One was bound to affect the other. As women worked like men, they demanded similar rights of employment, but attitudes towards women's 'proper sphere', the importance or otherwise of motherhood, was bound to affect a woman's overall status. The Women's Movement promoted the general position of women which was already changing for other reasons – it was a question of politics commanding a developing situation. Nineteenth-century and early twentieth-century feminism urged civic, employment, educational and, to an extent, sexual rights. Christabel Pankhurst had campaigned for Votes for Women and Chastity for Men but it was the later twentieth-century Women's Movement that most fully articulated changing sexual rights and a sexual morality on a par with men's, made more possible by relatively safe and easy contraception and abortion being brought within women's control. The CSA and the protest against it are one particular culmination of a process of change in domestic relations of which the feminist movement has clearly been part.

In the struggles centring on the CSA, it is often women who have borne the brunt of accusations for what is in fact a wider social crisis. That they should be especially targeted by such organizations as the Cheltenham Group is both predictable and ironic. It is predictable because women who are coping for better or worse without men are labelled 'feminist men-haters' in a culture which finds threatening the independence of the conventionally weak and dependent; it is ironic because an early thrust of feminism in the 1960s and 1970s was the demand for fathers to share in child care, involving them in, not ejecting them from, the family. The earlier feminist slogan of 'whatever a man can do, a woman can do too' was supplemented by 'whatever a woman can do, a man can do too' – and child-rearing was just that. 'Shared parenting' was, and is, a feminist slogan *par excellence*, which has now been taken up by divorced men. But shared parenting after divorce is difficult. It presents many practical problems which are affected by the relationships between the separated parents. Paternal violence is on the increase and few mothers would wish to leave the child alone with what the mother may fear is a potentially abusive father.

So, behind the hatred of government interference in private lives and accusations of the Agency's inefficiency lies a familiar scapegoating of marginal women: ex-wives, non-married mothers, lone women on benefit, lesbian mothers – any woman who is not the wife (today often the second wife), who is not attached to a man.

The majority of first wives already receiving maintenance from the absent parent have benefited from the Agency. It has been recognized that clean-break settlements do not put meals on the table and the cost of raising children has been far more realistically assessed. In many cases maintenance payments have more than doubled, provoking yet greater resistance from men. Whether a reluctance to pay is generated by actual or imagined restrictions of access, by the father's rejection of old attachment, and his attachment to new ones, or by his display of aggressive behaviour, it tends to justify itself by a demonization of the former partner in a manner that may take the form of seeing male interests as threatened by feminism. Women have paid for any improvement by being demonized as 'feminists', by ex-partners as well as by some elements in the wider population:

Feminism is certainly responsible for discrimination against men . . . By their hostility to traditional marriage and motherhood, feminists committed themselves to the alternatives, which, outside the delusional realm of feminist utopia, are – when not childlessness – single motherhood, cohabitation, divorce, day care, and full-time employment outside the home.[40]

Feminism is a political movement trying to stimulate underlying social and economic change in a way that ensures 'equality' for women. It is also an easy target as well as a symptom of this change.

In this connection both the creation of the CSA and the violence of the opposition make one want to ask tentative but disturbing questions. It is a commonplace of studies of industrial societies that the child is, at least as a child, an emotional but no longer an economic support. This has become increasingly true with the relative detachment of the elderly from dependence on a kin network; people do not expect to be supported by their children in old age. The Marxist-feminist group CACSA argues that children are the future workers of the capitalist system. But does society really want these future workers, or want all of them?

The anti-feminist fathers against the CSA blame what are seen as today's destructive, deracinated male youth on the absence of a prospect of becoming a husband and father. This tends to ignore the fact that there is also an absence of the prospect of employment (which affects girls as well as boys), which gives rise to a feeling that education has failed. Is structural unemployment leading away from the notion of a mass well-educated, well-cared-for workforce and towards a new version of the 'two nations' in which a certain percentage of children may be surplus to requirements?

This question seems to indicate the presence of a particular form of ambivalence towards children. In no society can the division into either economic or emotional asset be a neat one – infants everywhere both must be a drain on resources and at the time a source and focus of love. Perhaps, however, in situations and periods when the net economic return seems low, the higher valorization of the emotional aspect may put a strain on the system. Does it lead to more hate as well as to more love as one emotion always contains the possibility of the other? Whether there is really an increase in child abuse or just a greater awareness and a wider definition of abuse is debatable. Whatever the case, abuse would be the other side of the coin of protective legislation – in this instance the earlier concern for the best custody for the child, now for its most effective support.

What has been happening increasingly is that many mothers, by being or becoming lone mothers, have slipped from the middle-class hegemonic centre into the insecurity or impoverishment of the 'margins', producing the so-called 'feminization of poverty'. Poverty apart, the evidence for the achievement of children of lone mothers or of lesbian mothers is ambiguous, but this is not the image that is conveyed. All societies produce their illegitimate margins. Hence it would seem as though there is an effort (perhaps unconscious) to produce an image which welds the problem child, drug-taking, riotous and soon to be unemployed, on to the problem woman – the woman without a man.

One thing that does emerge is that socio-economic status persists as the biggest divider.[41] Previously middle-class women and their children by becoming 'lone' mothers are pushed down the socio-economic scale. The CSA sought to prevent this by trying to see that children should not live at a level lower than that of the absent parent. The success or otherwise of this endeavour is still very much in the balance. As it stands in our society the category of lone mothers is often associated with the prediction that their children may 'fail'. If this does happen the evidence linking failure with family structure is ambiguous. What is incontrovertible is that poverty causes both social and 'achievement' problems.

The Child Support Act is trying both to help and to unload the lone mother in her various social forms; the protest against it likewise wants both to recognize and assist but also to eliminate her. The particular social crisis illustrates a far more general problem about the nature of male–female and parent–child relationships in contemporary family structures.

Combating the Backlash: How Swedish Women Won the War

AGNETA STARK

*The history of men's opposition to women's emancipation
is more interesting perhaps than the story of that emancipation itself.*
A Room of One's Own, VIRGINIA WOOLF

The theme proposed by the editors for this chapter was: 'How Swedish women won the war.' As I write, this suggested theme leaves a somewhat bitter taste.

In editorial pages, news reports, on radio and television, Swedish feminists in 1995 are accused of betraying democracy, being paid off by powerful interests and fighting for women only as a pretext to promote their own personal career interests. Replies are refused. The caricatures on editorial pages are deeply and personally insulting, as they are meant to be. Creativity seems to consist of making up and repeating strange stories in which few facts are checked.

The price for feminist struggle is – as ever – smear campaigns, hate mail, modest careers lost, promised work opportunities suddenly disappearing, and private disappointment, even grief. The only novelty is that the process is extremely public, and perhaps that is also significant. The message to women is clear: 'These are the consequences of feminist activities. This is what will happen if you speak out.'

No, we have not won the war. It is still going on, and as we have touched on and challenged power, power is fighting back. There is nothing strange or surprising in that. We expected it. To some extent, we were prepared for it. However, preparation does not diminish the impact of the blows.

I am not embittered, far from it. Angry, yes. Sometimes exhausted, but as a feminist and a social scientist, fascinated by the
process in which I have now taken part for many years. More
importantly than any smear campaign, I am moved and cheered
by the many signs of support I and many others receive from
people we have never met before. The old lady at the bus stop
pats my arm and says: 'I am all for what you're doing.' A postcard
of lovely bluebells: 'I am a young unemployed woman, and I just
want you to know that I support you. I have started a network
of young women where I live. Please suggest a book on economic
problems we could study!'

Sweden of the mid-1990s cannot deliver any comforting or
optimistic example for feminists in other countries of a war won
once and for all. But women in Sweden, and in Scandinavia, have
come quite a long way, even very far in comparison with many
countries. The Gender-related Development Index (GDI), constructed by UNDP (1995), puts Sweden first, with Finland, Norway and Denmark following, in a survey of 140 countries. The
GDI, however, is crude, as very few factors are included, and the
weighting of these factors within the index is problematic.[1] The
Gender Empowerment Measure (GEM), also computed by the
UNDP, ranks Sweden first, followed by Norway, Finland and
Denmark, among 116 countries for which comparable data could
be produced.[2]

The gender pay differential in the Nordic countries is smaller
than in most countries, although it seems to be increasing. Traditional 'women's issues' are more frequently part of mainstream
politics; the political representation of women is higher than elsewhere. Over 80 per cent of women are in paid work, the main
difference between Sweden and other Western countries being
that a much higher proportion of women with only compulsory
education are found on the labour market in Sweden.[3] Child care
is more available, it is of quite good quality and comes at a more
reasonable cost to parents.[4] Rape is a crime in Sweden, but also,
since 1962, if committed within marriage; police procedures when
rape is reported have been improved even if they are still not

satisfactory. Abortion is available, within the National Health Service, and at all hospitals. The proportion of poor among the elderly is smaller than in most similar countries.

It must always be remembered that problems facing Swedish and Nordic women are very different from those with which women in India, China, Somalia, Afghanistan or Bosnia have to struggle. Some of the mechanisms behind discrimination or abuse of women may be similar, but the effects in their countries are of a different nature and infinitely worse. We are not faced with problems such as dowry deaths, systematic abortion of girl foetuses, genital mutilation of girls, the effects of extreme poverty when scarce resources mainly go to men taking part in war activities, and rape as a systematic part of so-called ethnic cleansing.

Sweden has now been at peace for almost 200 years and is a prosperous country. The history of that prosperity has not always been a proud one: Sweden is the world's tenth exporter of arms, our traditional policy of political neutrality has at times been based on quiet compliance rather than on firm and explicit principles.

Sweden has to be judged in a global perspective: a geographically large European country with a small population and a very high standard of living, in which women as everywhere fare less well than men. So much still remains to be changed, and at present progress seems remote.

During the first half of the 1990s, Sweden has experienced economic decline, a rise in unemployment from 2–3 per cent to 8 per cent (with an additional 5 per cent of the workforce in special training and re-training programmes), a severe financial crisis, high interest rates and cuts in welfare benefits. In the mid-1990s, the Swedish economy is divided into two. The export industry is booming, with record profitability. The home market is still in a recession owing to lack of purchasing power and increased savings, due to a decline of trust in public systems. In the public sector, it appears that health care, education, child care, care of the old and welfare systems are all going to face more severe cuts in the future.

During this difficult period many Swedish women with very

different backgrounds and aims, different political views, from different parts of the country have united in a common struggle for political power.

In the 1991 parliamentary elections, the proportion of women elected to parliament fell for the first time since 1919, when Swedish women first acquired the right to vote. This decrease from 38 per cent to 33 per cent could have been foreseen, but as gender issues at the time were almost completely absent from the media, for many people it came as a surprise.[5] On the morning of election day, the editorial of *Svenska Dagbladet*[6] stated that we should now put an end to this old-fashioned discussion of gender equality by quotas and numbers. 'Real competence, that is utterly individual competence, must be given greater weight; generalized arguments, such as alternate positions as, for instance, the position of president of a court of appeal, dean or chimney sweep should be a woman, with every year that passes have become increasingly divorced from reality.'

The Greens, 50 per cent of whom are women, lost their parliamentary seats, while a new, male-dominated conservative populist party gained entry. The new party, called New Democracy, had a manifesto and a campaign based on severe restrictions on immigration and sharp cuts in public spending and services. These services were described as a drain on the economy and as filled with people who did little but harass the ordinary citizen; one main target of the New Democrats was female traffic wardens.

The campaign preceding the election had been dominated by a strange mixture of economic technicalities (should state pension funds have the right to invest more on the stock exchange, so that the ordinary worker could benefit from the apparently everlasting economic boom?), aggressive criticism of the public health system and schools. Cutbacks in public spending, privatization and lower taxes were promised. Environmental topics which had dominated the elections of 1988 were totally forgotten.

The Social Democratic government lost the election and a coalition of Conservatives, Liberals, the Centre Party and Christian Democrats formed the new government. In this new government the first Swedish woman Minister of Finance was appointed, Anne Wibble of the Liberals. The new Minister of Foreign Affairs was a Conservative woman, Margareta af Ugglas. The Deputy Prime Minister was Bengt Westerberg, the chairman of the Liberal Party, a committed male feminist and also Minister of Social Services. As he had also taken a strong stand on the rights of immigrants, he was criticized and ridiculed more than any minister or indeed any politician during the following three-year period.

In the autumn of 1991, there were a number of arson attacks on refugee centres in various parts of Sweden. Few of the perpetrators were found. A frightening series of armed attacks, several in the dark, on foreign-looking people resulted in one man being killed and ten wounded. The economy slumped. Unemployment rose.

Since the 1970s Maria-Pia Boëthius, a well-known feminist journalist, has been writing extensively on rape and violence towards women, and in early October 1991 she invited nine other women to a discussion. We were of different ages and backgrounds, with varying political views. Sitting round her kitchen table, we followed the tradition of the women's movement and spoke in the order we were sitting, one by one without interruption. We were worried, depressed, as politics seemed to be moving away from what we considered to be basics: solidarity, care for the needy, support for children and the elderly, visions of a society in which burdens and benefits were shared. The change in politics we saw was not limited to one or a few parties, but more or less dominated the whole political agenda.

Maria-Pia Boëthius pointed out that Swedish women had had the vote for more than seventy years; if politics was not what we, and many other women, thought it should be, then no one but us should or could change that.

Three weeks later we met again, each one of us bringing four other women we thought might be interested, creative and useful. Squeezed together in one perfectly ordinary sitting-room, fifty women made plans, wrote lists of ideas, shared silly jokes and offered special knowledge, contacts, equipment or their spare time.

The Support Stockings

The name the 'Support Stockings' was chosen for the network, honouring the intellectual Blue Stockings of the nineteenth century, and the political Red Stockings of the 1970s, but also reflecting our aims: to support women who were already engaged in politics. The name also had a down-to-earth, middle-aged, non-glamorous appeal. Many of the women who bore the brunt of economic cutbacks were constantly on their feet: women cashiers, care workers, nursing assistants, cleaners.

We wanted to disturb, to be difficult to track down or define once the network became a target for public scrutiny and the attacks which we knew would come sooner or later. The arts activists, the Guerrilla Girls, were a source of inspiration, as was a Swedish network successfully agitating in the 1960s for child care and separate taxation for married couples.

The format of our meetings was based on experiences from the women's movement. We decided to have a different chair at each meeting, to ensure that everyone had a say and no one dominated. Each meeting would have one main theme and a short time set aside for news, information and proposed activities. Meetings would not last longer than two hours. We decided – after long and careful deliberation – to keep the network secret and closed.[7]

The simple rule that emerged in practice was that anyone could say, 'I am a Support Stocking,' but not that anyone else was. It would be a personal decision, as the consequences would be personal. (Eventually women who never took part said, 'Of course I am a Support Stocking!' which helped spread the mystery.)

The actual limit of the size of the network was the size of the meeting room: we met at least monthly during the next three years in a bare basement in a suburb of Stockholm, symbolically squeezed in between a child-care centre and a communal laundry.

Pragmatism prevailed. We wanted to change the Swedish political climate before the 1994 election[8] – an ambition we laughed about but took seriously. That meant focusing on a few essential problems and leaving many important things aside. We did not have time for lengthy discussions on definitions of feminism or ideology, but chose subjects and aspects we could agree on. Tough discussions and disagreements naturally occurred, but the brevity of our meetings helped to keep them focused on important issues. If we could not agree on an approach to a problem, or on an issue, we dropped it. There was no shortage of urgent problems.[9]

As a last resort, and only if we could not bring about changes in existing political parties, we would form a Women's List[10] and stand for parliament ourselves. But this was not our aim, for two main reasons. Most importantly, existing parties in a democracy ought to be parties for both women and men, and should provide evidence of that, which would be much more effective than a women's party. Also, the complications of a Women's List negotiating coalitions in parliament would inevitably entail severe disappointments, and might actually mean that feminist issues and perspectives on problems would be marginalized.

This restricted aim of our work, supporting women already active in party politics, made the secrecy strategy less problematic. As we were not promoting specific politicians or any single party and as we were not trying to gain power for ourselves, we were acting only as citizens in a democracy are expected to, forming opinions and spreading information. However, if we were forced to form a party and stand for parliament, we agreed that such a party would require a completely different approach and method of work. Then maximum openness, a declaration of intent and a programme would be necessary to make very clear who we were and what we stood for.

The 1980s have often been described as a period when the women's movement in Sweden was dead. Many Support Stockings had a completely different experience. We had lectured in schools and libraries, visited networks, taken part in women's seminars and symposia,[11] written, read, listened to women all over the country. One characteristic in common was that the meeting rooms were always too small. Women came in crowds to bleak school canteens or cosy public libraries on cold winter nights to discuss 'care in the future', 'prostitution', 'women and economics', 'violence against women', 'women and addiction', to listen to analyses of women writers or other results of feminist research, to find out how pension schemes worked, and to set up networks of their own. The best evenings were those when sports events were on television as baby-sitting would not then be a problem – fathers and elder brothers would be at home. These lectures, meetings and seminars were organized by women in local banks, trade unions, adult education organizations, networks, groups of business women, local women politicians cooperating over party lines, clubs, churches and youth groups.

Thus when the Support Stockings started, we had hundreds of informal contacts and addresses we could use. We knew of hundreds of active, competent and dissatisfied women in companies, in the public sector, in trade unions, in minor political positions, researchers, pensioners, activists. Many of them started network activities of their own or just continued what they were already doing. They aimed at promoting women, changing political decisions and introducing new aspects into the political agenda. Quite a few worked in secret; I know of one small bowling club which just quietly stopped bowling and started discussing pay discrimination against women instead. Cooperation between networks was never formally organized. Information spread, ideas were exchanged quickly along hundreds of informal channels.

We tried to find out what proposals and plans were prepared in companies, public bodies, in political parties or local authorities early, before the plans were ready and made public. The Stockings engaged in the project then analysed it for a meeting, which finished with the meeting deciding what action to take, and finding a small group which would coordinate action.

Government plans for cutting down on contraceptive advice to teenagers were leaked by spreading information of the plans to politicians, local papers, women's groups and also by using specific data to show that this would entail increased costs in other parts of the health service. Women substance abusers gradually had fewer and poorer services. Ideas to involve men more in the care of their children were developed by the Minister for Social Services, and we supported that. A new pension scheme was presented which had a considerably lower pension for people who worked part time over a number of years – all women. In trade unions, men's working conditions and problems had been discussed and improved, much more than women's. Gender-related pay differentials increased. In the aftermath of the Swedish banking crisis, men responsible for the enormous losses kept their jobs or were promoted, while competent women who had argued against the risks were dismissed.[12]

We wrote articles and letters, phoned, fed crucial ideas to journalists, took up subjects at work or when we were invited to speak, used all the networks, contacted politicians and offered help. Slowly new issues crept into the public agenda. Much of the change was possible because of energetic, resourceful women journalists, who welcomed the possibilities of presenting problems and aspects they considered important.

One strategic tool was gender-based statistics. Swedish women had the highest labour market participation of women in the OECD;[13] at the same time Sweden had the highest birth rate in Western Europe, after Ireland and Iceland. We used these figures, and crime statistics, health statistics, statistics about gender-based pay differentials, time use, pensions, etc., to spread the idea to women that statistics and facts were their tools and could be used systematically, also by women who usually considered official statistics to be abstract and difficult. A small booklet, *Women and Men in Sweden*, published every two years in Swedish and English by Statistics Sweden, was of crucial importance in this campaign.

Rumours started spreading about these strange 'Support Stockings'. The name was declared silly, the ideas – most of which were misrepresented – old-fashioned and backward. But other Stockings started to organize: Net Stockings, Woollen Stockings, even a male group called the Sports Socks. The women's organizations in political parties took an interest and started cooperating on a small scale across party lines. This was highly controversial, as it meant challenging the ever-repeated slogan: 'Party differences/ class differences are always greater and more important than gender differences!' The Swedish TUC women's network used these new opportunities to intensify their work of highlighting the situation of low-paid women with very demanding work and high rates of occupational risk.

Work along these lines had been going on for a long time. Swedish women in the 1990s were in a better position than twenty years earlier. They were in news rooms, negotiated pay deals, were in political positions, were better organized, had access to gender-based statistics in many areas, were able to form new alliances and were increasingly questioning the assumption that men were the norm and women the troublesome exception. Without this painstaking work, the Support Stockings could never have been the symbol they eventually became, a symbol which all these women could use to increase the effects of what they were already doing.

To celebrate 8 March, International Women's Day, on 6 and 7 March 1993 the Support Stockings arranged a women's tribunal in Stockholm. Four themes were chosen: education and research, the economy, violence and sex, and health care. Eight hundred women took part and for every theme a set of demands was formulated, directed at the political parties. Musicians, writers, adult education students, women working against child prostitution, researchers, poets, doctors, photographers, teachers, midwives, economists and trade unionists, some of them Support Stockings but many not, all worked to show what was happening in Swedish society. The media showed very little interest, but the effects spread through the many networks. A paperback with the contents of the tribunal was published.[14]

It is interesting that during a period when much media interest centred on the Support Stockings – Who were they? What did they want? – remarkably few journalists took the opportunity to find out by visiting the tribunal, which was quite public. A second women's tribunal was held one year later in Umeå (in the far north of Sweden), arranged by several networks there. The four themes analysed were: economy, pornography, immigrant women and young women.

We concentrated on a few areas which we summarized: we wanted women to have fair political representation, that is 50 per cent of political posts. Gender-based pay discrimination must be abolished. We coined a slogan: 'Half of the power – all of the pay!' Violence against women and children must cease. Health issues must be based on two biological sexes, not on research and actions geared to men. And, finally, all decision-making must be analysed for possible effects on women and men, of different ages and backgrounds.

Backlash – or Just Sensation Seeking?

The media again and again misrepresented events. But it must also be emphasized that the media did some very important high-quality clarifying work as well. The media are to some extent a distorting mirror of society, exaggerating what is already there.

Blaming women, creating divisions between women and portraying men as victims of women are frequent strategies. We knew when we started the Support Stockings that the ideal of traditional media and a common strategy of male dominance is to arrange shouting matches between women, or to portray women as unable to agree. Women disagree or agree no more or less than men, or than any other oppressed group. We decided that we would not take part in these pre-arranged conflicts. Neither would we allow ourselves to be used as weapons against other women's groups or organizations if we could possibly avoid it. But that did not mean denying differences of opinions or priorities.

A horrifying example of misrepresentation and blaming women was that of a young army officer, a second lieutenant, who one summer night in 1994 shot and killed a whole group of young people in a small Swedish town. He had been depressed and unbalanced for some time and his colleagues had encouraged him to seek psychiatric help. That night he was drunk and had quarrelled with a former girlfriend. He returned to his military quarters, put on his uniform, took his gun and ammunition, which – against the rules – he had kept together in his room, and he left his quarters without anyone stopping him. He then shot at and killed anyone he happened to meet.

The media version of this tragedy was of a small boy abandoned very early by his mother and brought up by his father. When the boy was rejected by the former girlfriend, it brought back memories of his early separation from his mother. The father was pitied, the mother and the girlfriend blamed. Headlines screamed about day-care centres fostering mass murderers. Several Support Stockings were invited to take part in discussions on the theme: day care for children and its violent consequences. We declined. The fact, pointed out early on, that the US has a higher frequency of mass murderers than any other country, and that day care there twenty years ago cannot have been an important factor as it was very rare, did not impress those taking part in the debate.

Gradually, over many months, a very different story emerged. The father, described early on as 'a respected arms dealer', had given his son five gun licences as a birthday present when the son was twenty-one (the minimum legal age in Sweden for such licences). The mother, who allegedly abandoned the boy, in fact stayed at home until the boy was nine. He never was in a day-care centre. After the divorce, the mother moved only a few hundred yards away in order not to lose daily contact with her son. A very troubled young man, with a fascination for firearms, and in need of psychiatric treatment for depressions and imbalance, had been allowed full access to guns, although he had been violent on several occasions. (His violent outbreaks had contributed to the girlfriend breaking up with him.) In addition, regular army security practices had been routinely ignored. This other story did not make the headlines. No discussions of military responsibility for arming unstable young men, or the responsibilities of arms dealers took place. Headlines screaming, 'The Army Fostering Mass Murders' did not appear. Debates on military service for young men and the price paid in violence were not set up.

The largest Swedish evening paper in late 1993 reported an opinion poll, showing that 40 per cent of voters would consider voting for a Women's List, headed by Maria-Pia Boëthius, if such a party was set up. The high proportion included both women and men, and the comparatively strong male support for gender aspects of politics came as a surprise.

The Support Stockings also experienced the media not reporting events, but creating them, and the media trying to pressure us into decisions of a very political nature. A well-known talk show host, who in a live broadcast had more or less created the populist party, New Democracy, eight months before the 1991 elections, wished to repeat this feat with the Support Stockings/Women's List. His producer said that if we did not appear on his programme in January 1994, he would devote a full hour of prime-time television to us anyhow. Three of us 'chose' to appear. In the live broadcast we were faced with opinion polls acquired by the talk show that claimed that 23 per cent of voters would vote for us if we started a Women's List, and that about 15 per cent wanted Maria-Pia Boëthius as prime minister. He then repeatedly tried to make us form the party on the spot. We did not.

Four days later, I was asked to quit the bi-monthly column I had written for a major daily paper for almost ten years. The reason given, which the paper published at my request, was that the obvious rules of the paper for independent columnists prevented my writing during an election year. I was the only columnist to whom these rules were ever applied, and the rules, however obvious, have never been explained. Male columnists, active in existing parties and actually campaigning in the election, kept their columns. Maria-Pia Boëthius, who had been unanimously nominated for the chair of the prestigious Publicistklubben was declared ineligible as she was 'too political'. The third Support Stocking in the talk show, Ebba Witt-Brattström, a feminist researcher in comparative literature, met with ever-increasing hostility at work (as well as strong support from her students), and was showered with hate mail, which reached a depressing climax when pornographic magazines were sent to her anonymously through the university internal mail and in official university envelopes.

Maria-Pia Boëthius was an obvious public face for the network. Ebba and I were chosen as two others, as for several reasons we risked less from hostile publicity than many other members did.

Ignorance as a Strategic Backlash Tool

Recent stories of management and leadership at work stress again and again how important it is to clarify demands if the workforce is to be able to fulfil them. Employees, too, should be encouraged to define clearly what they want from their employer. The message can be summarized as: 'People are not mind-readers, and you alone are responsible for letting others know what you think and want.'

But the very same men most likely to have been to expensive seminars on clear communications maintain that women should not create trouble, i.e., should not clarify what they want to achieve and with what they are dissatisfied. If women start causing a stir about wages and working conditions, the manager may very well lose enthusiasm for gender equality work. (No, I didn't make that up. It was said in a Swedish business organization's commentary on proposals for a change in the law.)

Most of the men who maintain that wage differences and women's poor working conditions are the fault of feminists on the whole are not thoughtful advocates of discrimination. They simply don't know what they are talking about.

What wages do men and women earn, respectively, in the country as a whole, and in the particular workplace for which you are responsible? As a manager in a particular area, what do you know about the educational system from a gender point of view? In time, my patience with such ignorance has become shorter. Nowadays, I divide ignorance of basic conditions in society into two types: passive ignorance and active ignorance.

The passively ignorant are those to whom it has never occurred that societal problems, such as gender discrimination, exist, because they are lazy and never think very much about the world around them.

The actively ignorant are those who, with great and well-directed energy, make sure that they are never present when questions concerning women and men at their own workplace are being dealt with; who never read an article in the daily paper or specialist press if it looks as if it is about 'that'; who simply use their deliberate ignorance to ensure that no demands can be made on them; and who then throw up their hands, smile, and say: 'I don't understand that at all. I don't think there's such a thing as women's pay!' Or, as the man in the Big Bank said: 'In this bank, we are concerned with the individual. I never think about whether my colleagues are men or women.'

It is pertinent to mention that 70 per cent of his bank's staff were women, that there were significant wage differentials to the detriment of women (even when the work was equivalent), that there were no women in management and that his closest colleagues of the last twenty years had been exclusively men (with the exception of his right-hand woman 'who really decides everything' – his secretary). This was a bank which prided itself on its careful analysis of the world and of its own organization, and which stressed that analysis of this kind in a modern bank, as in other companies with high aspirations, is a key task of top management.

The actively ignorant have found a lasting strategy. They try to keep those with knowledge and interest occupied by requesting them to repeat the same things over and over again, while they themselves don't listen. Possibly, the person doing the repeating can eventually be accused of nagging.

Many, many times, I and others invited to various organizations have heard, after the lecture, from both women and men: 'This has been really thought-provoking. What a pity the people who need to hear it most aren't here.' The actively ignorant are always somewhere else.

The Elections

The television show on which we did not form a political party gave rise to a media storm. The elections in September were expected to be very evenly balanced. Whoever won would do so by a very narrow margin. Thus a new party could tip the balance.

Forming a new party in Sweden turned out to be very simple, not too expensive and could also be left until very near the elections.

We knew that the nominations of candidates on political party lists were crucial. The listing process, involving local party organizations all over the country, is slow and complex. We had to keep the pressure high by keeping the threat to form our own party alive for a long time. Women from all over the country phoned or sent messages: keep on, we can use it to promote women candidates. We were, willingly, used as witches to frighten: 'If we don't get more women on the lists, the Stockings will come and get you!' In public the political candidates distanced themselves from us. Secretly they used us. Battles over these lists were fought by politically active women, and many men, all over Sweden. This meant that men expecting seats in parliament as rewards for activities and work suddenly saw women – with long political experience but with no seat in parliament as their birthright – taking eligible places on the lists instead of them.

For some time, every other name on the Liberals' list was a woman, as was the case of Greens and the Left. The Centre Party had quite a high proportion of women. The Christian Democrats promoted women more than before, but they were a very small party. The Conservatives rejected the idea, and the New Democrats declared that it would be ridiculous. The Social Democrats now decided that as a party they would alternate women and men on their list.[15] As that is the largest party in Sweden, the decision had an enormous impact.

A different Women's Party, previously formed by a group of women who did not expect the existing party structure ever to represent women fairly, registered for the elections. The main difference between them and us was that they saw a permanent women's party as a desirable thing, while we wanted to avoid it and – if we formed a party – would have the closing down of that party at the top of the party manifesto.

The Support Stockings printed small stickers and buttons with two slogans: 'Half of the power – all of the pay! and 'Little Sister is watching'. The latter in particular was popular. Some found their way into the men's lavatories in the parliament buildings.

The existing parties joined in declaring that a Women's List was not necessary. We kept up the pressure on them to prove it. One effect of our work and of the media attention on us at a difficult time for many women in Sweden was that the projections of dreams and hopes onto the Support Stockings grew. One early morning a woman grabbed my arm in an underground train: 'If only you'd started a party, all our problems would be solved!' Letters with pleas came: 'Don't let us down now! Form a party!'

The key problem, which we identified early on, was the inevitable disappointment of women who pinned their hopes on us. If we formed the party, we would disappoint them by not being able to achieve much in a multi-party parliament in which we would have to compromise with other parties and political coalitions would be negotiated, since no absolute majority for one party could be expected. In such negotiations we would in all probability be pushed aside as soon as important issues were at stake. If we did not form the party, that in itself would be a disappointment.

The main purpose of the Support Stockings helped clarify our analysis. The real effect on politics would be much greater if most parties changed, than if one new party entered parliament. And the threat of forming a party remains as long as it is not formed.

In the elections, Social Democrats won about 46 per cent of parliamentary seats, the Greens came back into parliament, the populist New Democracy dropped out after internal turmoil. The representation of women in all political forums reached record levels, both nationally and internationally. The declaration of intent by the new government put gender equality top of their priorities. Out of the twenty-two ministers appointed, eleven were men. As in the former government, the deputy prime minister was responsible for gender equality issues.

Women held about 42 per cent of the 349 seats in parliament; 48 per cent of the 1,800 seats in county councils, and 41 per cent of just under 14,000 seats in municipal counties.

Women – any Women?

Why did we concentrate on women in politics? Because women, with far less access to economic resources, at least have votes. Power in the democratic process is more accessible than economic power. The next important area for women is economic power, but that will take much longer.

Should women promote women, just because they are women? Are not political differences as large between women as between men? Yes, political differences are just as large, but sometimes different. In Sweden today, women with different class and geographic backgrounds lead more similar lives than did women at the turn of the last century. Most children go to day care, partly financed by public money, and very often organized by local authorities. Most old people receiving organized help get it from local authorities. Women with prestigious and well-paid jobs give birth in the same clinics, take their children to the same day care and visit their old mothers living in the same apartments for the elderly as women in low-paid jobs do. This does not mean that social segregation does not exist. But since about 80 per cent of Swedish women have paid work, and since household help or private servants are extremely rare, we share much more of the daily struggle to make time stretch than our mothers and grandmothers did.

Political scientists in Sweden are at present researching into what women in politics want and achieve, and what women voters expect and want as compared to men. Women in Swedish politics, from the beginning, have worked with health care, education, social issues and with women's rights and safety in paid and unpaid work, much more so than men. They have not always agreed on methods, but their areas of concern are not that different. Their priorities differ from men's, too. Women in Swedish politics have gradually lowered society's tolerance of violence; what were once seen as ordinary drunken brawls are now considered assault and battery.

Women voters are significantly more concerned than men with

welfare issues, with the quality of child care and care of the elderly, and with education. They are less concerned with reducing taxes. They put a lower priority on defence spending.

These research results are not well received by the political establishment, since they support the view that gender does matter in politics, a view which has been strongly rejected by men in power for a long time. Men see themselves as genderless humans, and find the fact that they are male humans degrading.

Will it make any difference? Are women being used as hostages for making the electorate accept unpopular decisions during a period of serious economic difficulties? Are women allowed into positions of power because power is not there any more? We do not know yet. It does not look too promising. Established politicians have naturally tried to impose their ideas of political etiquette and proper work procedures on the newly elected women. The power struggles around them have been fierce, and as yet the newly elected women do not seem to have worked out very efficient strategies of their own.

What was unusual? I think that it was seen as a disturbance that the Support Stockings did exactly what we said we would do: promote women, and only start a party if the existing parties did not respond to women's demand for their fair share of political power. Certain men with a past in the revolutionary left of the 1970s, and who today have highly paid bank, financial advisory or media jobs, seem to have been very much provoked by this. Perhaps it did not accord with their own ambitions and experiences.

Maud Edwards, a political scientist, has studied the reactions which faced the Support Stockings, then compared them to reactions to the appearance of the New Democrats. Her findings indicate that the male-dominated New Democrats were very early on declared a new political force. Finding out what they wanted, and how they analysed problems, was important. The Support Stockings, on the other hand, were declared wrong from the very beginning. For women to organize was unfashionable, backward and undemocratic.

It was said that the issues we stressed – pay discrimination, violence, etc. – were already well known; as everyone agreed that these things were wrong, why did we insist on them? We were attacked for taking up the same boring old concerns, and not producing new and interesting problems. We retorted that we would continue pointing at the issues until the problems were solved and women had their fair share, which as regards pay discrimination was also their legal right, and that these problems were worsening.

Now, after the elections, the new government has arranged a series of gender seminars for all ministers, top civil servants and heads of departments and regional offices. The bishops, with the archbishop, and vice-chancellors of universities have also participated in the same type of seminar, arranged for them by the deputy prime minister.[16] State departments have, with varying degrees of enthusiasm, started to create and improve tools for routine gender analysis of all decisions. A committee on the economic power of women, as compared to men, has been appointed.

The political parties of Sweden have this election period to prove their unanimous claim that no women's party was necessary. If not, the possibility of starting one remains.

The coverage in the media of gender issues has continued, and might have a lasting effect. Women journalists are now much more successful in getting their definition of what is news and what is interesting to the general public accepted. The absence of women from important decision-making, from senior management and from analysis of economic and social affairs is a part of everyday reporting. But this new material, too, has met with strong resistance.

The most visible Support Stockings are now sometimes targeted for personal attacks. In 1992 I was asked in a crowded, lively discussion arranged by feminist students at Stockholm University: 'What will happen to you yourselves when you start all this?' I recently met a student who reminded me of her question and of my flippant reply, which I had forgotten: 'When you hear rumours that I am regularly eating babies for breakfast, then you will know that we are closing in on power.'

We are certainly not there yet. I myself will perhaps never see it. But I will continue to do what I, and so many, have done for a long time: pointing out that the human race, regardless of age, class, ethnicity, sexual orientation, religion, physical and mental ability, always consists of women and men. Women *and* men. There is no third alternative, no genderless 'we', 'the party', certainly no 'women and everybody else'.

To analyse and discuss society seriously from the point of view that both female and male humans exist, with equal rights, equal obligations and equal responsibilities and that there are no other humans except women and men is an enormous challenge. For it means depriving many men of their assumed right to forget their gender, and to lift off their shoulder the burden of being the only norm for humans.

I. GETTING CIVILIZED

1. Originally published in the *Fordham Law Review*, vol. LXIII, October 1992, p. 17–31.

2. 'The Nomination of Judge Clarence Thomas to be Associate Justice of the Supreme Court of the United States: Hearings Before the Senate Comm. on the Judiciary, 102d Cong., 1st Sess. 36 (1991)'. See generally, N. Y. McKay, 'Remembering Anita Hill and Clarence Thomas: What Really Happened When One Black Woman Spoke Out', in T. Morrison (ed.), T. M. Phelps and H. Winternitz, *Capitol Games: Clarence Thomas, Anita Hill, and the Story of a Supreme Court Nomination*, New York, Hyperion (1992).

3. C. Gilligan, *In a Different Voice: Psychological theory and women's development*. Cambridge, Mass., Harvard University Press (1982).

4. See 'Lecture XXXIII: Femininity', in trans. J. Strachey, *The Standard Edition of the Complete Psychological Works of Sigmund Freud*, London, Hogarth Press (1971); see also E. Erikson, *Identity, Youth and Crisis*, New York, W. W. Norton (1968), pp. 261, 263; J. Piaget, trans. Marjorie Gabain, *The Moral Judgement of the Child*, Glencoe, Free Press (1948), pp. 76–83. Lawrence Kohlberg, in a personal communication with Carol Gilligan, discussed why he did not include girls in his theory-building studies of moral development. He stated that their responses did not fit his schema or make sense in his terms.

5. See, e.g., D. J. Levinson, *The Seasons of a Man's Life*, New York, A. Knopf (1978), pp. 8–9; D. Offer, *The Psychological World of the Teenager: A Study of Normal Adolescent Boys*, New York, Basic Books (1969).

6. The term 'social perspective-taking' refers to the ability to take the point of view of other people.

7. Studies must conform to certain standards in order to receive federal funding or serve as grounds for academic promotion.

8. T. Randall, 'AMA Joint Commission to Urge Physicians to Become Part of Solution to Family Violence Epidemic', *Journal of the American Medical Association* (1991), 266:2524.

9. For example, more men have recently been able to come forth and proclaim that they were sexually abused, many by their boyhood priests. See, e.g., L. Matchan, 'Town secret: the case of James Porter,

who has been charged with sexually abusing children in his parish in the 1960s, *Boston Globe*, 29 August 1993; J. Rakowsky, 'Vermont Probes Hingham Priest: 3 Men Allege Sex Abuse', *Boston Globe*, 14 June 1993.

10. M. Belenky *et al.*, *Women's Ways of Knowing: The Development of Self, Voice and Mind*, New York, Basic Books (1986).

11. S. Ruddick, *Maternal Thinking: Toward a Politics of Peace*, Boston, Beacon Press (1989).

12. K. Pollit, 'Are Women Morally Superior to Men?' *Nation*, 28 December 1992.

13. 'Equality feminism' refers to equal access for women to those privileges from which they have been traditionally barred because they are women. See C. A. MacKinnon, *Feminism Unmodified*, Cambridge, Mass., Harvard University Press (1987), pp. 32–4.

14. By contrast to 'equality feminism', whereby women seek equality to males, 'difference feminism' emphasizes that women and men have different points of view, and thus different voices. See M. Minow, *Making All the Difference: Inclusion, Exclusion, and American Law*, Ithaca, Cornell University Press (1990), pp. 377–8; C. A. MacKinnon, op. cit., pp. 32–3. For a general discussion of difference feminism, see C. A. MacKinnon, 'Sexual Harassment as Sex Discrimination', in (ed.) *Sexual Harassment of Working Women: A Case of Sex Discrimination*, New Haven, Yale University Press (1979).

15. See J. B. Miller, *Toward a New Psychology of Women*, Boston, Beacon Press (1976); C. Gilligan, *In a Different Voice*, Cambridge, Mass., Harvard University Press (1982).

16. Compare J. Shibley and M. C. Linn, *The Psychology of Gender: Advances through Meta-analysis*, with E. E. Maccoby, C. N. Jacklin, *The Psychology of Sex Differences* (1974).

17. D. Tannen, *You Just Don't Understand: Women and Men in Conversation*, New York, Morrow (1990).

18. I. Kant, trans. Humphrey Palmer, *Critique of Pure Reason*, Lewiston, E. Mellen (1992).

19. Ibid., pp. 1–2.

20. Ibid.

21. See C. Gilligan (1982) op. cit.; J. B. Miller, op. cit.

22. Lecture XXXI, 'The Dissection of the Psychical Personality', in trans. J. Strachey, op. cit.

23. M. Belenky *et al.*, op. cit.
24. D. C. Jack, *Silencing the Self: Women and Depression*, Cambridge, Mass., Harvard University Press (1991).
25. S. Ruddick, op. cit.
26. J. R. Martin, *Reclaiming a Conversation: The Ideal of the Educated Woman*, New Haven, Yale University Press (1985).
27. The Harvard Project on Women's Psychology and Girls' Development is an outgrowth of the Center for the Study of Gender, Education and Human Development. Research undertaken for the Harvard Project has uncovered the onset of dissociative processes in girls at adolescence and also girls' resistance to disassociation as they enter adolescence and continue into adulthood.
28. J. L. Herman, author of *Father-Daughter Incest*, Cambridge, Mass., Harvard University Press (1981) and *Trauma and Recovery*, New York, Basic Books (1992), and M. Harvey run the Victims of Violence Program.
29. See L. M. Brown and C. Gilligan, *Meeting at the Crossroads: Women's Psychology and Girls' Development*, Cambridge, Mass., Harvard University Press (1992); C. Gilligan *et al.*, *Making Connections: The Relational Worlds of Adolescent Girls at Emma Willard School*, Cambridge, Mass., Harvard University Press (1990); C. Gilligan *et al.*, *Women, Girls and Psychotherapy: Reframing Resistance*, New York, Harrington Park Press (1991); L. M. Brown, 'A Problem of Vision: The Development of Voice and Relational Knowledge in Adolescent Girls Ages Seven to Sixteen', *XIX Women's Studies Quarterly* 1 & 2, The Feminist Press at the City University of New York (1991); A. G. Rogers, 'Voice, Play and a Practice of Ordinary Courage in Girls' and Women's Lives', *Harvard Educational Review*, Fall 1993, pp. 265–95; J. M. Taylor, C. Gilligan and A. Sullivan, *Between Voice and Silence: Women and Girls, Race and Relationship*, Cambridge, Mass., Harvard University Press (1995).
30. See C. G. Heilbrun, *Toward a Recognition of Androgyny*, New York, A. Knopf (1973).
31. See L. M. Brown and C. Gilligan, op. cit.
32. J. L. Herman, *Trauma and Recovery*.
33. W. E. B. DuBois, *The Souls of Black Folk*, New York, Dodd, Mead and Co. (1979).
34. V. Woolf, *Three Guineas* (1938).
35. E. Snee, *Split Vision: Psychological Dimensions of Authority for Women*,

Unpublished Ph.D. dissertation, Harvard University Graduate School of Education (1994).

36. Ibid.

37. E. Snee, unpublished paper (1991); see also B. Zimlicki, *Speaking of Love: From a Study of Relationships in Crisis*, Unpublished Ph.D. dissertation, Harvard University Graduate School of Education (1991).

38. Emily's List is a non-partisan fundraising organization to support female political candidates.

39. Take Our Daughters to Work is a nationwide initiative sponsored by the Ms Foundation in an effort to invite girls into the workplace and help them broaden their visions of their future work possibilities.

40. The Company of Women is an all-woman theatre company created to join the work of Carol Gilligan and Kristin Linklater and to bring women's and girls' voices into the world.

41. L. M. Brown and C. Gilligan, op. cit.

42. W. Kaminer, 'Feminism's Identity Crisis', the *Atlantic*, October 1993, pp. 51, 68.

43. Ibid., p. 62.

44. 410 US 113 (1973).

45. Virgil, *The Aeneid*, trans. R. Fitzgerald, New York, Random House (1983).

46. *The Congressional Yellow Book*, summer 1994, 1–5, pp. 1–125. The seven women senators are: Barbara Boxer, Dianne Feinstein, Kay Bailey Hutchinson, Nancy Landon Kassebaum, Barbara A. Mikulski, Carol Moseley-Braun and Patty Murray.

47. T. Morrison, *The Bluest Eye*, New York, Holt, Rinehart and Winston (1970).

48. Ibid., p. 9.

49. Ibid.

50. Aristophanes, *Lysistrata*, trans. G. Seldes, New York, The Limited Editions Club (1934).

51. V. Woolf, op. cit.

2. A BRIEF HISTORY OF GENDER

1. T. Laqueur, *Making Sex: Body and Gender from the Greeks to Freud*, Cambridge, Mass., Harvard University Press (1990), p. 22.

2. L. Jordanova, *Sexual Visions: Images of Gender in Science and Medicine*

Between the Eighteenth and Twentieth Centuries, Hemel Hempstead, Harvester Wheatsheaf (1989), p. 14.

3. S. Firestone, *The Dialectic of Sex: The Case for Feminist Revolution*, London, Paladin (1972), p. 14.

4. Ibid., p. 192.

5. G. Greer, *The Female Eunuch*, London, MacGibbon and Kee (1970).

6. K. Millett, *Sexual Politics*, London, Rupert Hart-Davis (1969), p. 29.

7. R. Stoller, *Sex and Gender*, New York, Science House (1968), pp. viii–ix.

8. N. Oudshoorn, *Beyond the Natural Body: An Archaeology of Sex Hormones*, London, Routledge (1994), p. 152.

9. Shorter Oxford English Dictionary.

10. J. Archer and B. Lloyd, *Sex and Gender*, Harmondsworth, Penguin (1982), p. 22.

11. C. N. Degler, 'Darwinians Confront Gender: Or, There is More to it than History', in D. L. Rhode (ed.), *Theoretical Perspectives on Sexual Difference*, New Haven, Yale University Press (1990), p. 35.

12. B. Friedan, *The Feminine Mystique*, London, Gollancz (1963).

13. A. Oakley, *Sex, Gender and Society*, London, Temple Smith (1972).

14. L. Segal, *Is the Future Female? Troubled Thoughts on Contemporary Feminism*, London, Virago (1987), p. 119; M. Komarovsky, 'The New Feminist Scholarship: Some Precursors and Polemics', *Journal of Marriage and the Family* (1988), 50:585–93, p. 592; Oudshoorn, op. cit., p. 2.

15. A. Oakley, *Women Confined: Towards a Sociology of Childbirth*, Oxford, Martin Robertson (1980).

16. N. Chodorow, *The Reproduction of Mothering: Psychoanalysis and the Sociology of Gender*, Berkeley, California, University of California Press (1978).

17. C. Lasch, *Haven in a Heartless World: The Family Besieged?*, New York, W. W. Norton (1977).

18. C. Lasch, *The Culture of Narcissism: American Life in an Age of Diminishing Expectations*, London, Abacus Press (1980).

19. G. F. Gilder, *Sexual Suicide*, New York, Quadrangle Books (1973).

20. G. Gilder, *Naked Nomads: Unmarried Men in America*, New York, Quadrangle Books (1974).

21. B. Berger and P. Berger, *The War Over the Family*, Harmondsworth, Penguin (1983).

22. S. A. Hewlett, *A Lesser Life: The Myth of Women's Liberation in America*, New York, Warner Books (1986).
23. B. Friedan, *The Second Stage*, London, Michael Joseph (1982).
24. G. Greer, *Sex and Destiny*, London, Secker and Warburg (1984).
25. C. H. Sommers, *Who Stole Feminism? How Women Have Betrayed Women*, New York, Touchstone Books (1994).
26. R. Coward, *Our Treacherous Hearts: Why Women Let Men Get Their Way*, London, Faber and Faber (1992).
27. Segal, op. cit.
28. N. Wolf, *Fire with Fire*, London, Chatto and Windus (1993).
29. K. Roiphe, *The Morning After: Sex, Fear and Feminism*, London, Hamish Hamilton (1994).
30. R. Denfield, *The New Victorians*, London, Simon and Schuster (1995).
31. On Camille Paglia, see M. Walters, this volume.
32. Chodorow, op. cit.
33. Lasch, *Heaven in a Heartless World*, p. vxi.
34. Berger and Berger, op. cit., p. 64.
35. A. Etzioni, *The Spirit of Community*, London, Fontana (1995), pp. 54–5.
36. Ibid., p. 61.
37. T. Parsons and R. F. Bales, *Family: Socialization and Interaction Process*, London, Routledge and Kegan Paul (1956).
38. I. Illich, *Gender*, London, Marion Boyars (1983), p. 14.
39. L. Segal, *Straight Sex: The Politics of Pleasure*, London, Virago (1994).
40. M. Freely, *What About Us? An Open Letter to the Mothers Feminism Forgot*, London, Bloomsbury (1995), p. 17.
41. J. Neuberger, *Whatever's Happening to Women?* London, Kyle Cathie (1991), p. 3.
42. N. Davidson, *The Failure of Feminism*, New York, Prometheus Books (1988), p. 1.
43. Ibid., p. 39.
44. R. Pool, *The New Sexual Revolution*, London, Hodder and Stoughton (1993).
45. Etzioni, op. cit.
46. J. Doane and D. Hodges, *Nostalgia and Sexual Difference: The Resistance to Contemporary Feminism*, New York, Methuen (1987).
47. J. Stacey, 'Are Feminists Afraid to Leave Home? The Challenge of Conservative Pro-family Feminism', in J. Mitchell and A. Oakley (eds.) *What is Feminism?* Oxford, Basil Blackwell (1986).

48. J. B. Elshtain, *Public Man, Private Woman: Women in Social and Political Thought*, Oxford, Martin Robertson (1981).
49. Greer, *Sex and Destiny*, p. 25.
50. Stacey, op. cit.
51. G. Steinem, *Revolution from Within*, London, Bloomsbury (1992), p. 247.
52. Steinem also had breast cancer, which is more common among older women and may be another factor leading to a different awareness of the body.
53. Sommers, op. cit., p. 16.
54. Ibid., p. 230.
55. Ibid., p. 44.
56. Ibid., p. 18.
57. C. Paglia, *Sex, Art and American Culture*, Harmondsworth, Penguin (1992), p. 50.
58. M. B. Belenky, B. M. Clinchy, N. R. Goldberger and J. M. Tarule, *Women's Ways of Knowing*, New York, Basic Books (1986).
59. N. Denzin, *On Understanding Emotion*, San Francisco, Josey Bass (1987).
60. C. Gilligan, *In a Different Voice: Psychological Theory and Women's Development*, Cambridge, Mass., Harvard University Press (1982).
61. S. Ruddick, *Maternal Thinking*, New York, Ballantine (1989).
62. See e.g. J. Finch and D. Groves (eds.), *A Labour of Love: Women, Work and Caring*, London, Routledge and Kegan Paul (1983); C. Merchant, *The Death of Nature: Women, Ecology and the Scientific Revolution*, New York, Harper and Row (1980).
63. M. French, *Beyond Power*, London, Jonathan Cape (1986).
64. G. Steinem, 'What if Freud were Phyllis? Or, the Watergate of the Western World', in *Moving Beyond Words*, London, Bloomsbury (1984).
65. S. L. Bem, *The Lenses of Gender*, New Haven, Yale University Press (1993), p. 127.
66. Degler, op. cit., p. 34.
67. See A. Oakley, *Public Visions, Private Matters*, London, Institute of Education (1995).
68. Coward, op. cit., p. 1.
69. Segal, op. cit., p. ix.
70. Ibid.

71. Ibid., p. 2.
72. Wolf, op. cit., p. xvii.
73. Ibid., p. 134.
74. Ibid., p. 147.
75. Roiphe, op. cit.
76. Paglia, op. cit.
77. Roiphe, op. cit., p. 5.
78. Denfield, op. cit., p. 11.
79. See e.g. Denfield, op. cit., pp. 62–80.
80. Segal, op. cit., p. xv.
81. Ibid., p. 141.
82. Laqueur, op. cit., p. 7.
83. Ibid., p. 11.
84. V. L. Bullough and B. Bullough, *Cross-dressing, Sex, and Gender*, Philadelphia, University of Pennsylvania Press (1993).
85. Ibid., p. 7.
86. Oudshoorn, op. cit.
87. S. Ortner, 'Is Female to Male as Nature is to Culture?' in M. Z. Rosaldo and L. Lamphere (eds.), *Woman, Culture and Society*, Stanford, California, Stanford University Press (1974), p. 87.
88. Bem, op. cit.
89. B. Thorne, 'Children and Gender: Constructions of Difference', in Rhode (ed.), op. cit., p. 105.
90. Ibid., p. 278.
91. Oudshoorn, op. cit., p. 9.
92. C. A. MacKinnon, 'Legal Perspectives on Sexual Difference' in Rhode (ed.), op. cit., p. 214.
93. C. A. MacKinnon, *Feminism Unmodified: Discourses on Life and Law*, Cambridge, Mass., Harvard University Press (1987), p. 2.
94. Ibid., p. 9.
95. C. A. MacKinnon, *Toward a Feminist Theory of the State*, Cambridge, Mass., Harvard University Press (1989), p. x.
96. Ibid., p. xiii.
97. 'Scientists Detect Gender in Sperm', *Independent*, 11 November 1993.
98. 'Doctors reject right to choose babies' gender', *Independent*, 30 June 1993.
99. J. Mitchell, 'Women: The Longest Revolution', *New Left Review*, no. 40.

100. P. Rose, *Parallel Lives: Five Victorian Marriages*, London, Chatto and Windus (1984).

101. See K. Figes, *Because of Her Sex: The Myth of Equality for Women in Britain*, London, Pan Books (1994).

I would like to thank Gill Bendelow for help with the research for this chapter.

3. AMERICAN GOTHIC

1. See P. Brooks, *The Melodramatic Imagination*, New Haven and London, Yale University Press (1976).

2. See J. Mitchell and A. Oakley (eds.), *The Rights and Wrongs of Women*, Harmondsworth, Penguin (1976), pp. 307–29.

3. Quoted in N. Strossen, *Defending Pornography*, London, Abacus (1996), p. 22.

4. M. French, *The War against Women*, London, Hamish Hamilton (1992), p. 166.

5. G. Greer, *The Female Eunuch*, London, MacGibbon and Kee (1970), p. 67.

6. L. Segal, *Straight Sex*, London, Virago (1994), p. 65.

7. Ibid., p. 66, p. 62.

8. S. Brownmiller, *Against Our Will*, New York, Bantam Books (1976), p. 5.

9. S. Griffin, 'Rape: The All-American Crime' in *Pornography and Silence*, London, The Women's Press (1971).

10. R. Morgan, 'Theory and Practice: Pornography and Rape' in L. Lederer (ed.), *Take Back the Night*, New York, Bantam Books (1980), pp. 125–32.

11. A. Dworkin, *Letters from a War Zone*, New York, E. P. Dutton (1988), p. 119.

12. A. Dworkin, *Intercourse*, London, Secker and Warburg (1987), pp. 194, 189, 133–4.

13. A. Dworkin, *Pornography: Men Possessing Women*, London, The Women's Press (1981), p. 223.

14. A. Dworkin, *Ice and Fire*, New York, Weidenfeld and Nicolson (1987), p. 84.

15. Quoted C. Bennett, *Guardian*, 28 May 1994, p. 20. See also K.

Roiphe's account of a MacKinnon lecture in *The Morning After*,
London, Hamish Hamilton (1994), pp. 149–50.
16. C. MacKinnon, *Feminism Unmodified: Discourses on Life and Law*,
Cambridge, Mass., Harvard University Press (1987), p. 205.
17. 'Pornography, Civil Rights and Speech', in Catherine Itzin (ed.),
Pornography: Women, Violence and Civil Liberties, Oxford, OUP
(1993), p. 456.
18. C. Paglia, *Sex, Art and American Culture*, London, Penguin (1993).
19. C. MacKinnon, *Only Words*, London, HarperCollins (1995), p. 3.
20. C. MacKinnon, *Feminism Unmodified*, p. 7.
21. C. MacKinnon, *Towards a Feminist Theory of the State*, Cambridge,
Mass., Harvard University Press (1989), p. 151. *Only Words*, p. 40.
22. J. Mitchell, *Psychoanalysis and Feminism*, London, Allen Lane (1974),
p. xxii.
23. The one reference to Freud in *Towards a Feminist Theory of the State*
cites Masson; the only footnoted reference in *Feminism Unmodified*
cites, on p. 279, Masson again, and Florence Rush, *The Best Kept
Secret: Sexual Abuse of Children*.
24. C. MacKinnon, *Towards a Feminist Theory of the State*, p. 152, p. 138.
25. C. Paglia, *Sexual Personae: Art and Decadence from Nefertiti to Emily
Dickinson*, New York, Vintage Books (1991), p. 24. *Vamps and
Tramps*, London, Viking (1994), p. 111.
26. A. Carter, *The Sadeian Woman*, London, Virago (1979). Susan Sontag,
'The Pornographic Imagination' in *Styles of Radical Will*, London,
Secker and Warburg (1966), pp. 35–73.
27. J.W.'s Foreword in Margaret Reynolds (ed.), *Erotica: An Anthology
of Women's Writing*, London, Pandora (1991), pp. ixx–xx.
28. MacKinnon, *Only Words*, p. 13.
29. Quoted in Katie Roiphe, op. cit., p. 141.
30. Sontag, op. cit., p. 66.
31. MacKinnon, *Only Words*, p. 5.
32. Strossen, op. cit., especially pp. 229–40.
33. B. Williams, 'Drawing Lines', *London Review of Books*, 12 May 1994,
pp. 9–10.
34. Strossen, op. cit., pp. 75–9.
35. Paglia, *Vamps and Tramps*, p. 108.
36. Paglia, *Vamps and Tramps*, p. 32 and *Sexual Personae*, p. 4.

NOTES

37. The first chapter of Paglia's *Sexual Personae, passim.* Paglia, *Sex, Art and American Culture*, p. xi.
38. MacKinnon, *Only Words*, p. 24. Paglia, *Sexual Personae*, pp. 20–21.
39. Paglia, *Vamps and Tramps*, p. 32.
40. Paglia, *Sexual Personae*, p. 13.
41. Paglia, *Vamps and Tramps*, pp. 63–71.
42. Paglia, *Vamps and Tramps*, p. 59.
43. Paglia, *Sex, Art and American Culture*, pp. 15–16; p. 9.
44. Ibid., p. 51.
45. 'Now Hear This', *Guardian*, 23 March 1995, Section 2, pp. 6–7.
46. Paglia, *Sex, Art and American Culture*, pp. 38–45.
47. Paglia, *Sexual Personae*, p. 85.
48. Ibid., p. 445; p. 673.
49. S. de Beauvoir, *The Second Sex*, London, Jonathan Cape (1953), p. 91, p. 643.
50. Brooks, op. cit., p. 54, and the chapter called 'The Text of Muteness', pp. 56–80. See also the article by Mark Cousins and Parveen Adams, 'The Truth on Assault', *October*, Winter 1995, pp. 93–102.
51. MacKinnon, *Only Words*, p. 5, p. 28, p. 40.

4. WOMEN, ETHNICITY AND EMPOWERMENT

1. See e.g. A. Gorz, *Farewell to the Working Class*, London, Pluto Press (1982); H. Wainwright, *Labour, A Tale of Two Parties*, London, Hogarth Press (1985); H. Cain and N. Yuval-Davis, ' "The Equal Opportunities Community" and the Anti-racist Struggle', *Critical Social Policy*, Autumn 1990.
2. F. Fanon, *Black Skin, White Masks*, London, Pluto Press (1986).
3. P. Freire, *The Pedagogy of the Oppressed*, Harmondsworth, Penguin Books (1972).
4. J. M. Bystydzienski, *Women Transforming Politics: Worldwide Strategies for Empowerment*, Bloomington, Indiana University Press (1992).
5. E.g. A. Bookman and S. Morgen, *Women and the Politics of Empowerment*, Philadelphia, Temple University Press (1988); J. R. Macy, *Despair and Personal Power in the Nuclear Age*, Philadelphia, New Society Publishers (1983); N. Harstock, 'Political Change: Two Perspectives on Power', in C. Bunch et al. (eds.), *Building Feminist*

Theory: Essays from the Quest, New York, Longman Press (1981).

6. P. Hill Collins, *Black Feminist Thought: Knowledge, Consciousness and the Politics of Empowerment*, Boston, Unwin Hyman (1990), p. 222.

7. A. Gorz, op. cit.

8. I. M. Young, *Justice and the Politics of Difference*, Princeton, Princeton University Press (1990); N. Yuval-Davis, 'Citizenship Debate: Women, the State and Ethnic Processes', *Feminist Review*, Autumn 1991; F. Anthias and N. Yuval-Davis in association with H. Cain, *Racialized Boundaries: Race, Nation, Gender, Colour and Class and the Anti-racist Struggle*, London, Routledge (1992), Chapter 6.

9. H. K. Bhabha (ed.), *Nation and Narration*, London, Routledge (1990).

10. H. K. Bhabha in *Challenging Racism in London*, Report of a conference held on 12 March 1983, London, Greater London Council (1984).

11. P. Gilroy, *There ain't no Black in the Union Jack*, London, Hutchinson (1988).

12. H. Cain and N. Yuval-Davis, op. cit.; A. Phillips, *Engendering Democracy*, Cambridge, Polity Press (1991).

13. F. Anthias and N. Yuval-Davis, op. cit.

14. B. Bottomley, 'Culture, Ethnicity and the Politics/Poetics of Representation', *Diaspora*, (1) 3:302–320 (1991).

15. A. Chhachhi in D. Kandiyotti (ed.), *Women, the State and Islam*, London, Macmillan (1992).

16. A. Brah, 'Difference, Diversity, Differentiation', in S. Allen, F. Anthias and N. Yuval-Davis (eds.), *Gender, Race and Class*, special issue of *International Review of Sociology* (1991) 2:53–72, p. 58.

17. J. Bourne, *Homelands of the Mind: Jewish Feminism and Identity Politics*, Race and Class Pamphlet, 11 (1987).

18. H. Cain and N. Yuval-Davis, op. cit.

19. K. Mercer (ed.), *Black Film/British Cinema*, ICA documents, British Film Institute (1988).

20. Ibid., p. 12.

21. A. Rattanzi, 'Changing the Subject? Racism, Culture and Education', in D. James and A. Rattanzi (eds.), *'Race', Culture and Difference*, London, Sage (1992); F. Anthias and N. Yuval-Davis, op. cit.; G. Sahgal and N. Yuval-Davis (eds.), *Refusing Holy Orders: Women and Fundamentalism in Britain*, London, Virago (1992).

22. N. Glazer and P. Moynihan, *Beyond the Melting Pot*, Cambridge, Mass., MIT Press (1965); N. Glazer and P. Moynihan, *Ethnicity*,

Theory and Experience, Cambridge, Mass., Harvard University Press (1975); S. Wallman, *Ethnicity at Work*, London, Macmillan (1979); J. Watson, *Between Two Cultures*, Oxford, Blackwell (1977).

23. G. Sahgal and N. Yuval-Davis, op. cit.

24. Ibid.

25. H. Afshar, *Three Generations of Muslim Women in Bradford*, paper presented at the CSE Conference, London (1989); N. Yuval-Davis, 'Jewish Fundamentalism and Women's Empowerment', in G. Sahgal and N. Yuval-Davis, op. cit.

26. G. C. Spivak, 'Reflection on Cultural Studies in the Post-colonial Conjuncture', in *Cultural Studies: Crossing Borders*, special issue of *Critical Studies* 3(1):63–78 (1991).

27. R. Johnson, 'Frameworks of Culture and Power: Complexity and Politics in Cultural Studies', *Cultural Studies*, op. cit., p. 17.

28. M. Foucault, 'Truth and Power', in C. Gordon (ed.), *Power/Knowledge: Selected Interviews and Other Writings 1972–1977*, Brighton, Harvester Press (1980).

29. N. Yuval-Davis, 'The Bearers of the Collective: Women and Religious Legislation in Israel', *Feminist Review*, 3 (1980); N. Yuval-Davis and F. Anthias, *Woman – Nation – State*, London, Macmillan (1989); S. Walby, 'Woman and Nation', in *International Journal of Comparative Sociology*, 32:1–2, January–April 1992; N. Yuval-Davis, *Gender and Nation*, London, Sage (1997).

30. C. Pateman, *The Sexual Contract*, Cambridge, Polity Press (1989); U. Vogel, 'Is Citizenship Gender Specific?', paper presented at the Political Science Association Annual Conference, April 1989.

31. D. Kandiyotti (ed.), *Women, the State and Islam*, London, Macmillan (1991).

32. Especially of the lower classes – e.g. E. Wilson, *Women and the Welfare State*, London, Tavistock (1977); A. Showstack Sassoon (ed.), *Women and the State*, London, Hutchinson (1987).

33. T. H. Marshall, *Citizenship and Social Class*, Cambridge, Cambridge University Press (1950); T. H. Marshall, *Social Policy in the Twentieth Century*, London, Hutchinson (1965); T. H. Marshall, *The Right to Welfare and Other Essays*, London, Heinemann Educational (1981).

34. b. hooks, 'Sisterhood, Political Solidarity between Women', in Sneja Gunew (ed.), *Feminist Knowledge: Critique and Construct*, London, Routledge (1990), p. 29.

35. J. Kimble and E. Unterhalter, '"We opened the road for you, you must go forward": ANC/Women's Struggles 1912–1982', *Feminist Review*, 12 (1982); F. Anthias and N. Yuval-Davis, 'Contextualizing Feminism: Gender, Ethnic and Class Divisions', *Feminist Review*, 15 (1984); E. Spelman, *The Inessential Woman*, London, The Women's Press (1988); P. Hill Collins, op. cit.; N. Yuval-Davis, *Gender and Nation*, London, Sage (1997).

36. See the critique of M. Barrett and M. McIntosh, 'Ethnocentrism in Socialist Feminism', *Feminist Review*, 20 (1985); and of F. Anthias and N. Yuval-Davis, 'Contextualizing Feminism: Gender, Ethnic and Class Divisions', *Feminist Review*, 15 (1984).

37. G. C. Spivak, op. cit., p. 65.

38. S. Hall, 'Minimal Selves', in *Identity, the Real Me*, London, ICA document 6 (1987), p. 44.

39. Caryn McTighe Musil in L. Albrecht and R. Brewer (eds.), *Bridges of Power, Women's Multicultural Alliances*, Philadelphia, New Society Publishers (1990), p. vi.

40. G. Pheterson, 'Alliances between Women – Overcoming Internalized Oppression and Internalized Domination', in L. Albrecht and R. Brewer (eds.), op. cit.

41. Ibid., p. 3.

42. N. Yuval-Davis, 'Zionism, Anti-semitism, and the Struggle against Racism', *Spare Rib*, 18–22 September 1984.

43. L. Gordon, *On Difference Genders*, 10, spring 1991: 91–111, p. 103.

44. B. Thornton Dill, 'The Dialectics of Black Womanhood', in S. Harding (ed.), *Feminism and Methodology*, Indiana, Bloomington (1988), p. 106.

45. R. Brunt, 'The Politics of Identity', in S. Hall and M. Jacques (eds.), *New Times*, London, Lawrence & Wishart (1989).

46. Ibid., p. 150.

47. Ibid., p. 158.

48. P. Hill Collins, op. cit.

49. Ibid., p. 236.

50. E. Barkley Brown, 'African-American Women's Quilting: A Framework for Conceptualizing and Teaching African-American Women's History', *Signs* 14(4):921–9, p. 922.

51. M. Walker, 'Sisters Take the Wraps Off the Brothers', *Guardian*, 6 May 1993.

52. A. Bookman and S. Morgen, op. cit.
53. G. Bottomley, op. cit., p. 309.
54. A version of this appeared in *Feminism and Psychology*, 4(1):179–97 (1994).

5. THOUGHTS OF A LATECOMER

1. D. Merkin, 'A Closet of One's Own: On Not Becoming a Lesbian', *Tikkun*, 10(6):21 (1995).
2. J. Kramer, 'The Invisible Woman', *New Yorker*, 26 February & March 1996, pp. 145–7 (n.b. 'the invisible woman' of the title is not a lesbian, although, given the remarkable lack of lesbian presence in an issue devoted to the current status of feminism in the United States, one might easily have made that assumption.)
3. *The Book of Discipline* of the United Methodist Church, paragraph 402.2.
4. From an interview with Alison Bernstein.
5. *The New York Times*, 22 May 1995, p. A13.
6. R. Robson, 'Mother: The Legal Domestication of Lesbian Existence', in M. A. Fineman and J. Karpin (eds.), *Mothers in Law: Feminist Theory and the Legal Regulation of Motherhood*, New York, Columbia University Press (1995).
7. *The New York Times*, 22 December 1995, p. A24.
8. *The New York Times*, 22 May 1995, p. A13. Writing for the majority, Justice A. Christian Compton said: 'Living daily under conditions stemming from active lesbianism practised in the home may impose a burden upon a child by reason of the "social condemnation" attached to such an arrangement, which will inevitably afflict the child's relationships with its peers and with the community.' The law may couch its opinion more elegantly, but its rhetoric of backlash sanctions the grandmother's.
9. F. Rich, 'Bashing to Victory', *The New York Times*, 14 February 1996, p. A21.
10. *Denver Post*, 10 October 1995. Article included in fundraising literature from The Gay and Lesbian Task Force.
11. P. Robertson, quoted by Terry Castle in *The Apparitional Lesbian: Female Homosexuality and Modern Culture*, New York, Columbia University Press (1993), pp. 5–6.

12. As Lillian Faderman tells the rest of the story, 'Millay answered with the nonchalance requisite for a true bohemian: "Oh, you mean I'm homosexual! Of course I am, and heterosexual too, but what's that got to do with my headache?"' *Odd Girls and Twilight Lovers: A History of Lesbian Life in Twentieth-Century America*, New York, Columbia University Press (1991), p. 82.

13. S. Lipsitz Bem, *The Lenses of Gender*, New Haven, Yale University Press (1993), p. vii.

14. A. Rich, 'Compulsory Heterosexuality and Lesbian Existence', in Elizabeth Abel and Emily K. Abel (eds.), *The SIGNS Reader: Women, Gender, and Scholarship*, Chicago and London, University of Chicago Press (1983), p. 156.

15. M. Wittig, 'One Is Not Born a Woman', in Henry Abelove, Michele Aina Barale and David M. Halperin (eds.), *The Lesbian and Gay Reader*, New York and London, Routledge (1993), p. 105.

16. Although it might become legally possible in the very near future: in August 1996 a court in Hawaii will hear a case that could possibly lead to the legal recognition of same-sex marriage in that state. Horrified by that possibility, a Republican-dominated Congress passed the Defense of Marriage Act this summer; it has already been signed by President Clinton. The Defense of Marriage Act provides for the first time a federal definition of marriage as a contract between a man and a woman. It also grants states the power not to recognize same-sex marriages performed in other states. If Hawaii passes its bill and states exercise their power of non-recognition, a series of constitutional challenges will have to be initiated on behalf of people who, yet again, only want the same rights to be extended to them as are guaranteed to the rest of the population in the United States. The backlash continues.

6. THE END OF A LONG MARRIAGE

1. M. Bodkin, *Archetypal Patterns in Poetry*, Oxford University Press, London (1948).

2. L. Trilling, Introduction to Jane Austen's *Emma*, New York, Houghton Mifflin (1957).

3. E. Moers, *Literary Women*, New York, Doubleday (1976).

4. L. Trilling, *The Liberal Imagination*, New York, Viking (1951).

5. J. Atlas, *Battle of the Books: The Curriculum Debate in America*, New York, W. W. Norton (1992).

6. C. Jordan, *Renaissance Feminism: Literary Texts and Political Models*, Ithaca, Cornell University Press (1990).

7. W. Booth, 'Bakhtin and the Challenge of Feminist Criticism', *Critical Enquiry* (1992).

8. Clark, Emerson and Channing (eds.), *Memoirs of Margaret Fuller*, vol. 1, Boston, Simpson (1852).

9. G. Green and C. Kahn (eds.), *Changing Subjects: The Making of Feminist Literary Criticism*, New York, Routledge (1993).

10. Toni Morrison (ed. with an introduction), *Race-ing Justice, Engendering Power: Essays on Anita Hill, Clarence Thomas and the Construction of Social Reality*, New York, Pantheon Books (1992).

11. E. Walsh, *Divided Lives*, New York, Simon and Schuster (1995).

7. HOMOPHOBIA AND HEGEMONY

1. S. Freud, *Three Essays on the Theory of Sexuality*, Standard Edition, vol. 7 (1905), pp. 123–245.

2. K. Lewes, *The Psychoanalytic Theory of Male Homosexuality*, London, Quartet (1989).

3. N. O'Connor and J. Ryan, *Wild Desires and Mistaken Identities: Lesbianism and Psychoanalysis*, London, Virago and New York, Columbia University Press (1993).

4. C. W. Socarides, *The Overt Homosexual*, New York, Grune and Stratton (1968).

5. C. W. Socarides, 'The Erosion of Heterosexuality', *Washington Times*, 5 July 1994.

6. K. Lewes, op. cit.

7. I. Rosen, *Sexual Deviation*, Oxford, Oxford University Press (1979).

8. J. Rayner, 'Shrink Resistant', *Guardian*, 25 April 1995.

9. The Letter of Concern was initiated by Andrew Samuels, myself and Mary Lynne Ellis, following discussion at one of the planning meetings of PCSR, Psychotherapists and Counsellors for Social Responsibility, a broadly based group set up to address issues of social and political concern.

10. A. M. Smith, 'Hegemony Trouble: The Political Theories of Judith Butler, Ernesto Laclau and Chantal Mouffe', in J. Weeks (ed.), *The*

Lesser Evil and the Greater Good, London, Rivers Oram Press (1994).

11. A. M. Smith, 'Resisting the Erasure of Lesbian Sexuality: A Challenge for Queer Activism', in K. Plummer (ed.), *Modern Homosexualities: Fragments of Lesbian and Gay Experience*, London, Routledge (1992).

12. For a full account of this see V. Carter, 'Abseil Makes the Heart Grow Fonder: Lesbian and Gay Campaigning Tactics and Section 28', in K. Plummer (ed.), op. cit.

13. P. Romans, 'Daring to Pretend? Motherhood and Lesbianism', in K. Plummer (ed.), op. cit.

14. N. O'Connor and J. Ryan, op. cit.

15. J. McDougall, *Plea for a Measure of Abnormality*, New York, International Universities Press (1980). For a critique of McDougall's theories about lesbianism, see N. O'Connor and J. Ryan, op. cit.

16. J. Chasseguet-Smirgel, *Creativity and Perversion*, London, Free Association Books (1984).

17. For a review of this literature, see C. Kitzinger, *The Social Construction of Lesbianism*, London, Sage (1987).

18. C. W. Socarides, *The Overt Homosexual*.

19. J. McDougall, 'The Dead Father: On Early Psychic Trauma and Its Relation to Disturbance in Sexual Identity and in Creative Activity', *International Journal of Psychoanalysis*, 70:205–19 (1989).

20. S. Freud, 'Psychogenesis of a Case of Female Homosexuality', Standard Edition, vol. 18 (1920), pp. 145–72.

21. M-L. Ellis, 'Lesbians, Gay Men and Training', *Free Associations* (4) 32 (1994). See also article in the *Independent on Sunday*, 25 August 1994.

22. K. Lewes, op. cit.

23. H. P. Hildebrand, 'A Patient Dying with Aids', *International Review of Psychoanalysis*, 19:457–69 (1992). M. Burgner, 'Working with the HIV Patient: A Psychoanalytic Approach', *Psychoanalytic Psychotherapy* (8)3:201–13 (1994).

24. J. Rose, 'Hannah Segal Interview', in *Women: A Cultural Review* (1)2, Oxford, Oxford University Press (1990).

25. J. Padel, 'The Ego in Current Thinking', in G. Kohon (ed.), *The British School of Psychoanalysis: The Independent Tradition*, London, Free Association Books (1986).

26. For a general review of such studies, see C. J. Patterson, 'Children of Lesbian and Gay Parents', *Child Development*, 63:1025–42 (1992).

27. S. Golombok, S. Spencer and M. Rutter, 'Children in Lesbian and

Single-parent Households: Psychosexual and Psychiatric Appraisal', *Journal of Child Psychology and Psychiatry* (24)4:551–72 (1983).

28. R. Greenson, 'On Homosexuality and Gender Identity', *International Journal of Psychoanalysis*, 7:217–19.

29. H. Segal in E. H. Baruch and L. J. Serrano (eds.), *Women Analyze Women*, New York, New York University Press (1988), p. 250.

30. See J. Rayner, op. cit.

31. C. W. Socarides, 'The Erosion of Heterosexuality'.

32. H. P. Hildebrand, op. cit.

33. John Bowis, Under-Secretary for Health, in a speech to a MIND conference, as reported in the *Observer*, 18 June 1995.

34. J. Laplanche and J.-B. Pontalis, *The Language of Psychoanalysis*, London, Hogarth Press (1973).

35. R. D. Hinshelwood, *A Dictionary of Kleinian Thought*, London, Free Associations Books (1989).

36. The letter, which was mainly circulated after the date of the lecture, did not in any way suggest it should be prevented. The cancellation of the lecture in response to alleged threats (never proved) from activist groups outside the profession was not part of our aim or strategy.

8. (ANTI)FEMINISM AFTER COMMUNISM

1. Except in the indirect sense of a nineteenth-century legacy reinterpreted and exploited via Marxism.

2. See P. Watson, 'Civil Society and the Politicization of Difference in Eastern Europe', in J. W. Scott and C. Kaplan (eds.), *Transitions, Environments, Translations: The Meanings of Feminism in Contemporary Politics*, New York, Routledge (1997).

3. The last two East–West meetings of feminists which I have attended (one at the Institute for Advanced Study, Princeton, in April 1995, the other a meeting of the Central European University Gender and Culture Group at the University of Essex in November 1995) culminated in practically identical scenes. At the end of the formal sessions, which were mostly concerned with Eastern Europe, the issue of 'the crisis of Western feminism' was raised informally; this was a completely new idea which stunned the East European women present.

4. J. W. Scott, *Only Paradoxes to Offer*, Cambridge, Harvard University

Press (1996). The motive of 'paradox' which runs through the present chapter derives from Joan Scott's work.

5. I. Grewal and C. Kaplan (eds.), Introduction to *Scattered Hegemonies: Postmodernity and Transnational Feminist Practices*, Minneapolis, University of Minnesota Press (1994).

6. M. Adamik, 'Feminism in Hungary', *East European Reporter* (1991), 4(4):26–7.

7. See, e.g., M. Grünell, 'Feminism Meets Scepticism: Women's Studies in the Czech Republic', *European Journal of Women's Studies* (1995), 2(1):101–11; M. Molyneux, 'Women's Rights and the International Context: Some Reflections on the Post-communist States', *Millennium: Journal of International Studies* (1994), 23(2):287–313; P. Chamberlayne, 'Gender and the Private Sphere: A Touchstone of Misunderstanding between Eastern and Western Germany', *Social Politics* (1995), 2(1):25–36 A. Snitow, 'Feminist Future in the Former East Bloc', *Peace and Democracy News*, VII (1994), 1(1):40–44; B. Einhorn, *Cinderella Goes to Market: Citizenship, Gender and Women's Movements in East-Central Europe*, London, Verso (1993); G. Waylen, 'Women and Democratization: Conceptualizing Gender Relations in Transition Politics', *World Politics*, 46, April 1994, pp. 327–54; M. Ferree, 'Patriarchies and Feminisms: The Two Women's Movements of Post-Unification Germany', *Social Politics* (1995), 2(1):10–24; N. Funk, 'The Fate of Feminism in Eastern Europe', *Chronicle of Higher Education*, 2 February 1994.

8. de Seve, 'Youth Dissent and Transition: Gender's not so Silent Part', p. 2. Paper given at the ESRC Research Seminar on Class, Gender and Ethnicity in Post-communist States, London University Institute of Latin American Studies, 15 October 1995. This is a reference to a remark made by Jiřina Šmejkalová-Strickland.

9. Ibid., pp. 22–3.

10. B. Einhorn, op. cit., p. 183.

11. Fontaine, quoted by R. Dahrendorf, *Reflections on the Revolution in Europe*, London, Chatto and Windus (1990).

12. Quoted by B. Einhorn, op. cit., p. 204.

13. N. Funk, op. cit.

14. Lipovskaya, quoted by B. Einhorn, op. cit., p. 202.

15. J. Siklova, 'McDonalds, Terminators, Coca Cola Ads – And Feminism? Imports from the West', in S. Trnka (ed.), *Bodies of Bread*

and Butter: Reconfiguring Women's Lives in the Post-Communist Czech Republic, Praha, Prague Gender Studies Centre (1993), p. 10.

16. The exception was Romania.

17. J. W. Scott, 'Gender: A Useful Category of Historical Analysis', in E. Weed (ed.), *Coming to Terms: Feminism, Theory, Politics*, New York and London, Routledge (1989), p. 98.

18. J. Heinen and J. Kiss, 'The Second "No": Women in Hungary', *Feminist Review* (1991), 39:53. For an analysis of reproduction issues in Hungary, Romania and Poland, see S. Gal, 'Gender in the Post-socialist Transition: The Abortion Debate in Hungary', *East European Politics and Societies* (1994) 8(2):256–286; G. Kligman, 'The Politics of Reproduction in Ceaucescu's Romania: A Case Study in Political Culture', *East European Politics and Societies* (1992), p. 6; and A. Matuchniak-Krasvska and J. Heinen, *L'Avortement en Pologne: la croix et la bannière*, Paris, L'Harmattan (1992).

19. Personal communication. 'That is one thing I really do hold against my son,' said his elderly mother. 'After all, what is an abortion? It's such a little thing.'

20. See P. Watson, 'Gender Relations, Education and Social Change in Poland', *Gender and Education* (1992), 4(1–2): 127–47.

21. Bielicki, quoted by P. Watson, 'The Rise of Masculinism in Eastern Europe', *New Left Review* (1993), 198:71–82.

22. Stankevich, quoted by T. Klimenkova, 'What Does Our New Democracy Offer Society?', in A. Posadskaya (ed.), *Women in Russia*, London, Verso (1994), p. 24.

23. Personal communication, November 1994.

24. T. Klimenkova, op. cit., p. 24.

25. Personal communication.

26. M. S. Fong and G. Paull, *The Changing Role of Women in Employment in Eastern Europe*, Washington, World Bank, February 1992, p. 19.

27. *Europe Express*, 7 May 1993.

28. C. Hann, 'After Communism: Reflections on East European Anthropology and the "Transition"', *Social Anthropology* (1994), 2(3):229–49, p. 245.

29. A. Reading, *Polish Women, Solidarity and Feminism*, Basingstoke, Macmillan (1992).

30. Quoted in ibid., p. 15.

31. I. Grewal and C. Kaplan, op. cit., p. 7; see also S. P. Mohanty, 'Us

and Them: On the Philosophical Bases of Political Criticism', *Yale Journal of Criticism* (1989), 2(2):1–31.

32. A. Rattansi and S. Westwood, *Racism, Modernity and Identity: On the Western Front*, Cambridge, Polity Press (1994).

33. J. Alexander, *Fin de Siècle Social Theory: Relativism, Reduction and the Problem of Reason*, London, Verso (1995).

34. Ibid., p. 39.

35. B. Einhorn, op. cit., pp. 256–7. See also A. Milić, 'Women and Nationalism in the Former Yugoslavia', in N. Funk and M. Mueller (eds.), *Gender Politics and Post-Communism: Reflections from Eastern Europe and the Former Soviet Union*, New York, Routledge (1993), p. 111: 'In the power struggle between communism and anticommunism, nationalism has won out and democracy was again the loser.' Similarly, T. Rener and M. Ule (n.d.), 'Nationalism and Gender in Postsocialist Societies – Is Nationalism Female?' Unpublished MS, p. 7, note that the 'advocacy of "the return of women to the family" is closely related to national–ideological rhetoric, since according to such conceptions only women, who have dedicated themselves exclusively to their families, are capable of preserving traditional values and the national consciousness of new generations . . . What is new about it is that the postsocialist societies following national ideologies [do not] notice the historical shift of the position and perception of women which has taken place in developed European societies [whereby a woman] confines her life, work and needs less and less to her gender identity and . . . her family role.' See also R. Tsagarousianou, 'God, Patria and Home: "Reproductive politics" and Nationalist (Re)definitions of Women in East/Central Europe', *Social Identities* (1993), 1(2):283–95; S. L. Mayhall, 'Gendered Nationalism and "New" Nation-states: "Democratic Progress" in Eastern Europe', *Fletcher Forum of World Affairs* (1993), 17(2):91–100; F. Millard, 'The Catholic Church and Women in Poland', Paper presented to Women and Gender Relations in Russia, the Former Soviet Union and Eastern Europe Seminar, Centre for Russian and East European Studies, University of Birmingham, 15 November 1995.

36. K. Verdery, 'From Parent-state to Family Patriarchs: Gender and Nation in Contemporary Eastern Europe', *East European Politics and Societies* (1994), 8(2):225–55.

37. Ibid., p. 254, n. 92.

38. Ibid., p. 254. A similar link between communism and nationalism is made by R. Pearson, 'The Geopolitics of People Power: The pursuit of the Nation-state in East Central Europe', *Journal of International Affairs* (1992), 45(2):499–518, p. 499, who writes: 'Within the East European context, the scene was set for a twentieth century in which the nation-state was pursued with a passion all the more consuming because of its successive encouragement and then frustration through external intervention.' Likewise, Michael Walzer has written that the 'tribes have returned, and the drama of their return is greatest where their repression was most severe' (M. Walzer, 'The New Tribalism: Notes on a Difficult Problem', *Dissent*, spring (1992):164–71, p. 164).

39. See, for example, S. Gal, op. cit., K. Verdery, op. cit., G. Kligman, op. cit., J. Govan, *The Gendered Foundations of Hungarian Socialism: State, society and the anti-politics of anti-feminism, 1949–1990*, Ph.D. Dissertation, University of California (1993).

40. Christian Joppke suggests that East Germany was the exception in this regard. (C. Joppke, 'Intellectuals, Nationalism and the Exit from Communism: The Case of East Germany', *Comparative Studies in Society and History*, 37, April 1995, pp. 213–41.)

41. A. Arato, 'Civil Society Against the State: Poland 1980–1981', *Telos* (1981), 47:23–47.

42. See, for example, J. Staniszkis, *The Ontology of Socialism*, Oxford, Clarendon Press (1992); M. Marody, 'Social Stability and the Concept of Collective Sense', in J. Koralewicz, I. Bialecki and P. Watson (eds.), *Crisis and Transition: Polish Society in the 1980s*, Oxford, Berg Publishers (1987). The material and psychological importance of the family under state socialism is reflected in the fact that mortality trends among the married and non-married were quite different for the Eastern European countries for which data are so far available (see P. Watson, 'Explaining Rising Mortality among Men in Eastern Europe', *Social Science and Medicine* (1995), 41(7):923–34). Data from Hungary, the former GDR and Poland show that rising mortality among men between the mid-1960s and 1990 was overwhelmingly concentrated among the non-married.

43. S. Nowak, 'Values and Attitudes of the Polish People', *Scientific American* (1981) 245 (1):23–31.

44. See P. Watson, 'Gender Relations, Education and Social Change in

Poland', p. 139; I. Dölling, 'Between Hope and Helplessness: Women in the GDR', *Feminist Review*, 39:3 – 15.

45. P. Watson, 'Eastern Europe's Silent Revolution: Gender', *Sociology* (1993), 27 (3):471 – 87.

46. I owe this phrasing to Ann Snitow.

47. See P. Watson, *Transitions, Environments, Translations*.

48. Verdery, op. cit., p. 255.

49. Renan, quoted by Tsagarousianou, op. cit.

50. See Alexander, op. cit.

51. Quoted in J. Szacki, *Liberalizm Po Komunizmie, Warszawa: Społeczny Instytut Wydawniczy Znak* (1994), p. 195. See also R. Gortat, 'Liberalizm jako Konstruktywizm', *Przeglad Społeczny*, 6 (1992); C. Offe, 'Capitalism by Democratic Design? Democratic Theory Facing the Triple Transition in East Central Europe', *Social Research* (1991), 48 (4):865 – 901.

52. P. Gowan, 'Neo-liberal Theory and Practice in Eastern Europe', *New Left Review* (1995), 213: 3 – 60, p. 46.

53. F. Fukuyama, *The End of History and the Last Man*, London, Hamish Hamilton (1992).

54. See J. M. Barbalet, *Citizenship*, Milton Keynes, Open University Press (1988), p. 17. Note: The argument which I present in the following paragraphs also appears in P. Watson (1997), op. cit.

55. Marshall, quoted by Barbalet, op. cit.

56. J. Heinen, 'Unemployment and Women's Attitudes in Poland', *Social Politics* (1995), 2(1):91 – 110.

57. Author's interview with Union representatives in Szczecin Shipyard, September 1994.

58. Ferree, op. cit., p. 16.

This chapter forms part of a larger project entitled *Civil Society and the Mobilization of Difference*, which is funded by the John D. and Catherine T. MacArthur Foundation.

9. 'DAMNED IF YOU DO AND DAMNED IF YOU DON'T'

1. I chose abortion because it is a worldwide emergency, and the situation of working mothers because it is one of my main fields of interest. I chose to ignore the new reproductive technologies, not

because the question was irrelevant here, but because there is already a great deal of feminist literature on the subject.

2. A. Smyth, 'A (Political) Postcard from a Peripheral Pre-postmodern State (of Mind) or How Alliteration and Parenthesis can Knock You Down Dead in Women's Studies', *Women's Studies International Forum* (1992), 15 (3):331–7.

3. According to a recent national survey carried out by the SWG Research Institute, Trieste, 1993 (unpublished). Thanks to Chiara Perini of the SWG for showing me these data.

4. N. Rasmussen and P. Moss, *L'emploi des parents et la garde des enfants*, Copenhagen, Ministère des Affaires Sociales (1993).

5. ISTAT, *Rapporto Annuale, La Situazione del Paese*, Rome, ISTAT (1994).

6. Five cases were reported between April and July 1995.

7. Personally, I do not believe that Italian males are 'worse' than their other occidental counterparts. Patriarchy and machismo assume different forms in different cultures, and it is not easy to assess the degree of oppression men exert on women in different countries. This kind of assessment would be a very worthy comparative research project.

8. M. J. Saurel-Cubizolles, P. Romito and J. Garcia, 'Description of Maternity Rights in France, Italy and in the United Kingdom', *European Journal of Public Health* (1993), 3 (1):48–53.

9. Another Italian paradox: a virulently anti-communist coalition in a country where communists are almost extinct.

10. G. Letherby, 'Mother or Not, Mother or What? Problems of Definition and Identity', *Women's Studies International Forum* (1994), 17 (5): 525–32, p. 527. See also A. Rich, *Of Woman Born*, New York, Norton and Comp (1996); S. Ruddick, 'Maternal thinking', *Feminist Studies* (1980), 6 (2):342–67; C. Gilligan, *In a Different Voice: Psychological Theory and Women's Development*, Harvard, Mass., Harvard University Press (1992).

11. See J. Stacey, 'Are Feminists Afraid to Leave Home? The Challenge of Conservative Pro-family Feminism', in J. Mitchell and A. Oakley (eds.), *What Is Feminism?* Oxford, Blackwell (1986); L. Segal, *Is the Future Female? Troubled Thoughts on Contemporary Feminism*, London, Virago (1987); C. Delphy, 'Changing Women in a Changing Europe. Is "Difference" the Future of Feminism?' *Women's Studies International Forum* (1994), 17 (2/3):187–201.

12. L. Passerini, 'The Interpretation of Democracy in the Italian Women's Movement of the 1970s and 1980s', *Women's Studies International Forum* (1994), 17 (2/3):235–9.

13. Libreria delle Donne di Milano (ed.), *Non credere di avere dei diritti. La generazione della libertà femminile nell'idea e nelle vicende di un gruppo di donne*, Torino, Rosenberg e Sellier (1987).

14. See J. Travers, 'Il femminismo e il pensiero della differenza', *Il paese delle donne* (1992), 27–9:3–4.

15. This group has several things in common with that of Antoinette Fouque in France: the psychoanalytic origins; the central role of an authoritative female guru; and the active opposition to many feminist campaigns, such as those to defend the abortion law. See C. Delphy, 'Les origines du Mouvement de libération des femmes en France', *Nouvelles Questions Féministes* (1991), 16–18:137–48.

16. L. Irigaray, *Il tempo della differenza*, Rome, Editori Riuniti (1989).

17. Ibid., p. 62.

18. Ibid., pp. 4–5.

19. For a critique, see M. Guerlais, 'Vers une nouvelle idéologie du droit statutaire: Le temps de la différence de Luce Irigaray', *Nouvelles Questions Féministes* (1991), 16–18:63–92.

20. See M. Mafai, 'Mamma è più bello . . . La capriola delle donne PDS', *La Repubblica*, 10 January 1992, and I. Dominijanni, 'Mamma è bello. Maternità, aborto, autodeterminazione. Un convegno', *Il Manifesto*, 10 January 1992.

21. See R. Tatafiore, 'Potenza materna e bandiere elettorali', *Il Manifesto*, 16 January 1992, and E. Donini, 'Non tutte madri, non solo madri', *Il Manifesto*, 31 January 1992.

22. This heartfelt concern for families is, however, limited to Italian ones. As for non-EU immigrants and refugees, despite the existence of legislation allowing for families to be reunited it is extremely difficult for them to see this right recognized and have their spouses and children with them.

23. C. Delphy, 'Changing Women in a Changing Europe', p. 195.

24. A. Oakley, A. McPherson and H. Roberts, *Miscarriage*, London, Fontana (1984), p. 191.

25. G. Letherby, op. cit., p. 525; see also A. Woollett, 'Having Children: Accounts of Childless Women and Women with Reproductive Problems', in A. Phoenix *et al.* (eds.), *Motherhood: Meanings, Practices and Ideologies*, London, Sage (1991).

26. See C. Delphy, 'Changing Women in a Changing Europe' and G. Letherby, op. cit.

27. The full title of the law is 'Measures Regarding the Social Protection of Motherhood and the Voluntary Termination of Pregnancy'.

28. R. Salemi, *Sulla pelle delle donne*, Milan, Rizzoli (1989).

29. The Pope is much softer on capital punishment: he thinks it should be avoided whenever possible, except when absolutely necessary for the protection of society. He had never advised young men to refuse to fight in the various wars going on around the world, or even to be conscientious objectors in peacetime (which is the way to avoid national service in Italy, albeit far more difficult to do than object to abortion). Speaking to young conscripts in 1989, he said that war 'may be justified' on certain occasions and that military service 'is by its very nature, very dignified, very beautiful, very kind' ('Il Papa ai soldati: La guerra può essere giustificata', *Corriere della Sera*, 3 April 1989).

30. 'Cattolici si, ma non in farmacia', *La Repubblica*, 7 April 1995.

31. G. Erdenet, 'RU 486, le chiffre de la Bête. Le mouvement contre le droit des femmes à l'avortement en France', *Nouvelles Questions Féministes* (1992), 13 (3):29–43.

32. 'Aborto "consentito" dal parroco', *Il Piccolo*, 30 May 1995.

33. See S. Faludi, *Backlash*, London, Chatto and Windus (1991); J. Hoff, 'Comparative Analysis of Abortion in Ireland, Poland and the United States', *Women's Studies International Forum* (1994), 17 (6):621–46.

34. H. Jankowska, 'The Reproductive Rights Campaign in Poland', *Women's Studies International Forum* (1993), 16 (3):291–96; J. Hoff, op. cit.

35. R. Dixon-Mueller, 'Abortion Policy and Women's Health in Developing Countries', *International Journal of Health Services* (1990), 20 (2):297–314.

36. Thanks to Geneviève Cresson for this information.

37. T. Sheldon, 'Dutch Contraceptive Plan Attracts Criticism', *British Medical Journal* (1995), 310:487.

38. See R. Salemi, op. cit., and more recently in 1995 the proposition put forward by D'Alema, the secretary of PDS.

39. See, for example, the article by C. Mancina, 'L'errore delle donne', *La Repubblica*, 2 July 1995.

40. With a few exceptions: see C. Cacciari, 'Il rito dell'aborto', in C. Cacciari and F. Pizzini (eds.), *La donna paziente*, Milan, Unicopli (1985).

41. L. Evans, 'Italy has Europe's Highest Caesarean Section Rate', *British Medical Journal* (1995), 310:487.

42. The same trend has been observed in the United States. See M. Shearer, 'Maternity Patients' Movements in the United States' in I. Chalmers, M. Enkin and M. J. N. C. Keirse (eds.), *Effective Care in Pregnancy and Childbirth*, Oxford, Oxford University Press (1989).

43. Istituto Superiore de Sanità, quoted by *La Repubblica*, 5 May 1995.

44. All the known instances involve a male doctor. See, for example, the recent case of an objector gynaecologist who raped his patients after the operation. 'Stupra la donna che fa abortire', *La Repubblica*, 20 May 1995.

45. R. Salemi, op. cit.

46. C. Delphy, 'Egalité, équivalence et equité: La position de l'Etat français au regard du droit international', *Nouvelles Questions Féministes* (1995), 16 (1):5–58.

47. P. Lunneberg, *Abortion: A Positive Decision*, New York, Bergin and Garvey (1992).

48. Ibid., p. 106.

49. These differences can be explained by the instrument used to evaluate depression and the characteristics of the women studied. For a review see P. Romito, 'Postpartum Depression and the Experience of Motherhood', *Acta Obstetrica et Gynecologica Scandinavica*, Supplement 154 (1990).

50. S. Henshaw, 'Induced Abortion: A World Review, 1990', *Family Planning Perspectives* (1990), 22:76–89.

51. J. Lanman, S. Kohl and J. Bedell, 'Changes in Pregnancy Outcome after Liberalization of the New York State Abortion Law', *American Journal of Obstetrics and Gynecology* (1974), 15:485–92; J. Parker and F. Nelson, 'Factors in the Unprecedented Decline in Infant Mortality in New York City', *Bulletin of the New York Academy of Medicine* (1974), 50 (7):839–67.

52. H. David, 'Born Unwanted: Longterm Developmental Effects of Denied Abortion', *Journal of Social Issues* (1992), 48 (3):163–81.

53. These responses were given in a research project on 'Work and the Health of Mothers after the Birth of a Child' carried out in a northeast region of Italy. Data were collected from mothers on three occasions: in hospital shortly after birth, and when their babies were five and twelve months old. A total of 820 mothers provided inform-

ation after birth, and 772 and 738 at the next two stages. The data are still being analysed. The study was part of a collaborative project involving France (co-ordinator M. J. Saurel-Cubizolles of INSERM, Paris) and Spain (co-ordinator V. Escribà of IVESP, Valencia).

54. J. Astbury, S. Brown, J. Lumley and R. Small, 'Birth Events, Birth Experiences and Social Differences in Postnatal Depression', *Australian Journal of Public Health* (1994), 18 (2):176–84; A. Oakley, *Women Confined*, Oxford, Martin Robertson (1980); A. Oakley and L. Rajan, 'Obstetric Technology and Maternal Emotional Well-being', *Journal of Reproductive and Infant Psychology* (1990), 8:45–55; P. Romito, 'La naissance du premier enfant', *Etude psychosociale de l'expérience de la maternité et de la dépression post-partum*, Lausanne, Delachaux et Niestlé (1990); A. Stein, *et al.*, 'Social Adversity and Perinatal Complications: Their Relation to Postnatal Depression', *British Medical Journal* (1989), 298:1073–4; H. Williams and A. Carmichael, 'Depression in Mothers in a Multi-ethnic Urban Industrial Municipality in Melbourne', *Journal of Child Psychology and Psychiatry* (1985), 26 (2):277–88.

55. J. Holland, C. Ramazanoglu, S. Scott, S. Sharpe and R. Thomson, 'Sex, Gender and Power: Young Women's Sexuality in the Shadow of Aids', *Sociology of Health and Illness* (1990), 12 (3):336–48.

56. M. le Doeuff, 'Problèmes d'investiture (de la parité, etc.)', *Nouvelles Questions Féministes* (1995), 16 (2):5–80; C. Delphy, 'Egalité, équivalence et equité'.

57. S. Hite, *The Hite Report: A Nationwide Study of Female Sexuality*, New York, Macmillan (1976).

58. Equal Opportunities Unit, *Mothers, Fathers and Employment 1985–1991*, Brussels, Commission of the European Communities, March 1993.

59. L. Roveri, 'I dati sull'infanzia nelle indagini multiscopo sulle famiglie effettuate dall'ISTAT' in T. Musatti (ed.), *La giornata del mio bambino*, Bologna, Il Mulino (1992).

60. Equal Opportunities Unit, op. cit.

61. M. Kempeneers and E. Lelievre, *Famille et emploi dans l'Europe des Douze, Eurobaromètre*, Bruxelles, Commission des Communautés Européennes (1991).

62. P. Romito, M. J. Saurel-Cubizolles and M. Cuttini, 'Mothers' Health after the Birth of the First Child: The Case of Employed Women in an Italian City', *Women and Health* (1994), 21 (2/3):1–22.

63. See note 53.
64. M. J. Saurel-Cubizolles *et al.*, 'Description of Maternity Rights in France, Italy and in the United Kingdom'.
65. S. McRae, 'Returning to Work after Childbirth: Opportunities and Inequalities', *European Sociological Review* (1993), 9 (2):125–37.
66. S. McRae and W. Daniel, *Maternity Rights in Britain: First Findings*, London, Policy Studies Institute (1991).
67. P. Moss, *I servizi per l'infanzia nella Comunita Europea 1985–1990*, Bruxelles, Commissione delle Comunità Europee, 31 August 1990.
68. S. McRae, op. cit.
69. What follows would have been superfluous a few years ago, but at a time of backlash such as this it needs to be said. Critics might point out that not all mothers want to go back to work; some actually 'prefer' to stay at home and look after their children full time. Numerous studies show, for example, that there is no association between mothers' mental health and whether they 'work' or not. The important factor is the congruence between their preferences and what they actually do: women who 'work' when they would prefer to stay at home are depressed; women who stay at home when they would rather go out to work are even more depressed (J. Brannen and P. Moss, *Managing Mothers: Dual Earner Households after Maternity Leave*, London, Unwin Hyman (1991); C. Ross, J. Mirowsky, J. Huber, 'Dividing Work, Sharing Work and in between: Marriage Patterns and Depression', *American Sociological Review* (1983), 48:809–23). Regardless of whether women want to go out to work or not, the alternative is total dependence on a man, or on the welfare state (where this still exists).
70. P. Romito and M. J. Saurel-Cubizolles, 'Fair Law, Unfair Practices? Benefiting from Protective Legislation for Pregnant Workers in Italy and France', *Social Science and Medicine* (1992), 35 (12):1485–95.
71. P. Moss, op. cit.
72. P. Ghedini, 'Politiche sociali, famiglia e servizi per i più piccoli', in T. Musatti, op. cit.
73. See note 53.
74. S. Faludi, op. cit.
75. *Il Piccolo*, 29 January 1993.
76. *L'Unità*, 28 January 1993.
77. *La Suisse*, 2 May 1993.

78. A. Poerksen and D. Petitti, 'Employment and Low Birthweight in Black Women', *Social Science and Medicine* (1991), 33:1281–6; M. J. Saurel-Cubizolles and G. Gestin, 'Housewives, Unemployed and Employed Women: Why Different Risks of Preterm Delivery? A French Study', *International Journal of Health Sciences* (1991), 2:83–91; see also M. J. Saurel-Cubizolles and T. M. Kaminski, 'Work in Pregnancy: Its Evolving Relationship with Perinatal Outcome (A Review)', *Social Science and Medicine* (1986), 22 (4):431–42.

79. E. Gold, B. Lasley and M. Schenker, 'Reproductive Hazards: State-of-the-art Reviews', *Occupational Medicine*, 9 (3), Philadelphia, Hanley and Belfus, July–September 1994.

80. P. Romito *et al.*, 'Work and Health in Mothers of Young Children', *International Journal of Health Services* (1994), 24 (4):607–28.

81. La Lèche League International, *L'arte dell'allattamento materno*, Brescia, Opera Pavoniana (1990). The original version, *The Womanly Art of Breastfeeding*, is published by La Lèche League International, PO Box 1209, Franklin Park, Illinois, USA (1987).

82. Ignorant or heedless of the fact that sleep deprivation has well-documented negative effects on mental and physical well-being, and is used as a form of psychological torture.

83. P. van Esterik and T. Greiner, 'Breastfeeding and Women's Work: Constraints and Opportunities', *Studies in Family Planning* (1981), 12 (4):184–97.

84. P. Romito and M. J. Saurel-Cubizolles, 'Working Women and Breastfeeding', *Journal of Reproductive and Infant Psychology* (1996), 14:145–56.

85. See Ibid. for a review of the relevant literature.

86. See J. Brannen and P. Moss, op. cit.

87. K. Moore, D. Spain and S. Bianchi, 'The Working Wife and Mother', *Marriage and Family Review* (1984), 7:77–98.

88. A. Clarke-Stewart, 'Infant Day Care. Maligned or Malignant?' *American Psychologist*, February 1989, 266–73; A. Clarke-Stewart, 'Does Day-care Affect Development?' *Journal of Reproductive and Infant Psychology* (1991), 9:67–78; I. Hoffman, 'Effects of Maternal Employment in the Two-parent Family', *American Psychologist* (1989), 44 (2):283–92; B. Tizard, 'Employed Mothers and the Care of Young Children', in A. Phoenix *et al.* (eds.), op. cit.

89. 'Il bimbo sta meglio nella propria casa', *Il Piccolo*, 11 March 1990.

90. P. Romito et al., 'Mothers' Health after the Birth of the First Child: The Case of Employed Women in an Italian City'; P. Romito and M. J. Saurel-Cubizolles, 'Fair Law, Unfair Practices?'

91. P. Romito, 'The Practice of Protective Legislation for Pregnant Workers in Italy', *Women's Studies International Forum* (1993), 16 (6):581–90.

92. ISTAT, *Indagine sulle strutture e i comportamenti familiari*, Rome, ISTAT (1985); ISTAT, *Tempi diversi*, Rome, ISTAT (1994).

93. See note 53.

94. ISTAT, *Tempi diversi*.

95. P. Moss, G. Bolland and R. Foxman, *Transition to Parenthood*, Research Report, London, Department of Health and Social Security (1982); A. Oakley, *Women Confined*; P. Romito, 'La naissance du premier enfant'; D. Tierney, P. Romito and K. Messing, 'She Ate Not the Bread of Idleness: Exhaustion is Related to Domestic and Salaried Working Conditions among 539 Quebec Hospital Workers', *Women and Health* (1990), 16 (1):21–42.

96. See G. Cresson, *Le travail domestique de santé*, Paris, L'Harmattan (1995); A. Oakley, *Women Confined*; P. Romito, 'La naissance du premier enfant'.

97. M. C. Lennon, G. Wasserman and R. Allen, 'Infant Care and Wives' Depressive Symptoms', *Women and Health* (1991), 17 (2):1–23; P. Romito, 'La naissance du premier enfant'; C. Ross et al., op. cit.; C. Ross and J. Mirowsky, 'Child Care and Emotional Adjustment to Wives' Employment', *Journal of Health and Social Behavior* (1988), 29:127–38.

98. *Le donne cambiano i tempi. Una legge per rendere più umani i tempi del lavoro, gli orari delle città, il ritmo della vita.* Sezione femminile del PCI, via delle Botteghe Oscure 4, Rome.

99. P. Romito et al., see note 90.

100. See note 98.

101. C. Delphy, 'Egalité, équivalence et equité'.

102. D. Kergoat, 'Les femmes et le travail à temps partiel', Paris, Ministère du Travail, Service des études et de la statistique (1984).

103. C. Delphy, 'Egalité, équivalence et equité'.

104. J. Fagnani, 'L'allocation parentale d'éducation: effets pervers et ambiguités d'une prestation', *Droit Social* (1995), 3:287–95.

105. S. Perry, 'Part-time Work and Returning to Work after the Birth of a Child', *Applied Economics* (1990), 22:1137–48.

106. H. Davies and H. Joshi, 'The Forgone Earnings of European Mothers. Paper Prepared for EAPS Symposium on the Costs of Children', Barcelona, Spain, October 1990.

107. While the lack of a partner may be a financial and emotional strain, it is associated with a significant reduction in the time mothers spend in housework (ISTAT, *Tempi diversi*; M. Proulx, *Five Million Women: A Study of the Canadian Housewife*, Ottawa, Canadian Advisory Council on the Status of Women (1978).

108. See note 53.

109. M. Dew, R. Bromet and L. Penkower, 'Mental Health Effects of Job Loss in Women', *Psychological Medicine* (1992), 22:751–64; E. Hall and J. Johnson, 'Depression in Unemployed Swedish Women', *Social Science and Medicine* (1988), 27 (12): 1349–55.

110. M. Piazza and S. Biadene, 'Donne, lavoro e famiglia', *Famiglia Oggi*, May 1995: 42–63.

111. Ministero del Lavoro e della Sicurezza Sociale, *Rapporto 93–94, Lavoro e politiche dell'occupazione in Italia*, Rome, Ministero del Lavoro e della Sicurezza Sociale (1994).

112. A. Oakley, 'The Cries and Smiles of Babies', in A. Oakley (ed.), *Essays on Women, Medicine and Health*, Edinburgh, Edinburgh University Press (1993), pp. 89–90.

113. A last-minute note: there has been a move in the right direction. The newspapers report that this year as many as 30,000 children, mostly from ex-Yugoslavia and the Chernobyl region, will be spending their summer holidays here with Italian families ('Prestiti d'amore. Le famiglie italiane ospitano oltre trentamila bambini dell'Est', *La Repubblica*, 19 June 1995).

I am grateful to Ann Oakley, who gave me the occasion to write this chapter; to the many friends – Geneviève Cresson, Cynthia Cockburn, Augusta De Piero Barbina, Christine Delphy, Elisabetta Donini and Marie-Josèphe Saurel-Cubizolles – who read and commented on previous versions of this paper; to Judy Moss, who not only made my English more English, but also challenged many of my ideas; and to Livio Lanceri, who, as always, offered support, love, and help with software.

IO. DANGEROUS DESIGN

1. See K. K. Bhavnani and M. Coulson, 'Transforming Socialist Feminism: the Challenge of Racism', in *Socialist Feminism – Out of the Blue*, a special issue of *Feminist Review* (1988), 23:81–92; V. Amos and P. Parmar, 'Resistances and Responses: The Experiences of Black Girls in Britain', in A. McRobbie and T. McCabe (eds.), *Feminism for Girls*, London, Routledge (1981); C. Mohanty, 'Cartographies of Struggle: Third World Woman and the Politics of Feminism' and 'Under Western Eyes', in *Third World Women and the Politics of Feminism*, Bloomington, Indiana University Press (1991); P. Parmar, 'Gender, Race and Class: Asian Women in Resistance' and H. Carby, 'White Woman Listen: Black Feminism and the Boundaries of Sisterhood', in *The Empire Strikes Back*, London, Hutchinson (1982), and K. K. Bhavnani and A. Phoenix (eds.), *Shifting Identities and Shifting Racisms*, London, Sage, (1994). Two significant feminist-women-of-colour anthologies are: B. Bryan, S. Dadzie and S. Scafe, *Heart of the Race: Black Women's Lives in Britain*, London, Virago (1985) and Grewal, Shabnum, Kay, Jackie, LiLiane Landor, Lewis, G. and P. Pratibha (eds.), *Charting the Journey: Writings by Black and Third World Women*, London, Sheba Feminist Press (1988). In the USA feminist-women-of-colour anthologies broke new ground in contesting white feminist conceptualizations of the lives of women of colour. These include: C. Moraga and G. Anzaldua, *The Bridge Called My Back: Writings by Radical Women of Color*, Watertown MA, Persephone Press (1983), and Asian Women United of California (eds.), *Making Waves: An Anthology of Writings by and about Asian American Women*, Boston MA, Beacon Press (1989).

2. See A. Brah, 'Difference, Diversity and Differentiation', in J. Donald and A. Rattansi (eds.), *Race, Culture and Difference*, London and Milton Keynes, Sage and Open University (1992); and 'Women of South Asian Origin in Britain: Issues and Concerns', *South Asia* 7(1); A. Phoenix, 'Narrow Definitions of Culture: The Case of Early Motherhood' and P. Bhachu, 'Apni Marzi Kardhi: Home and Work: Sikh Women in Britain', in S. Westwood and P. Bhachu (eds.), *Enterprising Women: Ethnicity, Economy and Gender Relations*, London, Routledge (1991); P. Bhachu, 'Culture, Ethnicity and Class among Punjabi Sikh Women in 1990s Britain' (1988), in *New Community* (1991), 17

(3):401–12; and S. Westwood, 'Racism, Mental Illness and the Politics of Identity', in *Racism, Modernity, Identity on the Western Front*, Cambridge, Polity Press (1994).

3. See P. Bhachu, *Twice Migrants: East African Sikh Settlers in Britain*, London and New York, Tavistock (1985); P. Bhachu, 'Work, Marriage and Dowry among East African Sikh Women in United Kingdom', in R. J. Simon and C. B. Brettell (eds.), *International Migration: The Female Experience*, Totowa, New Jersey, Rowman and Allanheld (1988); I. Light and P. Bhachu, *Immigration and Entrepreneurship: Culture, Capital and Ethnic Networks, Transactions*, New Brunswick, Rutgers University Press (1993); P. Bhachu, 'Identities Constructed and Reconstructed: Representations of Asian Women in Britain', in G. Buijs (ed.), *Migrant Women: Crossing Boundaries and Changing Identities*, Oxford, Berg Publishers (1994); and P. Bhachu, 'The Multiple Landscapes of Transnational Asian Women in the Diaspora', in V. Amit-Talai and C. Knowles (eds.), *Re-Situating Identities: The Politics of Race, Ethnicity, Culture*, Canada/USA, Broadview Press (1996).

4. These politically charged cultural and consumer processes are explored by K. Mercer, 'Black Hair/Style Politics', in *Welcome to the Jungle: New Positions in Black Cultural Studies*, London, Routledge (1994) and in A. Mcrobbie (ed.), *Zoot Suits and Second Hand Dresses: An Anthology of Fashion and Music*, London, Macmillan (1989), notably in S. Cosgrave, 'The Zoot Suit and Style Warfare'.

5. *Euronews*, 26 June 1996.

6. *Daily Star*, 26 March 1996.

7. See S. Westwood, 'Workers and Wives: Continuities and Discontinuities in the Lives of Gujarati Women', in S. Westwood and P. Bhachu (eds.), *Enterprising Women: Ethnicity, Economy and Gender Relations*, London, Routledge (1988).

8. See L. Back, 'X Amount of Sat Siri Akal: Apache Indian, Reggae Music and Intermezzo Culture', in R. Sunquist (ed.), *Cultural Studies and Discourses on Ethnicity*, Sweden, Umea University Press (1995).

9. *Daily Express*, 23 February 1996.

10. *Sunday Times*, 27 February 1994.

11. See S. Hall, 'New Ethnicities', in K. Mercer (ed.), *Black Film, British Cinema*, BFI/ICA Documents 7 (1988); S. Hall, 'The Local and the Global: Globalization and Ethnicity' and 'Old and New Ethnicities', in A. D. King (ed.), *Culture, Globalization and the World System*,

London, Macmillan (1991); and A. Brah, 'Reframing Europe: Engendered Racisms, Ethnicities and Nationalisms in Contemporary Europe', in *Feminist Review*, 45 (1994).

12. See the interview with Gurinder Chadha by G. Bhatacharia and J. Gabriel, in *Third Text*, April 1995; also '"Ruptured and Sutured" Identities: Gurinder Chadha and Parminder Bhachu Discuss their Lives and Work', in *Sojourner*, August 1996.

13. *Guardian*, 6 April 1996, pp. 13−16.

14. See I. Grewal and C. Kaplan (eds.), *Scattered Hegemonies: Postmodernity and Transnational Feminist Practices*, Minneapolis, University of Minnesota Press (1994).

I am really grateful to my US colleagues at Clark University – Marcia Butzel, Lois Brynes, Cynthia Enloe and Jim Gee – for commenting on drafts of this chapter. My close friend Jane Singh at the University of California, Berkeley, helped me think through the themes of this paper. In Britain my special thanks go to my friends John Solomos at Southampton University and Les Back at Goldsmiths' College, London University, for discussing the 'multiplicities of my thoughts and writings' in all their various stages. Final thanks are due to my dear and very 'trendy' *salwaar-kameezed* pal, Shaista Farruki-Hickman, who has for years helped me track and decipher the various *salwaar-kameez* suit styles and trends in Britain and Pakistan.

II. FEMINISM, FATHERHOOD AND THE FAMILY IN BRITAIN

1. We are grateful to the Nuffield Foundation for the award of a research grant and to the Social Science Research Unit of the Institute of Education, University of London and St John's College, Cambridge for space and facilities. We received help from the DSS, CSA and various voluntary organizations. Our thanks are due to Xavier Ribas and Polly Rossdale for help in reporting a demonstration.

2. M. Speed, J. Crane and K. Rudat, *CSA National Client Satisfaction Survey 1993*, HMSO (1994), pp. 129−30.

3. Hansard 1990−1991, 526:809.

4. The legislation speaks of 'absent *parents*', not wishing to pre-empt the question of who raises the children. Clearly most absent parents,

but not all, are fathers. Some mothers do leave children with their fathers and a few fathers claim and receive care and custody. As the legislation does not distinguish we have adopted the same terminology, while we recognize that here and elsewhere most upbringing, even in two-parent families, continues to be done by women, whatever the attitudes to sharing work. Of the 10 per cent of lone parents who are men, 25 per cent are widowers who may well use extensive child-care facilities. In France the comparable figure is 85 per cent mothers as carers.

5. The basic elements of the CSA formula are: the maintenance requirement of the children (based on income support rates); the assessable income of the absent mother or father (net income after allowances for day-to-day expenditure); the deduction rate (50 per cent of assessable income until the maintenance requirement is met); and the additional element (levied at a lower rate on the balance of assessable income after the maintenance requirement is met). Under this formula it is absent parents in the middle income bracket who will generally be paying the highest percentage (up to a limit of 30 per cent) of their net income in maintenance.

6. W. Mantle, *Child Support: The New System Explained*, London (1993), p. 1.

7. This is the figure in the Government paper, *Children Come First*, 1990, vol. 1. Precise figures are hard to establish as different sources make their calculations in different ways. According to a report of the Family Policy Studies Centre, 39 per cent of lone parents had received some payment, but only 29 per cent received it regularly.

8. In 1961, one in six lone parents claimed supplementary benefit; by 1987 over two-thirds claimed it; K. Kiernan and M. Wicks, *Family Change and Future Policy*, London, Family Policy Studies Centre (1990), p. 33.

9. What we have called serial families are referred to by other names, post-modern, divorce-extended or recombinant, reconstructed families, J. Stacey, *Brave New Families: Stories of Domestic Upheaval in Late-twentieth-century America*, New York (1990), or reconstituted families, K. Kiernan and M. Wicks, op. cit.

10. C. Hill, *The World Turned Upside Down: Radical Ideas during the English Revolution*, London (1972), pp. 306ff.

11. See, for example, the case described in the *Independent*, 29 January

1996 of a record producer who lived in a £300,000 house, owned a Porsche and two BMWs, employed a cleaner and a gardener, and produced audited accounts for the CSA showing he earned only £14,340 a year.

12. *Sunday Telegraph*, 6 November 1994, p. 2.

13. Wages for housework/motherhood is now being considered in France – but with the aim of combating the ever lower birth-rate and male infertility, presumably assuming a psychological factor to the latter.

14. The sociologist Evelyne Sullerot has listed eighteen associations in France for the defence of fathers, one of which is called SOS-Papa (*Le Nouvel Observateur*). The change in men's position, not only of absent fathers, is illustrated by the fact that in France on 4 June 1970, the day of General de Gaulle's death, a law was passed putting an end to the notions of '*chef de famille*' and '*autorité paternelle*'.

15. J. Campion, *Families Come First: The Case against the Child Support Agency*, Midhurst, Family Law Action Group (1994).

16. M. Melli and S. Zink, 'Alternatives to Judicial Child Support and Enforcement: A Proposal for a Child Support Tax', in J. M. Eekelaar and S. N. Katz (eds.), *The Resolution of Family Conflict: Comparative Legal Perspectives*, Toronto (1984), p. 516.

17. H. D. Krause, 'Child Support in the United States: Reporting Good News', in J. M. Eekelaar and S. N. Katz, op. cit., p. 544.

18. J. Roll, *Lone Parent Families in the European Community: The 1992 Report to the EC*, London, Family Policy Studies Centre (1992).

19. J. Bradshaw and J. Millar, *Lone-parent Families in the UK*, London, HMSO (1991), found a figure of 43 per cent. For a sensitive discussion see R. Simpson, P. McCarthy and J. Walker, *Being There: Fathers after Divorce*, Newcastle, Relate Centre for Family Studies (1995).

20. S. Faludi, *Backlash: The Undeclared War against American Women*, New York (1991), p. 24.

21. For example, one-person households had increased from 11 per cent in 1961 to 25 per cent in 1987; K. Kiernan and M. Wicks, op. cit., p. 17.

22. Ibid., p. 12. The rate has levelled off since 1981.

23. Ibid., p. 14; L. Burghes, *Lone Parenthood and Family Disruption: The*

Outcome for Children, London, Family Policy Studies Centre (1994), pp. 50–51 (see Table 1, on p. 214).

24. *Guardian*, 14 December 1994.

25. *Le Monde*, 29 July 1995, p. 3, reporting on Eurostat figures.

26. *Guardian*, 16 October 1995.

27. B. Hill, 'The Marriage Age of Women and the Demographers', *History Workshop Journal*, 28 (1989), pp. 129–47.

28. K. Kiernan and V. Estaugh, *Cohabitation: Extra-marital Childbearing and Social Policy*, London, Family Policy Studies Centre (1993), p. 10.

29. See E. Kingdom, 'Lawyers will Draft Anything: Attitudes to Cohabitation Contracts', *Issues in Sociology and Social Policy*, paper 5, Liverpool, University of Liverpool (1994).

30. W. Seccombe, *A Millennium of Family Change: Feudalism to Capitalism in Northwestern Europe*, London (1992), p. 226.

31. See L. Roper, *The Holy Household: Women and Morals in Reformation Augsburg*, Oxford (1989).

32. The links between family break-up and academic achievement of children are contested. It is not easy to control statistically for intervening variables (especially social class, income and housing). For a summary, see J. Elliot and M. Richards, 'Children and Divorce: Educational Performance and Behaviour before and after Parental Separation', *International Journal of Law and the Family*, 5 (1991), pp. 258–76.

33. Interviews of J. M. with X. D. and Y. B.

34. The figure for married women in employment was 10 per cent in 1931, by 1987 it was 60 per cent (mostly part time).

35. But already during the English Revolution among some protestant sects; C. Hill, op. cit.

36. Statutes, 2–3 Victoria, cap. 54.

37. Statutes, 15–16 George 5, ch. 45.

38. W. Seccombe, *Weathering the Storm: Working Class Families from the Industrial Revolution to the Fertility Decline*, London (1993), pp. 203–4.

39. See the account in W. Seccombe, ibid.

40. M. Levin, 'Children and Feminism', *Quest* (1994).

41. The re-analysis of mortality statistics by K. Judge and M. Benzeval, 'Health Inequalities: New Concerns about the Children of Single Mothers', *British Medical Journal*, 306 (1993), pp. 677–80.

12. COMBATING THE BACKLASH

1. The GDI is based on the relation between women's and men's life expectancy, adult literacy, education and share of earned income. The methodology used imposes a penalty for inequality.

2. The GEM is also a very crude index, based on the proportion of women in parliament, among administrators and managers, among professional and technical workers and women's share of earned income.

3. A contributing factor to the high level of women with low education in paid work is that the Swedish labour market's pay structure is comparatively compressed, thus the gap between the highest and lowest levels of pay is smaller than in other countries.

4. Child care is, or should be, an issue for both men and women, and especially something which concerns children as citizens. However, in most parts of the world, including Scandinavia, it is seen mainly as a service for women.

5. Sweden has a system of proportional representation with a minimum requirement of 4 per cent of national votes for a party to be represented in parliament. Seven parties were represented in 1995: Moderate Party (Conservatives), Centre Party, Liberal Party, Christian Democrats, Green Party, Social Democratic Party and Left Party (Socialists).

6. *Svenska Dagbladet*, the second largest Stockholm morning paper, is independent conservative.

7. We also later decided not to include women in political posts, as that was considered to give some parties an advantage in knowing beforehand what we planned. This caused resentment among a few excluded women, and it also resulted in the only attempt by anyone at a meeting to harm the network, after more than three years of networking: one excluded woman published members' names and topics discussed, using it to promote her own political and private interests.

8. The election period in Sweden was three years, but is now four (thus the next election will be in 1998). Election day is the third Sunday in September.

9. One example of an issue we dropped was that of whether Sweden should join the European Union or not. A referendum was held in

November of 1994. The result was 52 per cent Yes and 47 per cent No. Support Stockings campaigned on both sides, but not in the name of the network.

10. *Kvennalistin*, the Women's List, is an Icelandic party with a feminist programme which has existed since 1983 in its present form, and which is represented in *Alltinger* (Icelandic parliament).

11. Every two years a special women's fair is held, in which seminars on women's issues are combined with a trade fair. Women in trade unions, politics, large and small companies, business women, women in research and education, lunch ladies in schools, care workers etc. all arrange lectures, meetings and exhibitions; 50,000–60,000 women take part in these fairs.

12. A ridiculous, but true example: when a restructuring of a large bank was carried out, paid for with taxpayers' money, the argument for sacking the women and promoting the men responsible for losses was that the women lacked experience in credit rating! That the men's 'experience' eventually cost the taxpayers around sixty billion Swedish crowns was considered irrelevant.

13. The labour participation rate in 1994 was 80 per cent; however, only 44 per cent was full-time, 26 per cent long part-time and 4 per cent short part-time work; 5 per cent were unemployed. Comparative figures for men are 84 per cent labour participation rate, 70 per cent full-time, 5 per cent long part-time and 2 per cent short part-time; 7 per cent were unemployed. (Statistics Sweden: Women and Men in Sweden, 1995.)

Swedish women's labour participation differs from that in other western countries in that a higher proportion of women with only compulsory education have paid jobs. The labour force participation for women from 25 to 64 years with only compulsory education in 1992 was 81 per cent in Sweden, 68 per cent in Denmark, 66 per cent in Finland, 55 per cent in Norway, 55 per cent in France, 54 per cent in the UK, 46 per cent in the USA, 46 per cent in Germany and 29 per cent in Ireland. The country mean value in the OECD was 50 per cent. The difference between male and female labour participation was smallest in Sweden. (OECD: *Education at a Glance. OECD Indicators*, 1995.)

14. The revenue from that book, and from a subsequent book (all the writers donated their work), together with the entrance fee to the

tribunals (twenty pounds for two days, with donations collected to pay for women who could not afford it; the major part of that money paid for the hall, and for lighting arrangements), was the only money we collected and used. Telephones, postage and stationery were paid for by Support Stockings with jobs.

15. However, the word 'quota' was politically impossible, so they invented a new Swedish term, which can be translated into 'layered' or 'sandwiched' lists.

16. It is interesting that so many foreign journalists have assumed, without asking, that only women have been invited to these seminars! In fact, there have been the same seminars for men only, on the initiative of men in senior positions and very much involved in gender issues.

I have been invited to lead these seminars together with Ms Birgitta Hedman, one of the founding mothers of the gender statistics in Statistics in Sweden. They comprise an overview of Sweden today in a gender perspective: health, crime, work, income, pay, power, education, smoking, conditions for the elderly etc. as well as international comparisons.

Notes on Contributors

Parminder Bhachu is Henry R. Luce Professor of Cultural Identities and Global Processes at Clark University, Massachusetts. She is widely published on both sides of the Atlantic. She is the author of *Twice Migrants: East African Sikh Settlers in Britain*, co-editor with Sallie Westwood of *Enterprising Women: Ethnicity, Economy and Gender Relations* and co-editor with Ivan Light of *Immigration and Entrepreneurship: Culture, Capital and Ethnic Networks*. She was Simon Senior Fellow at Manchester University for 1996, and is working on a book entitled *Dangerous Designs: Subversive Fashion Style and Images*.

Carol Gilligan is the author of *In a Different Voice: Psychological Theory and Women's Development* and Professor of Education at Harvard University. With her colleagues she founded a feminist research collaborative, the Harvard Project on Women's Psychology and Girls' Development, and co-authored or co-edited four books: *Making Connections* (with N. Lyons and T. Hanmer); *Meeting at the Crossroads* (with L. M. Brown): *Women, Girls, and Psychotherapy: Reframing Resistance* (with A. G. Rogers and D. Tolman); and *Between Voice and Silence: Women and Girls, Race and Relationship* (with J. M. Taylor and A. Sullivan). She is co-artistic director of the Company of Women, an all-women theatre company. In 1992 she was Pitt Professor at Cambridge University.

Jack Goody is currently a Jean Monnet Fellow at the European University, Florence. He was formerly William Wyse Professor of Social Anthropology at Cambridge, where he is also a Fellow of St John's College. He is the author of books on kinship, the family, flowers, food, literacy and representations.

Susan Heath was born and brought up in England and now lives with her partner in New York City, where she works as a freelance editor and writer and serves on the board of a battered-women's shelter. She received her M.Phil. in English Literature from Columbia University in 1984. With Beverly Guy-Sheftall, she produced *Women's Studies: A Retrospective*, a 1995 Ford Foundation report. She has four sons, two daughters-in-law and two grandsons.

Carolyn C. Heilbrun is the Avalon Foundation Professor in the Humanities Emerita at Columbia University. She is the author of *Writing a Woman's Life*, *The Education of a Woman: The Life of Gloria Steinem*, and eleven detective novels under the name of Amanda Cross.

Juliet Mitchell is a psychoanalyst and currently A. D. White Professor-at-large at Cornell University. She is a university lecturer in Gender and Society at Cambridge University and is also a Fellow of Jesus College. Her books include: *Women's Estate*, *The Selected Melanie Klein* (editor), *Psychoanalysis and Feminism*, *Women: The Longest Revolution* and *Rights and Wrongs of Women* (edited with Ann Oakley).

Ann Oakley is Professor of Sociology and Social Policy and Director of the Social Science Research Unit at the University of London Institute of Education. She has been researching and writing in the field of gender, the family and health for more than thirty years, and has published widely. Her books include: *Sex, Gender and Society*, *The Sociology of Housework*, *Subject Women*, *From Here to Maternity*, *The Captured Womb*, *Social Support and Motherhood*, an autobiography, *Taking it Like a Woman*, a biography of her parents, *Man and Wife*, and six novels.

Patrizia Romito is a feminist researcher in the Department of Psychology at the University of Trieste (Italy), where she teaches Methodology of Social Research and Social Psychology, and acts as adviser to the women's health research programme at the Burlo Garofolo Hospital in Trieste. She received a Ph.D. in psychology from the University of Geneva, and a Ph.D. in maternal and child health from the University of Trieste. Her main research interests are in the field of women's mental health, of the relationships between work, motherhood and health, and of male violence against women. She is the author of books on post-partum depression and on women's work during pregnancy.

Joanna Ryan is a psychoanalytic psychotherapist in practice in London. A life-long feminist, she has a Ph.D. in psychology from Cambridge

University. She trained as a psychotherapist at the Philadelphia Association, London, where she now teaches. She is author of *The Politics of Mental Handicap*, co-editor with Sue Cartledge of *Sex and Love: New Thoughts on Old Contradictions* and co-author with Noreen O'Connor of *Wild Desires and Mistaken Identities: Lesbianism and Psychoanalysis*.

Agneta Stark is Reader at the School of Business in Stockholm University. Since 1995 she has worked part time as an expert for the Swedish government's Committee for Gender Equality and has been a columnist on the *Svenska Dagbladet* since 1986. She has lectured extensively in Sweden and abroad and has written countless articles and books on gender aspects of economic matters. Agneta Stark is a founder member of the Support Stockings, which was set up in 1991.

Margaret Walters was born in Australia and now lives in London. Formerly a lecturer in English Literature at the University of Reading, since 1988 she has worked as a freelance writer, teacher and broadcaster. She was film critic for the *Listener*, reviews fiction for the *Sunday Times* and works regularly on arts programmes for the BBC, the World Service and Radio National, Australia. She has written a book on the male nude and is currently working on a book on women photographers and one on the myth of the *femme fatale*.

Peggy Watson is Senior Research Associate at the Faculty of Social and Political Sciences at Cambridge University. She has written widely on issues relating to gender/feminism, particularly from an East–West comparative perspective. Recent publications include: 'The Rise of Masculinism in Eastern Europe' in M. Threifall (ed.), *Mapping the Women's Movement*, 'Marriage and Mortality in Eastern Europe', in C. Hertaman *et al.* (eds.), *Environmental and Non-environmental Determinants of the East–West Life Expectancy Gap in Europe* and 'Civil Society and the Politicization of Difference in Eastern Europe', in J. W. Scott and C. Kaplan (eds.), *Transitions, Environments, Translations: The Meaning of Feminism in Contemporary Politics*. Her forthcoming book is entitled *Civil Society and the Mobilization of Difference in Eastern Europe*.

Nira Yuval-Davis is a professor and post-graduate course-director in Gender and Ethnic Studies at the University of Greenwich, London. She has written extensively on issues of nationalism, racism, fundamentalism and gender relations, especially in Israel and Britain. Among her recent books are *Racialized Boundaries, Refusing Holy Orders: Women and Fundamentalism in Britain, Unsettling Settler Societies: Articulations of Gender, Ethnicity, Race & Class* and *Gender and Nation.*